Fishing
Wyoming

Kenneth Graham

GUILFORD, CONNECTICUT
HELENA, MONTANA
AN IMPRINT OF THE GLOBE PEQUOT PRESS

FALCONGUIDES®

All black-and-white photos by Kenneth Graham.
Cover photo: Grand Teton National Park, by Michael Shedlock, New England Stock.

Library of Congress Cataloging-in-Publication Data

Graham, Kenneth Lee
   Fishing Wyoming / by Kenneth Graham.
      p.   cm.
   ISBN 978-1-56044-629-3 (pbk. : alk. paper)
   1. Fishing—Wyoming—Guidebooks. 2. Wyoming—Guidebooks.
   I. Title.
   SH565.G735 1998
   799.1'1'09787—dc21   98-28500
                                                                              CIP

Manufactured in the United States of America.
First Edition/Third Printing

To buy books in quantity for corporate use
or incentives, call **(800) 962–0973**
or e-mail **premiums@GlobePequot.com**.

The author and The Globe Pequot Press assume no liability for accidents happening to, or injuries sustained by, readers who engage in the activities described in this book.

Contents

Map Legend ix
Overview Map x
Introduction 1
How to Use This Guide 5
Fish Species of Wyoming 6

Northeast

1. Sand Creek 20
2. Cook Lake 21
3. Keyhole Reservoir 23
4. LAK Reservoir 26
5. Turner Reservoir 27
6. Muddy Guard Reservoir 2 28
7. Muddy Guard Reservoir 1 28
8. Middle Fork Powder River 30
9. Healy Reservoir 32
10. Lake DeSmet 33
11. North and South Fork Sayles Creek Ponds 34
12. North Fork Clear Creek 34
13. Middle Fork Clear Creek 36
14. Sherd Lake 36
15. Willow Lake 37
16. South Fork Clear Creek 37
17. North Fork Crazy Woman Creek 37
18. North Fork Powder River 39
19. Doyle Creek 41
20. Dull Knife Reservoir 41
21. Beartrap Creek 43
22. East Tensleep Lake 44
23. Meadowlark Lake 44
24. West Tensleep Lake 46
25. Golden Lakes 47
26. Tensleep Creek 47
27. Paintrock Creek 47
28. (Lower) Medicine Lodge Creek 48
29. Renner Reservoir 50
30. East Fork Big Goose Creek 51
31. Weston Reservoir 52
32. West Fork Big Goose Creek 52
33. Sawmill Lakes 54
34. Calvin Lake 54
35. East Fork South Tongue River 55
36. West Fork South Tongue River 55

37. Owen Creek 55
38. Tongue River 57
39. Sibley Lake 59
40. South Tongue River 61
41. Shell Creek 62
42. Shell Creek Reservoir 62
43. (Upper) Medicine Lodge Creek 64
44. Upper Medicine Lodge Lake 64
45. Lower Medicine Lodge Lake 65
46. Upper Paint Rock Lake 65
47. Lower Paint Rock Lake 66
48. North Fork Tongue River 66
49. Porcupine Creek 68

Northwest
50. Bighorn Lake 70
51. Lower Bighorn River 71
52. Upper Bighorn River 73
53. Wardell Reservoir 77
54. Lower Sunshine Reservoir 78
55. Upper Sunshine Reservoir 79
56. East Newton Lake 79
57. West Newton Lake 79
58. Buffalo Bill Reservoir 81
59. Shoshone River 82
60. North Fork Shoshone River 84
61. South Fork Shoshone River 86
62. Luce Reservoir 88
63. Hogan Reservoir 88
64. Lower Clarks Fork River 88
65. Dead Indian Creek 90
66. Sunlight Creek 91
67. Copper Lakes 93
68. Upper Clarks Fork River 93
69. Lily Lake 95
70. Beartooth Lake 95
71. Island Lake 96
72. Wind River Canyon 96
73. Boysen Reservoir 98
74. Lake Cameahwait 100
75. Ocean Lake 101
76. Pilot Butte Reservoir 102
77. Ray Lake 102
78. Bull Lake 104
79. Upper Wind River 104

80. Torrey Lake 105
81. Ring Lake 105
82. Trail Lake 107
83. Horse Creek 107
84. Wiggins Fork River 108
85. East Fork Wind River 109
86. Moon Lake 109
87. Lake of the Woods 109
88. Fish Lake 110
89. Pelham Lake 110
90. Brooks Lake 111
91. Upper Brooks Lake 111
92. Upper Jade Lake 112
93. Lower Jade Lake 112
94. Wind River Lake 112
95. Leidy Lake 113
96. Bridger Lake 113
97. Grassy Lake 115
98. Toppings Lake 115
99. Lower Slide Lake 118
100. Gros Ventre River 118
101. Flat Creek 120
102. Granite Creek 121
103. Hoback River 121
104. Snake River 122

Southwest
105. Greys River 128
106. Upper Salt River 130
107. Lower Salt River 132
108. (Upper) Green River 134
109. Fontenelle Reservoir 137
110. (Lower) Green River 139
111. North Piney Lake 140
112. Middle Piney Lake 140
113. LaBarge Creek 142
114. Pine Creek 142
115. Hobble Creek 143
116. Smith's Fork 145
117. Viva Naughton Reservoir 146
118. Kemmerer City Reservoir 146
119. Sulphur Creek Reservoir 148
120. Meeks Cabin Reservoir 150
121. Flaming Gorge Reservoir 150
122. New Fork Lakes 154

123. Duck Creek 155
124. Willow Lake 155
125. Soda Lake 157
126. Fremont Lake 158
127. Elbow Lake 159
128. New Fork River 159
129. Wall Lake 160
130. Upper Cook Lake 162
131. Lower Cook Lake 163
132. Half Moon Lake 163
133. Meadow Lake 164
134. Burnt Lake 164
135. Boulder Lake 165
136. Norman Lakes 165
137. Big Sandy Reservoir 166
138. Frye Lake 168
139. Worthen Meadows Reservoir 168
140. Fiddlers Lake 169
141. Little Popo Agie River 171
142. Louis Lake 172
143. Christina Lake 173
144. Rock Creek Reservoir 174
145. Sweetwater River 174

Southeast
146. (Upper) North Platte River 178
147. French Creek 181
148. Saratoga Lake 181
149. Encampment River 183
150. Hog Park Reservoir 185
151. Rob Roy Reservoir 186
152. Lake Owen 186
153. Sodergreen Lake 188
154. Meeboer Lake 189
155. Lake Hattie 189
156. Gelatt Lake 190
157. Twin Buttes Lake 190
158. Nash Fork Creek 191
159. Big Brooklyn Lake 191
160. Towner Lake 193
161. Libby Lake 193
162. Lewis Lake 194
163. Lookout Lake 194
164. Mirror Lake 196
165. Silver Lake 196

166. North Fork Little Laramie River 198
167. Sand Lake 198
168. Medicine Bow River 198
169. East Fork Medicine Bow River 200
170. Rock Creek 200
171. Diamond Lake 202
172. East Allen Lake 202
173. Pole Mountain 204
174. North Crow Reservoir 204
175. Granite Lake 206
176. Crystal Lake 209
177. Hawk Springs Reservoir 209
178. Wheatland Reservoir #3 211
179. Johnson Creek Reservoir 211
180. Grayrocks Reservoir 211
181. Seminoe Reservoir 213
182. North Platte River (Miracle Mile) 217
183. Dome Rock Reservoir 217
184. Alcova Reservoir 218
185. Pathfinder Reservoir 219
186. (Middle) North Platte River 220
187. LaBonte Creek 225
188. North Laramie River 225
189. Glendo Reservoir 227

Grand Teton National Park
190. Jackson Lake 231
191. Snake River 235
192. Two Ocean Lake 237
193. Cottonwood Creek 237
194. Leigh Lake 239
195. String Lake 242
196. Jenny Lake 242
197. Bradley Lake 243
198. Taggart Lake 243
199. Phelps Lake 244

Yellowstone National Park
200. Gardner River 248
201. Yellowstone Lake 250
202. Yellowstone River 252
203. Soda Butte Creek 256
204. Slough Creek 256
205. Lamar River 258
206. Gallatin River 259
207. Madison River 261

208. Firehole River 262
209. Gibbon River 263
210. Shoshone Lake 264
211. Lewis Lake 266
212. Lewis River 266
213. Heart Lake 268
214. Bechler River 268

Appendix 270
About the Author 273

Map Legend

Interstate		One Way Road	*One Way*
US Highway		Gate	
State or Other Principal Road		City or Town	Casper *or* Casper
Forest Road	000	Campground	
Interstate Highway		Cabin or Building	
Paved Road		Peak	5,281 ft.
Gravel Road		Pass	)(
Unimproved Road		Tunnel	}⋯{
Fishing Site	2	Overlook/Point of Interest	
Parking Area	P	National or State Forest/Park Boundary	
Lake, River/Creek, Waterfalls		Map Orientation	N
Bridge			
Marsh or Wetland		Scale	0 0.5 1
Trail/Route			Miles
Trailhead	T		
Railroad		Wind River Indian Reservation	

Overview Map

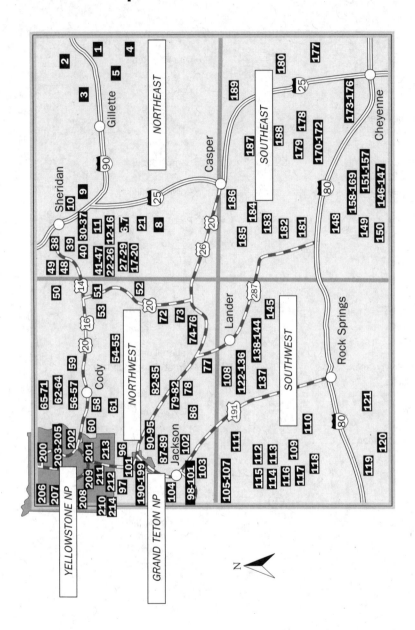

Introduction

As the sign at the border announces, Wyoming is like no place on earth. Wyoming has nine national forests, and the Bureau of Land Management maintains a good portion of the state, including four designated areas with fishing sites. Wyoming also offers fishing opportunities at state-managed locations. All of these separate agencies have their own individual offices and sources of information. This book is an attempt to combine information about Wyoming's diverse fishing locations from all of these sources into a statewide overview.

Trout are the most prominent gamefish in the state's waters. Most mountain streams and alpine lakes hold at least one of Wyoming's seven species of trout. Even as these coldwater rivers flow out of the majestic mountains and cross windy high desert country, trout, with few exceptions, remain the dominant gamefish in most rivers and reservoirs.

Northern pike live in the warmer waters of Keyhole Reservoir, in the northeastern part of Wyoming. To date, this is the only place in the state where pike are found. Tiger muskies inhabit scattered locations throughout the state. Anglers sometimes mistake them for northern pike, but they are actually a pike-muskellunge hybrid.

Walleye are also present in some warmer waters, predominantly at lower elevations. You will find most of these fish in the larger reservoirs. Catfish and sauger are caught in both warm-water rivers and reservoirs at selected areas.

Renner Reservoir is known for its largemouth bass. Not because of their trophy size, but because they are the only fish in the reservoir.

Wyoming has many lakes and streams, located in hard-to-reach backcountry, that are not reported in this book. There are 1,300 lakes in the Wind River Range alone, not to mention other rugged areas. All the same, there are some remote sites covered here with the adventurous angler in mind.

WYOMING'S WILDLIFE

Rattlesnakes top the danger list for me, though bears are probably more deadly. For the most part, the snakes I have encountered were more afraid of me than I was of them. Pay attention to where they go and don't follow them. In the early fall, it is not uncommon to find rattlesnakes warming themselves on the asphalt highways near sundown. At this time of year a rattlesnake is preserving all the energy it can and will not necessarily warn you by rattling its tail. They can also become contentious about their turf, so be wary of the not-so-dead snake on the road.

Large game animals are a welcome attraction if you treat them with common sense and respect. Antelope seem to dominate the otherwise desolate expanses of sagebrush. An antelope prefers to go under a fence as opposed to jumping over it, which can provide an interesting sideshow at times.

Deer are active during the darker parts of the day, when they become likely candidates to be hit by a vehicle. The most dangerous time for motorist and deer alike is in the early morning or late evening.

Elk, buffalo, and moose frequent roadsides in Yellowstone National Park. These large animals can and do charge when they feel threatened. Unfortunately, a large number of well-intentioned picture takers become a perceived threat when they try to take a close-up photograph.

Both grizzly and black bears are present in Wyoming. Grizzly bears inhabit the national forests and parks in the greater Yellowstone area. Black bears inhabit the same area, as well as the other national forests of Wyoming. Bears eat fish, among other things, and will often be fishing during spawning runs. Spring spawning, which occurs from May through July, draws the most bears, since they have just emerged from hibernation. Some fish species spawn in the fall, which also attracts hungry bears.

Even though the larger animals present potential dangers, the most annoying to me is the pesky mosquito. There are also ticks and horse and deer flies, although they don't buzz in my ear at night causing sleeplessness. Adequate bug repellent is of great value. There are a lot of miles between stores in Wyoming, so stock up before you leave home.

WYOMING'S WEATHER

Wyoming's high elevations result in a relatively cool climate. A hot sunny day will often require a coat by day's end. This is especially true of the high, mountain country surrounding the vast desert basins between ranges. The highest elevation in Wyoming is 13,804 feet—in the Wind River Mountain Range of the central western region, on top of Gannett Peak. Wyoming also boasts the highest point on Interstate 80 (Transcontinental Highway). The Summit reaches 8,640 feet in the southeast near Laramie. Wyoming's lowest elevation is located in the northeast corner at 3,125 feet. Average rainfall is only 14.5 inches per year, though it is not evenly distributed. The eastern portion of the state seems to get the greater share of moisture, while the southwestern parts look quite forsaken. When the dryer parts of Wyoming do get moisture, travel may become difficult, especially on unpaved roads.

Wyoming wind will leave a permanent impression on all first-time visitors. A story once circulated through a mining camp in central Wyoming about a local wind indicator. Supposedly, a half-inch log chain was left dangling just off the ground on a pole near a public gathering place. If the chain held steady at 45 degrees from the vertical it was an ordinary day. A truly windy day was when this chain stretched out at 90 degrees like a bicycle streamer on a downhill ride. There are days when it is easy to believe this story. The wind can also create very dangerous conditions for boaters. Keep in mind that if you happen to be capsized in one of the coldwater lakes, hypothermia sets in within minutes. Check with local authorities about conditions before tempting your fate with an unmerciful Mother Nature.

Storms can be fast and furious in any part of Wyoming, though they seem to be much more severe in the wide open desert. If your travels take you into some distant backcountry, it might be best to sit and wait out a storm. During the winter months, travelers should note that the gates on the highways are not for livestock. When those gates block the road, it is closed.

For the most part, summer weather will provide plenty of quality conditions for the persistent angler. Early morning is generally the quietest time, with wind intensity increasing in the early afternoon.

Wintery weather can move in quickly at any time in the high country, even in the summer. Be sure to have both rain gear and warm clothing when traveling into Wyoming's mountain country. A cap or hat of some kind is advisable, along with sunscreen to help avoid a blistered nose and strained eyes.

FINDING YOUR WAY

I have made every effort to provide accurate maps and mileage. The major problem is that even on freeways odometer readings will vary. Off-road travel creates a different set of circumstances that hinders accuracy as well. Therefore, take the mileage reported as approximate.

CATCH AND RELEASE

Points to Ponder: Most, if not all, anglers have an inner desire to catch a trophy fish. Obviously, any fish cooked for breakfast is through growing. With the following tips, an angler can provide bigger, more challenging fish for the future.

1. Land the fish as quickly possible.
2. Keep the fish in the water, even while removing the hook.
3. Don't squeeze the fish or put your fingers in it's gills.
4. Remove the hook gently. If this cannot be done, cut the line. The hook will decompose naturally.
5. If your catch is exhausted, hold it in an upright position facing upstream and move it back and forth. This will force water through its gills and help revive its strength. When the fish can hold itself upright, release your grip.
6. Released fish are 5 to 10 times more likely to survive when artificial flies or lures are used.
7. Barbless hooks make it easier to release fish.

HIKING

Getting to many of Wyoming's streams and lakes may involve some type of foot access. The following definitions will help identify levels of difficulty:
Easy: Mostly level, with short downhill/uphill parts, good trail surface, and few hazardous obstacles.

Moderate: Level to sloping, with longer downhill/uphill sections, a good trail surface, and few hazardous obstacles.

More difficult: Level to steep, with sustained downhill/uphill parts and fair to poor trail surface. Short stretches will have significant hazardous obstacles.

Most difficult: Mostly steep, with sustained downhill/uphill sections and a poor to nonexistent trail surface. Longer stretches will have significant hazardous obstacles.

BEST TIMES TO FISH

According to state biologists, there is a general tendency for fish to bite a day or two before, during, or after a full moon—or when there is no moon. Bright sunlight tends to make fishing less productive. Early in the morning or late in the evening is good in the lakes. During the day, stream fishing offers the most appeal.

REGULATIONS

Be sure to obtain and read a current copy of the *Wyoming Fishing Regulations*. Some restrictions are subject to change. Anglers should be aware that in Wyoming it is unlawful to use or possess corn while fishing.

How to Use This Guide

This book does not cover every fishing area in the state. Some areas are not advertised by local residents to safeguard fisheries that are perceived as delicate. I have attempted to avoid violating these sometimes unspoken desires. However, I've included plenty of other excellent fishing sites throughout Wyoming.

There are six sections in this book: They include Northeast, Northwest, Southwest, Southeast, Grand Teton National Park, and Yellowstone National Park. Entries for specific sites are numbered to correspond with the accompanying maps.

Each site description is organized as follows:

Number and name of site

Key species: At the top of every site description there is a list of the game fish found at the site.

Description: This section contains detailed information on the type of terrain and water present at each site. Any facilities available at the site, including boat ramps, toilet facilities, and camping information, are listed in this section. The description will also note whether it is necessary to hike into the site.

Tips: This section includes area-specific information with respect to the best time, lures, techniques, or other related material.

The fishing: Fish species present at the site are listed here along with where to find them, their average sizes, best angling techniques, and the time of year that fishing is best. Any special regulations will also be found in this section.

Directions: "Windshield" directions are given here, beginning at easy-to-find towns. These may not be the shortest or most direct routes.

Additional information: This is a catch-all category that provides extra bits of information, including access points, special difficulties, or the locations of nearby campgrounds.

Contact: This section provides the names of any government agencies or organizations that can give you information on current conditions at a site. Their addresses and phone numbers are listed in Appendix A.

Access points: Some sites have multiple access points due to size and/or distance involved.

Fish Species of Wyoming

BROOK TROUT (SALVELINUS FONTINALIS)

General description: This small-headed fish graduates from dark green on top to a white belly. The males have splashes of bright red on their bellies. The light spots on a dark background are joined by some red or pink spots with blue halos on the lower sides. Striking black-and-white borders are found on the lower fins and tail.

Distribution: Brook trout are abundant in streams and small lakes in the mountain ranges of Wyoming. These fish are native to the eastern United States and the upper Midwest. They have been introduced into Wyoming. Brook trout are predominant in waters at or above an elevation of 10,000 feet. Though the species may be found at lower elevations, they are usually the only fish found in the high mountain country. Some of the waters where these tasty fish reside include Beartrap Creek (site 21), Porcupine Creek (site 49), Sunlight Creek (site 66), Island Lake (site 71), and Silver Lake (site 165).

Points to ponder: Brook trout are easy to catch. Many anglers prefer to fish for them with light or ultralight gear. The most frequently used bait is a piece of worm attached to a size 12 to 14 hook. Rumors have circulated that these fish are so hungry they can be caught on a bare hook, though I have not tried it. The relative ease of catching these tasty morsels, combined with the majestic mountain scenery where they live, makes brook-trout fishing a most entertaining activity for families with young anglers. Brook trout spawn in the fall and fishing is good year-round.

Brook trout

Brown trout

BROWN TROUT (SALMO TRUTTA)

General description: This brown-colored fish may have olive hues on top, with yellow sides and a belly with black and red or maroon spots. In contrast to the cutthroat and rainbow trout, there are few spots on the tail.

Distribution: These fish are from Europe and western Asia. All of the brown trout present in North America have their roots in foreign waters. Brown trout are found in both streams and lakes in most of Wyoming. Some of the blue-ribbon waters with brown trout are Sand Creek (site 1), Middle Fork Powder River (site 8), North Platte River at the Miracle Mile (site 182), Sweetwater River (site 145), and the Green River (site 108).

Points to ponder: The brown trout has a hard-to-catch reputation which makes the pursuit a personal challenge. There are many ways to attempt hooking these beauties, though if the "big ones" are your choice, the hours of twilight or darkness will offer the best chances.

Live nightcrawlers are effective earlier in the season while using grasshoppers as bait in the late fall can provoke strikes that are almost violent. Anglers seeking to increase the challenge of fishing for brown trout prefer artificial flies and spinners. Be sure to research the fishing regulations—there are some places where only lures or artificial flies are allowed. Brown trout prefer spawning in the fast water of streams in fall. This provides for some excellent fishing at a very colorful time of year.

CUTTHROAT TROUT (ONCORHYNCHUS CLARKI)

General description: Except for the Snake River subspecies, which has a more uniform distribution of spots, these fish display a heavier concentration of black spots in the tail area. The black spots are either minimal or nonexistent on the head. There is a red or orange slash located under the jaw.

Distribution: This is the only trout native to Wyoming. The cutthroat trout is found in all the drainages west of the Continental Divide, though there are cutthroats in various places to the east. Some of the waters included east of the Continental Divide are the Madison River (site 207)), Yellowstone River (site 202), Big Horn River (site 52), and the Tongue River (site 38). The most popular, and perhaps the most well-known, site on the west side of the divide is the Snake River (site 104).

Points to ponder: There are five subspecies of cutthroat trout in Wyoming and many more methods of catching them. Fly fishing seems to be the most popular, though not the only method. Be sure to research the regulations in regard to where you are fishing.

All of the subspecies of cutthroat spawn in the early spring. Depending on which of these subspecies is present, spawning may begin as early as March and continue into July.

GOLDEN TROUT (ONCORHYNCHUS AGUABONITA)

General description: This colorful fish is topped with green and separated from a yellow-to-red hue on its bottom by a bright red lateral band. Large round black spots are abundant on the dorsal fin and tail.

Distribution: This species hails from California. Golden trout in Wyoming are found in high, remote alpine lakes. A large concentration of these colorful trout inhabit the rugged Wind River Mountains. Some of the backcountry lakes inhabited by golden trout include Golden Lakes (site 25), Copper Lakes (site 67), Elbow Lake (site 127), Wall Lake (site 129), and Norman Lakes (site 136). These are all wilderness waters where only non-motorized access is allowed.

Points to ponder: The golden trout is noted more for its beauty than as a food fish. These trout spawn in late spring or early summer depending on the quality of the water and elevation.

LAKE TROUT OR MACKINAW (SALVELINUS NAMAYCUSH)

General description: This gray or light green fish has light spots on a dark background from head to tail. An additional feature worth noting is its forked tail.

Distribution: The lake trout is native to Canada but there are also some in New England and northern Montana. In Wyoming, these fish live in large, deep coldwater lakes including Buffalo Bill Reservoir (site 58), Beartooth Lake (site 70), Flaming Gorge Reservoir (site 121), Fremont Lake (site 126), and Jackson Lake (site 190).

Points to ponder: Lake trout are sought after because of their large size. The record 50-pound mackinaw caught in Jackson Lake, by Doris Budge in 1983, challenges anglers to seek even bigger ones. Ice fishing is an effective and inexpensive method for catching lake trout. Trolling is another alternative,

Lake trout or mackinaw

however the cost of equipment can be limiting. In the fall, lake trout migrate to shallow water with gravel bottoms to spawn. This can offer some exciting fishing from shore.

RAINBOW TROUT (ONCORHYNCHUS MYKISS)

General description: This silvery-sided fish has an obvious red or pink lateral stripe. They have small, irregular black spots on their bodies and dark green to blue-green fins.

Rainbow trout

Distribution: Rainbow trout are native to western North America. These trout inhabit streams and lakes throughout Wyoming. They are more abundant in cooler, higher elevation waters. Some of these waters include LAK Reservoir (site 4), Lake DeSmet (site 10), Fontenelle Reservoir (site 109), and Lake Hattie (site 155).

Points to ponder: A variety of methods and equipment are used to catch this species. Not nearly as difficult to hook as the brown trout, they often end up in the skillet at a streamside camp. Although rainbow trout prosper in lakes, they are known to prefer fast-water streams. Spawning usually occurs between February and May, which makes early spring a good time for rainbow trout fishing.

SPLAKE (BROOK TROUT–LAKE TROUT HYBRID)

General description: These hybrids look like brook trout and eat like mackinaw. They are able to reproduce, unlike most hybrids, and tend to get larger than the average brook trout.

Distribution: Splake primarily occupy lake waters. Some of these lakes include Willow Lake (site 15), Upper Sunshine Reservoir (site 55), Torrey Lake (site 80), Rob Roy Reservoir (site 151), and Lewis Lake (site 162).

Points to ponder: Splake are often introduced into waters overpopulated by minnows, suckers, grayling, and/or yellow perch. As splake grow larger it is hoped they will prey on the smaller, overpopulating fish.

KOKANEE SALMON (ONCORHYNCHUS NERKA)

General description: This silvery fish has blue-green coloring along its top, with fine black spots on its back. During the spawning season these fish turn red.

Kokanee salmon

Distribution: These landlocked salmon are native to North America and Asian coastal waters. In Wyoming, kokanee are located in lakes and reservoirs primarily in the south. These waters include Flaming Gorge Reservoir (site 121), New Fork Lakes (site 122), Fremont Lake (site 126), Boulder Lake (site 135), Lake Hattie (site 155), Granite Lake (site 175), and Crystal Lake (site 176).

Points to ponder: Kokanee spawn in the fall in rocky bottoms along lake shorelines and in streams. They die after spawning.

ARCTIC GRAYLING (THYMALLUS ARCTICUS)

General description: This trout-like fish has an elongated body colored a bluish gray. Other features include a rainbow coloring toward the front and black spots both in front and above the lateral line. A conspicuously long dorsal fin with 18 to 21 rays is its most recognizable feature. During spawning the male's dorsal fin develops bright blue or violet spots with red borders. Grayling spawn in the spring and prefer clear mountain streams with pebble bottoms. Even though some stay in streams year-round, most grayling reside in high mountain lakes when they are not breeding. These fish are not known for their great size and average 12 inches or less in length.

Distribution: This coldwater salmonid is native to northern Canada and farther south to parts of extreme northwestern Wyoming and east to Michigan. Grayling have been introduced to various Wyoming lakes and provide a challenge all their own. Some of the lakes in which these teasers reside are Willow Lake (site 15), Weston Reservoir (site 31), Toppings Lake (site 98), and Meadow Lake (site 133).

Points to ponder: Grayling feed extensively on insects, making fly fishing an appealing technique. These deceptive fish are known to dart at artificial flies several times and then retreat into deeper water without taking the hook. Because a grayling's jaw bone is thin and weak, a hard jerk on your line will literally pull the hook out of its mouth.

Artic Grayling

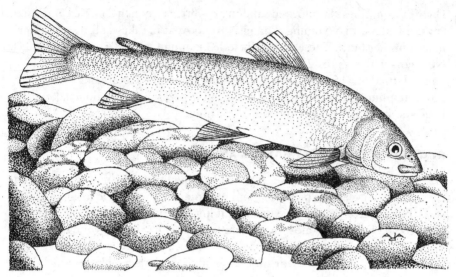

Mountain whitefish

MOUNTAIN WHITEFISH (PROSOPIUM WILLIAMSONI)

General description: This silvery-sided fish has a grayish blue to green top and a white belly. Its small pointed mouth also helps to identify this species.

Distribution: Mountain whitefish are native to Canada and the northwestern United States, as well as Colorado, Montana, and Wyoming. Some Wyoming rivers that hold mountain whitefish include the Tongue River (site 38), (Lower) Clark's Fork (site 64), Snake River (site 104), Salt River (sites 106 and 107), and the Green River (site 108).

Points to ponder: Many of the same techniques that catch trout will work on the mountain whitefish. Although whitefish are present in the same waters as trout, they are not as sought after by anglers and therefore not heavily harvested. These fish spawn in the late fall, predominantly in lakes.

WALLEYE (STIZOSTEDION VITREUM)

General description: This brassy-colored, white-bellied fish has large canine teeth and a silvery eye. Another unique feature of this fish is its double dorsal fin with the front one usually holding 13 to 14 spines. Other helpful identification marks include white markings on the lower tail and anal fins, and black membranes on the last few spines of the first dorsal fin.

Distribution: The walleye is native to southern Canada and the northern United States, ranging from the Dakotas east to the Atlantic Coast and south to Alabama and Georgia. These highly esteemed game fish are found in many of Wyoming's reservoirs, including Keyhole Reservoir (site 3), Boysen Reservoir (site 73), Grayrocks Reservoir (site 180), Seminoe Reservoir (site 181), and Glendo Reservoir (site 189).

Points to ponder: Walleye can get up to 18 pounds or more, so heavier equipment should be considered. Minnows are commonly used as bait. However, be sure to check current regulations for the area you fish; there are some restrictions on the species of minnows that may be used. Jigs perform exceptionally well when "popped" along the bottom while drifting. Walleye seem to prefer gravel stream beds for spawning, though they will also use rocky lake beds. They spawn early in the spring as the ice begins to melt off.

SAUGER (STIZOSTEDION CANADENSE)

General description: This fish is very similar to the walleye but has some distinct differences. The olive-gray coloring is contrasted with brassy to orange sides splattered with dark mottling. Unlike the walleye, it has rows of black half-moons on the first dorsal fin. The white markings found on the tail and anal fin of the walleye are absent.

Distribution: Sauger are native to southern Canada and the eastern United States, but range as far south as Arkansas and west to Montana and Wyoming. In Wyoming, these fish are located almost exclusively in Big Horn Lake (site 50) and the Big Horn River (site 51).

Points to ponder: Sauger will migrate into rocky streams or backwaters to spawn. Adult fish will seek out shallow water to deposit their eggs when water temperatures reach 40 to 50 degrees F.

NORTHERN PIKE (ESOX LUCIUS)

General description: This elongated fish looks like someone grabbed it by the mouth and tail and then yanked, almost pulling it apart. A pike's mouth looks

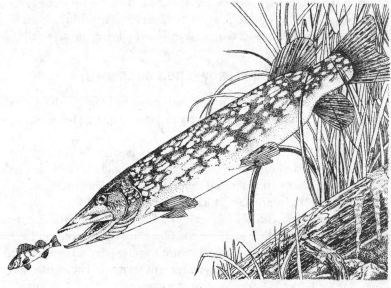

Northern pike

like a duck beak and is full of very sharp teeth giving it the nickname "toothy." Both the dorsal and anal fins are found toward the back of the body, adding to the stretched-out appearance. Pale blotches dot the greater part of the sides and there are stripes across the back on an olive background.

Distribution: Northern pike are native to both North America and parts of Eurasia. The only place pike are found in Wyoming is in Keyhole Reservoir (site #3).

Points to ponder: This fish likes weedy, warm to cool waters and spawns in the early spring shortly after ice melt. Pike are aggressive predators and will feed on fish, crayfish, frogs, and even ducklings. Females tend to be larger than the male northerns, reaching over 20 pounds. Shore anglers catch the majority of fish with bait, such as nightcrawlers and bacon rinds. Some lures are effective but difficult to use in the weedy areas where the larger fish are found. Pike have a reputation for being an ambush or attack-oriented feeder. This particular feature provides some explosive angling action.

TIGER MUSKY

General description: The tiger musky is a pike-muskellunge hybrid that is often mistakenly referred to as a northern pike. Tiger Muskies have a duckbill mouth and long body that are similar in appearance to the pike. Differences in coloration separates the two. Unlike pike, tiger muskies have dark bars on a lighter background. The males are sterile so stocking is required to maintain population levels. These fish, like the pike, are aggressive feeders and tend to grow quite rapidly.

Distribution: Since tiger muskies are hybrids there is no native area for them. These fish are primarily located in the southern portion of Wyoming. The future may find them in more waters, but for now tiger muskies are located in LAK Reservoir (site 4) and Grayrocks Reservoir (site 180).

Points to ponder: These fish are aggressive and grow quite rapidly.

SMALLMOUTH BASS (MICROPTERUS DOLOMIEU)

General description: Commonly greenish brown or olive with white along their lower portion. The mouth is relatively large with a large head and sharp, spiny segments on the dorsal fin.

Distribution: Smallmouth bass are native to eastern South Dakota, south to the Ozarks, east to north Georgia, and north to include the Great Lake States. In Wyoming, these fish are found in Keyhole Reservoir (site 3), Flaming Gorge Reservoir (site 121), and Grayrocks Reservoir (site 180).

Points to ponder: Artificial lures and/or live bait with spinning, baitcasting, and even fly rods and reels, are used. There are restrictions on the use of live minnows as bait in Wyoming, so be sure to research current regulations. Live worms are a popular bait for younger fisherman. These fish spawn when

Smallmouth bass

water temperatures are around 60 degrees F. Spawning times will vary with elevation and other factors. The smallmouth bass will seek cover, but can be found in shallower water when spawning.

LARGEMOUTH BASS (MICROPTERUS SALMOIDES)

General description: The usual color for this species is green with a bronze tint. A noticeable dark lateral band helps to identify this fish as well. They have a large mouth and head. As with the smallmouth bass, watch out for the spiny dorsal fin.

Distribution: Largemouth bass are native to southern Canada, from the Great Lakes area south to southeastern Mexico and east to Florida. The Wyoming Game and Fish Department trades trout eggs for bass from surrounding states with warm water fisheries, when stocking is authorized, to maintain or establish a population level at selected sites. Largemouth bass are restricted to the warmer waters found in some larger lakes and in farm ponds at lower elevations. Renner Reservoir (site 29), near Ten Sleep, is a hotspot for this species. These fish are also found in Boysen Reservoir (site 73), Hawk Springs Reservoir (site 177), and Grayrocks Reservoir (site 180).

Points to ponder: Spinning, baitcasting, and even fly rods and reels are used with artificial lures and/or live bait. The type of lure used depends on the kinds

Largemouth bass

of aquatic weeds present. Bright sunlight seems to drive the fish into darker or shaded areas. Shortly before sunset or just after sunrise are excellent times to work the shallows among the weeds. Spawning is similar to the smallmouth bass.

YELLOW PERCH (PERCA FLAVESCENS)

General description: This yellow or pale green fish has some dark vertical bands and orange or reddish pelvic fins. The moderately large mouth holds plenty of teeth, though they are not as large as the canine teeth of the walleye. Watch out for the spines.

Distribution: Yellow perch are native to parts of Canada, the eastern United States, and the upper Midwest south to Missouri. In Wyoming, this species has been stocked in many lakes and some streams, generally at lower elevations. Some of the waters include the Keyhole Reservoir (site 3), Boysen Reservoir (site 73), Ocean Lake (site 75), and Grayrocks Reservoir (site 180).

Points to ponder: These fish feed in schools, which creates a feast or famine for anglers. Bright jigs and spinner baits work well, as do worms and live minnows. Be sure to check the regulations concerning minnows. Spawning usually occurs in May and June in shallow water. During daylight hours, these fish are more likely to be found in deeper, shady waters.

BLACK CRAPPIE (POMOXIS NIGROMACULATUS)

General description: The large mouth on this mottled black, white, and olive colored fish is upturned in a sort of "pouting" fashion. Watch out for the spines on the dorsal fin.

Distribution: Black crappie are native to eastern Canada and most of the eastern United States. In Wyoming, this species is more likely to be found in rocky-bottom lakes at lower elevations, on the east side of the Continental Divide. These waters include Boysen Reservoir (site 73), Ocean Lake (site 75), Grayrocks Reservoir (site 180), and Glendo Reservoir (site 189).

Points to ponder: Light to ultralight rods are adequate to catch this popular game fish. A variety of baits and lures are effective, including minnows and artificial flies. Spawning occurs in May or June. Crappies are noted for being hungry all the time.

WHITE CRAPPIE (POMOXIS ANNULARIS)

General description: The dark olive color on top graduates to a silver on the sides that ends at a white belly. Some very distinct vertical bars are found on the sides as well. The white crappie does not have as many dorsal spines as the black crappie.

Distribution: White crappie are native to eastern South Dakota, east to the Great Lake States, and south to Texas. In Wyoming, this less popular, smaller fish has been stocked in lower elevation lakes and streams. Some of these waters include Keyhole Reservoir (site 3), Hawk Springs Reservoir (site 177), Grayrocks Reservoir (site 180), and Glendo Reservoir (site 189).

Points to ponder: The same methods and equipment used for black crappie work for white crappie as well.

CHANNEL CATFISH (ICTALURUS PUNCTATUS)

General description: This slender, scaleless fish is noted primarily for its "whiskers" or more technically, barbels. These long lateral features extend past the gill openings. The dorsal and pectoral fins have spines. The blue-gray coloring on top of the fish fades to white on the belly. Catfish prefer larger rivers and don't mind turbid waters. The Wyoming Fish and Game Department trades trout eggs for catfish from other states for stocking in Wyoming waters. Anglers in Wyoming catch catfish weighing over 20 pounds.

Distribution: Channel catfish are native to the eastern part of North America, including the prairie provinces of Canada and northern Mexico. Wyoming has catfish in several locations, including Bighorn Lake (site 50), Bighorn River (site 51), (Lower) Green River (site 110), and Flaming Gorge Reservoir (site 121).

Points to ponder: Catfish are recognized as "garbage eaters" that feed primarily on the bottom. Dead fish, nightcrawlers, and stink bait are effective for catching them. They avoid sunlight by staying in sheltered areas until night-fall, which is their feeding time.

LING OR BURBOT (LOTA LOTA)

General Description: The ling has a long eel-like body with a wide flat head containing a large mouth. A single "horn" or barbel is located in the middle of its lower jaw. The dorsal fin runs nearly the entire length of its back. This dark green fish is marbled with black blotches on top, which turn to yellow blotches on the bottom. Ling are not stocked in Wyoming. They grow up to 19 pounds.
Distribution: The ling or burbot is native to Canada and the northern United States. Ling are native to parts of northern Wyoming. They inhabit the Tongue River (site 38), Bighorn River (site 51), Boysen Reservoir (site 73), Ocean Lake (site 75), and Torrey Lake (site 80).
Points to ponder: Ling are classified as a game fish in Wyoming, but this status is not shared in other states. The colder waters that Wyoming ling inhabit are believed to produce a better tasting fish, creating the difference in classification. Ice fishing is a popular method for ling anglers, though not the only one. Night fishing is the most productive time to fish for ling.

Northeast

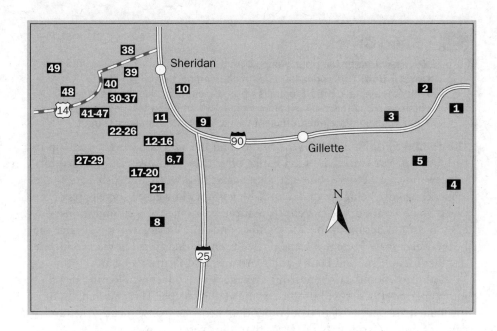

Northeast

1   Sand Creek

Key species: brown trout, rainbow trout
Description: This spring-fed stream courses north through the ponderosa pine–covered foothills of the Black Hills. High banks are common along this fairly shallow stream, which has a few deep pools.
Tips: Wading is the most efficient way to approach these wary trout.

The fishing: Fishing is open year-round, and the action starts to warm up in early May. Clear water and high banks offer these fish plenty of opportunity to view outside activity, but just about anything will catch fish here if the angler can avoid being spotted. Bait fishing is not allowed on some parts of the creek, so be aware of the current regulations. Grasshoppers or imitations generate plenty of action in the late summer and fall. Worms work well, but the heavy weed growth creates some difficulty in fishing them. Some productive dry flies include the Elk Hair Caddis, Adams, and Griffith's Gnat.

Both brown and rainbow trout average 8 to 12 inches. Floating dry flies into upper pool riffles will produce some action. A special regulation requires the immediate release of all trout other than browns. Consequently, the rarely-caught rainbow trout may be larger than the average brown.

Lightweight fly fishing gear is the easiest to use, especially with longer rods. If you choose bait fishing, one of the most productive methods is to drop your worm or grasshopper into the ripples and let it drift into a downstream pool. The pool should be far enough away for you to avoid being seen by your quarry.

Additional information: Primitive camping and outdoor restrooms are available on a first-come, first-served basis. There is some private land with no public access along the creek. Be alert for the posted areas and respect the wishes of the owners.

Contact: Wyoming Game and Fish Department, Sheridan.

1A. Ox Yoke Ranch

Description: Sand Creek meanders through the canyon floor on ranch property. Parking areas for fishing access only are clearly marked.
Directions: Take exit 205, the Ranch A exit, off I-90 just west of the South Dakota border. Follow the well-maintained gravel Sand Creek Road/FR 863 to the access sites, about 3 miles south.

1B. Wyoming State Land

Description: Parking areas are clearly marked along the road. There are about 2 miles of creek here with designated camping spots available.
Directions: The Ox Yoke Ranch borders state land.

1 Sand Creek

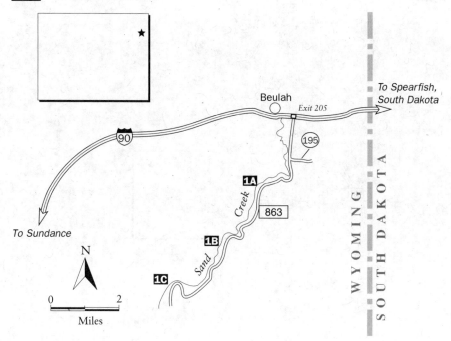

To Spearfish, South Dakota

Beulah

Exit 205

195

90

To Sundance

863

1A

1B

1C

N

Sand Creek

WYOMING | SOUTH DAKOTA

0   2
Miles

1C. Ranch A

Description: Ranch A is a former state fish hatchery in the process of changing hands within government agencies. Though no longer a hatchery, the change should not affect public access.

Directions: Take exit 205, the Ranch A exit, off I-90 just west of the South Dakota border. Drive south on Sand Creek Road/FR 863 about 6 miles.

2 Cook Lake

Key species: brown trout, rainbow trout

Description: Ponderosa pines and aspens cover the hills overlooking 30-acre Cook Lake, in the beautiful Bear Lodge Mountains north of Sundance. A 1-mile nature trail circles the lake. The Cliff Swallow Trail offers 3.5 miles of backcountry exploration.

Tips: Trout are usually in the deep water, at the drop-offs along the cliffs.

The fishing: Brown trout average 8 to 10 inches. Mepps spinners and an assortment of spoons work well in the shallow gravel-bottomed portions of the lake when these fish start spawning in late fall. Rainbow trout averaging 8 to 12 inches are stocked to outnumber the browns. Worms are the most commonly used bait when fishing from shore. Small spinners can be effective, although they don't produce as many trout. Fly fishers find that grasshopper imitations can create some explosive action later in the summer.

2 Cook Lake

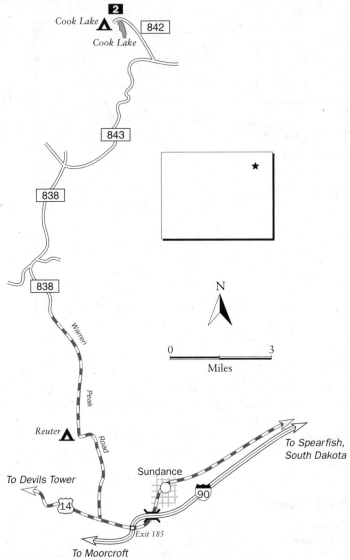

Directions: From Sundance, take I-90 to exit 185. Head west on US 14 and turn right onto Warren Peak Road/FR 838. After 7 miles, FR 838 becomes gravel near the Warren Peak Lookout. Continue on FR 838 about 5 more miles—a total of 13 miles from US 14. Turn right onto FR 843 and drive about 6 miles. Turn left onto FR 842 and drive 1 mile to Cook Lake.

Additional information: Motors are not allowed on Cook Lake. The Cook Lake Campground is a fee area with 34 units and a day use parking area open year-round; see Appendix A for campground reservations phone number.

Contact: Wyoming Game and Fish Department, Sheridan.

3 Keyhole Reservoir

Key species: catfish, northern pike, smallmouth bass, walleye, yellow perch
Description: The Keyhole Reservoir contains 7,500 surface acres of water along the edge of pine-covered hills; its backwaters stretch southwest into the Wyoming prairie.
Tips: Shore fishing for pike with worms is especially effective just after snowmelt, generally in late May or early June.

The fishing: This is the only place in Wyoming that offers northern pike. All northern pike less than 30 inches must be released. Both pike and walleye are stocked. Pike up to 15 pounds are most commonly caught from boat or shore in the shallower bays in the early spring. Shore anglers do well with worms and bacon rinds. Large Rapalas and other crankbaits work well when trolled near the weed beds along shore. Walleye average 12 to 20 inches and minnows are most effective with these fish. Try jigging the bottom.

Catfish weigh up to several pounds. Stink baits, worms, and sucker meat all work. Night fishing in the heat of the summer offers the greatest success. Smallmouth bass range from 8 to 16 inches. These feisty fish hang out in the rocks along the north shore. Spinner baits, jigs, and crayfish imitations develop plenty of activity. Yellow perch range from 3 to 9 inches, and just about anything will make these fish attack. Perch can be difficult to find; look in the shallower bays. Special regulations for ice fishing allow anglers to use up to 6 lines within certain guidelines. Check with state park officials.

Additional information: Keyhole State Park has boat ramps, camping, toilets, a motel, a restaurant, and a marina. Fee booths located at the entrances require payment ($2 to $4) for day use as well as overnight camping.

Contact: Keyhole State Park.

3A. Arch Rock Area

Description: This camping area at the upper end of Cottonwood Bay has tables and toilets.

Directions: Take I-90 west of Sundance for 20 miles to Exit 165, the Keyhole State Park exit. Drive north along Pine Ridge Road for 7 miles. Turn left and go through the park fee booth, then continue about 0.25 mile.

3B. Pronghorn Area

Description: This camping area at the lower end of Cottonwood Bay has tables, drinking water, toilets and a playground.

Directions: Follow the directions to the Arch Rock Area, site 3A. After passing through the fee booth, continue about 1.5 miles, staying to the right at the fork in the road.

3 Keyhole Reservoir

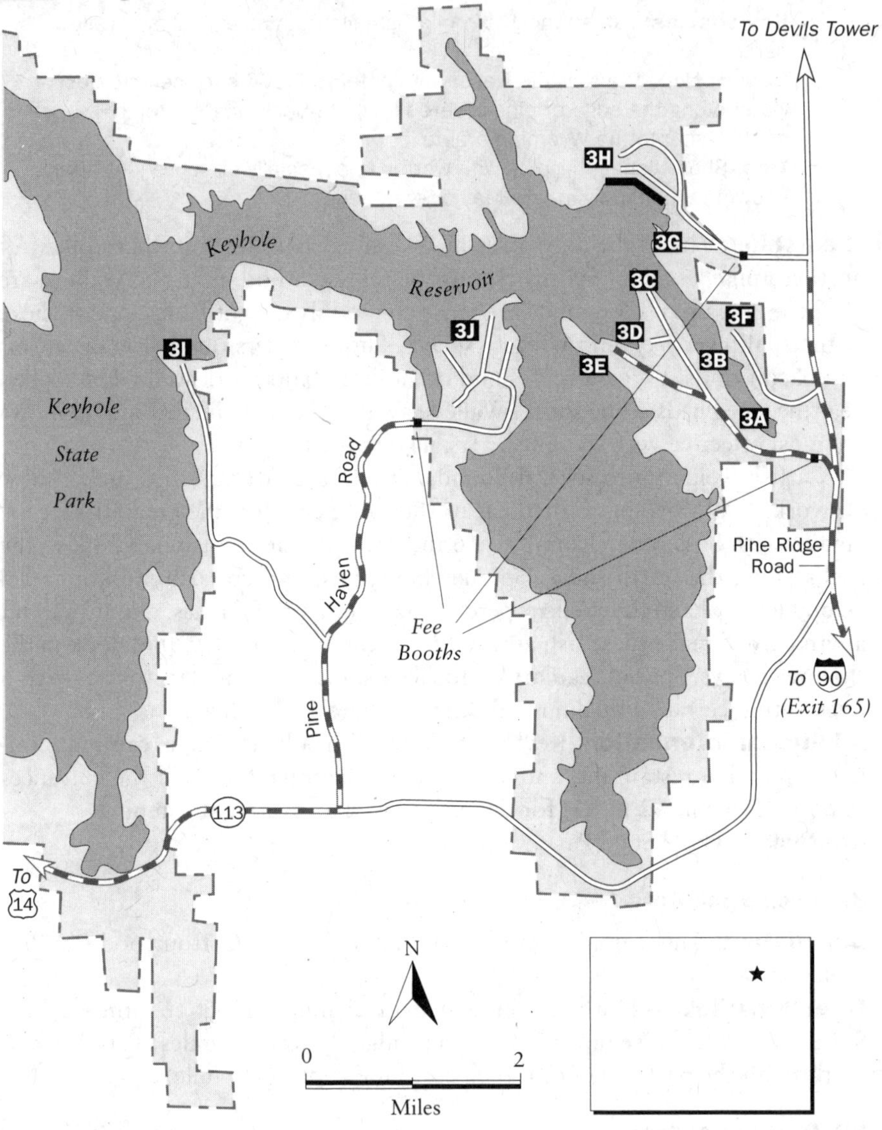

To Devils Tower
3H
3G
3C
3F
3D
3B
3E
3A
3J
3I
Keyhole
Reservoir
Keyhole
State
Park
Road
Haven
Pine
Fee
Booths
Pine Ridge
Road
To 90
(Exit 165)
113
To
14
N
0
2
Miles

3C. Beach Area

Description: This day use area has drinking water, tables, and toilets.
Directions: Follow the directions to the Arch Rock Area, site 3A. After passing through the fee booth, continue about 1.75 miles, staying to the right at the forks in the road.

3D. Keyhole Marina

Description: Along with a paved boat ramp, the marina offers camping, boat rentals, beverages, fishing equipment, fishing licenses, and a telephone.

Directions: Follow the directions to the Arch Rock Area, site 3A. After going through the fee booth, continue about 2 miles, staying to the right at the fork in the road.

3E. Pat's Point

Description: This camping area has drinking water, tables, group picnic shelters, a playground, and a boat ramp.
Directions: Follow the directions to the Arch Rock Area, site 3A. After passing through the fee booth, continue about 1 mile and turn left. Drive about 1 mile.

3F. Homestead Area

Description: This camping area has drinking water, tables, and toilets.
Directions: Take I-90 west of Sundance for 20 miles to Exit 165, the Keyhole State Park exit. Drive north along Pine Ridge Road for about 7.5 miles. Turn left onto the gravel road marked by a sign to the Homestead Access, and drive about 0.75 mile.

3G. Cottonwood Area

Description: This camping area on the north side of Cottonwood Bay has tables, group picnic shelters, toilets, and a playground.
Directions: Take I-90 west of Sundance for 20 miles to Exit 165, the Keyhole State Park exit. Drive north along Pine Ridge Road, about 8 miles. Turn left, go through the fee booth, and continue about 1.25 miles.

3H. Rocky Point

Description: This camping area is near the dam and has drinking water, tables, toilets, and a boat ramp.
Directions: Follow the directions to the Cottonwood Area, site 3G. After going through the fee booth, continue about 1.5 miles.

3I. Wind Creek Area

Description: This camping area has tables, toilets, and a boat ramp.
Directions: From Moorcroft, head east on US 14 for 6 miles to Wyoming 113. Turn right and drive 5 miles east to the Pine Haven turnoff. Turn left and drive 1.5 miles to the Wind Creek turnoff. Turn left onto this gravel road and drive 1.5 miles.

3J. Coulter Bay Area

Description: This camping area has tables, group picnic shelters, toilets, and a boat ramp. Hamburgers are available at the Pine Haven Bar and Grill along with groceries and fishing necessities.
Directions: From Moorcroft, head east on US 14 for 6 miles to Pine Haven Road/Wyoming 113. Turn right and drive 5 miles east to the Pine Haven turnoff. Turn left and drive about 2 miles to Pine Haven. Turn right at the Coulter Bay sign and drive 0.5 mile to the fee booth.

4 LAK Reservoir

Key species: rainbow trout, brown trout, largemouth bass, smallmouth bass, sunfish, tiger musky

Description: This 100-acre reservoir holds water from Stockade Beaver Creek, which flows out of the Black Hills. The narrow canyon has steep cliffs on the west side and scattered pine trees. Rolling, rocky ridges with plenty of sagebrush dominate the east side.

Tips: The deep water along the southwest corner is the most productive for rainbows.

The fishing: Tiger muskies and walleye were stocked here in the spring of 1996. The abundant sunfish will feed them well and should create some very nice-sized fish in the future. The walleye will probably dominate the reservoir in time. Rainbow and brown trout average 12 to 14 inches. Bottom-fishing nightcrawlers is the most productive method when you fish from shore. Trolling can be effective in the deeper waters; use cowbells and spinners with worms attached. A few large brown trout are caught here, usually late in the fall, but they are not very abundant. Largemouth and smallmouth bass can reach lengths of 15 inches.

Directions: Take US 16 east out of Newcastle about 5 miles. Turn left at the historical marker. County Road 5 is accessed from the historical marker, where the pullout is on the north side of the highway. The otherwise unmarked CR 5 starts at the west end of this pullout. Follow this gravel road for 1 mile.

Additional information: A concrete boat ramp is available. Overnight camping is not allowed. LAK Reservoir is on private land, so fishing here requires

The 100-acre LAK Reservoir was formed by damming Stockade Beaver Creek.

4, 5 LAK Reservoir, Turner Reservoir

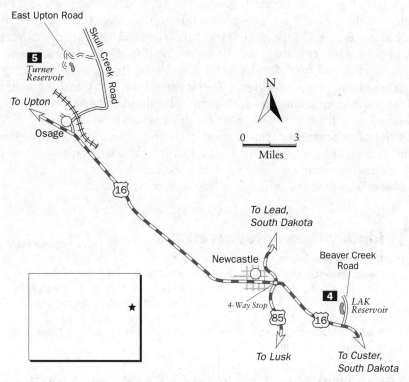

written permission from the landowner. This permit is available from Crums Department Store in Newcastle. The store is not open on Sundays or certain holidays, so make advance arrangements. You must have the permit before accessing the property.

Contact: Newcastle Chamber of Commerce.

5 Turner Reservoir

Key species: rainbow trout, largemouth bass

Description: This deep, 8-acre, manmade lake is blessed with an abundance of dead trees in the water and has some cattails scattered along the shallower areas. The wind here can be a concern, so be aware of weather conditions.

Tips: Look for the deep, shaded holes on either bank.

The fishing: Rainbow trout, averaging 10 inches, are stocked annually. Early morning or late evening, the trout tend to feast on the abundant insects. During the brighter part of the day, feeding activity moves toward the bottom. There are plenty of snags, however. Use bright, colorful spinners at the end of the day.

Directions: From Newcastle, take US 16 west for 12 miles to Osage. The Black Hills Power and Light Plant is on the north side of the highway. Continue past the power plant, about 0.25 mile, to the Osage turnoff. Turn right and drive 0.8 mile. Turn right onto a gravel road, which will cross two railroad tracks. After crossing, you will see the Skull Creek Road sign. Continue north on this road for 5.5 miles to the East Upton Road. Turn left onto this gravel road and travel 1.6 miles. The first part of the East Upton Road drops off the rim in a single lane that can become difficult driving when wet. Visibility is limited, so drive slowly and watch for other vehicles.

Additional information: This is a small lake that you can walk around with a little effort. Use the makeshift boat ramp at your own risk; the size of the lake makes launching a boat of any size questionable.

Contact: Wyoming Game and Fish Department, Sheridan.

6 Muddy Guard Reservoir 2

See map on page 31

Key species: brown trout, rainbow trout
Description: The Bighorn Mountains stand to the west of the grassy foothills around the lake. This manmade lake extends up to 36 surface acres, depending on the rainfall. Small sandstone cliffs dot the steep gumbo ridges.
Tips: Early morning and late evening are the most productive times, especially in the fall.

The fishing: Brown trout range from 8 to 12 inches, with a few exceeding 5 pounds. These trout tend to stay in deep water until late August. Spoons and spinners attract their attention when they move into the rocky shallows to spawn. Rainbow trout usually range from 8 to 12 inches.

Directions: From Buffalo, take WY 196 south about 12 miles. Turn right onto gravel Crazy Woman Canyon Road and drive 1.2 miles. Bear left onto Muddy Creek Road and drive 1.5 miles. Pass a large "No Trespassing" sign along the main road and a public access sign in the field to the right. Turn right onto the gravel public access road and travel 1 mile.

Additional information: Boats with less than 15 horsepower are allowed on this reservoir, but there is no boat ramp.

7 Muddy Guard Reservoir 1

See map on page 31

Key species: brown trout, rainbow trout
Description: Steep gumbo ridges enclose this 17-acre reservoir in grassy, windswept country with a limited view of the Bighorn Mountains.
Tips: Silver and gold spinners do well here and can be used on a windy day, of which there are plenty.

The fishing: Both brown and rainbow trout range from 15 to 22 inches here, but there is currently a limit of two fish if they are 18 inches or longer. You

An outhhouse sits beneath a bluff at the Muddy Guard Reservoir 2 parking area.

Muddy Guard Reservoir 2 is a 36-acre manmade lake east of the Bighorn Mountains.

must release any fish shorter than 18 inches, and only artificial flies or lures are allowed. Fly fishers will find that Hornbergs and Muddler Minnows are effective in the darker parts of the day, in the early morning or just before sundown. The wind can be a major problem, so bring a spinning rod with an assortment of spinners and spoons.

Directions: From Buffalo, take WY 196 south about 12 miles. Turn right onto gravel Crazy Woman Canyon Road and drive 4.5 miles. The road crosses Crazy Woman Creek after about 3.8 miles, and then climbs a steep hill. At the top of this hill you should be at the 4.5-mile point. Turn left onto the gravel access road and travel about 1 mile to the edge of the ridge overlooking the reservoir. The reservoir is about 1 mile downhill.

Additional information: Only boats with motors with less than 15 horsepower are allowed on this reservoir. Although there is no boat ramp, launching is easier here than at Muddy Guard Reservoir 2 because the banks are not as steep.

Contact: Wyoming Game and Fish Department, Sheridan.

8 Middle Fork Powder River

Key species: brown trout, rainbow trout
Description: This clear mountain river is 20 feet wide in places. Limestone cliffs on each side of the canyon flank multiple pools and

Muddy Guard Reservoir 2, Muddy Guard Reservoir 1, Middle Fork Powder River

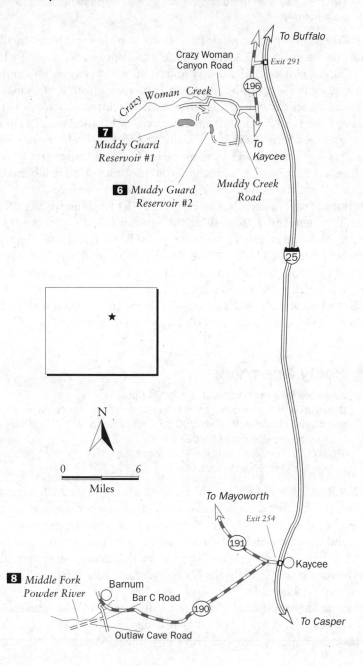

To Buffalo

Crazy Woman Canyon Road

Exit 291

196

Crazy Woman Creek

7
Muddy Guard Reservoir #1

To Kaycee

6 *Muddy Guard Reservoir #2*

Muddy Creek Road

I-25

N

0 — 6
Miles

To Mayoworth

Exit 254

191

Kaycee

8 *Middle Fork Powder River*

Barnum

Bar C Road

190

Outlaw Cave Road

To Casper

31

gentle stairstep rapids from the mountains to the desert prairie below. This area is steeped in history; Outlaw Cave once offered Butch Cassidy and other colorful characters a hiding place.

Tips: Be prepared to do some wading. A pair of tennis shoes is helpful on a hot day.

The fishing: Brown trout range from 10 to 16 inches and occasionally reach 5 pounds in the fall. Small Mepps spinners and spoons work well when fished deep. Caddis, mayfly, and stonefly imitations give better results in the shaded areas or early in the morning. Rainbow trout range from 8 to 16 inches. These trout outnumber the more wary browns. Early spring provides the fastest action, but poor road conditions can limit access. Floating dry flies in the riffles above any one of the many pools is the best way to find action. Grasshopper imitations work the best in late summer. There is a daily limit of 6 trout, of which only 1 may be over 16 inches. You must release all fish between 10 and 16 inches long, and you may use only artificial flies or lures.

Directions: From Kaycee, head west on WY 191 for 1 mile to WY 190/Barnum Road. Turn left and follow WY 190/Barnum Road for about ·15 miles to Barnum. At Barnum turn left onto the gravel Bar C Road and go 6 miles to the interpretive sign. At Outlaw Cave Road turn right. There are several access points as the road parallels the river/stream. The 800-foot climb down to the river from the canyon rim is steep.

Additional information: Camping and picnic areas with toilets are available.

Contact: Wyoming Game and Fish Department, Sheridan.

9 Healy Reservoir

See map on page 35

Key species: rainbow trout, cutthroat trout

Description: Badland ridges northeast of Buffalo conceal this small, manmade reservoir. It holds 200 surface acres of water, and some fluctuation results in muddy beaches.

Tips: Fly fishers are likely to catch some large fish by using streamers in late September and October.

The fishing: Rainbow and cutthroat trout average 10 to 18 inches. This is a popular spot for fly fishers, especially in late summer. Wading along the shoreline can be refreshing while you tempt big trout with large streamers. Early in spring and through summer, bottom fishing with nightcrawlers and Power Bait seems to be the most productive. The wind makes heavy fishing gear a necessity.

Directions: From Buffalo, take US 16 east for 5 miles. Healy Reservoir is on the left side of the road.

Additional information: A private family trust owns this reservoir, which allows public access but no boats or floating.

Contact: Wyoming Game and Fish Department, Sheridan.

10 Lake DeSmet

See map on page 35

Key species: rainbow trout, crappie

Description: You will see this large, treeless, prairie reservoir from I-90 long before you arrive. The scenic backdrop of the Bighorn Mountains adds to the appeal.

Tips: Power Bait can be very effective from the shore at either end of the lake in April and May.

The fishing: Rainbow trout average 12 to 20 inches. Early in spring, shore fishing with a variety of baits is productive on the south dam. Power Bait and worms commonly produce fish. A "No Trespassing" sign is on the fence along the dam, but the landowner has allowed fishing as long as the anglers stay in the dam area along the water. Another favorite spot for shore fishing is on the north end of the reservoir. Trollers consistently take the largest number of fish. You can find the most action along the drop-offs in deep water by pulling cowbells in front of a large, colorful streamer. Special regulations allow four trout per day or four in possession, and only one may be over 15 inches.

Crappies range from 6 to 8 inches. They were stocked in the past, and you can still find them in the shallower bays if the trout are uninterested in anything you offer. Worms and jigs are productive anytime you can find these fish.

Additional information: The Lake Stop Resort and Marina has camping, RV parking, cabins, groceries, a cafe, boat repair, sales, and rentals. Some of the access sites have toilets.

Contact: Wyoming Game and Fish Department, Sheridan.

10A. South Dam

Description: The Lake Stop Resort and Marina is located along the route to the dam. The earthen dam is a driveway for local residents, so park accordingly.

Directions: From Buffalo, take I-90 west 5 miles to exit 51, the Lake DeSmet exit. Take Monument Road for 1 mile and bear left to Lake DeSmet Road. Turn right onto this paved road and drive past the store to the dam and boat ramp access 2.5 miles away.

10B. Monument Access

Description: You can launch boats here along the sloping shoreline, when the water level and weather conditions are right.

Directions: From Buffalo, take I-90 west for 9 miles to exit 47, the Shell Creek Road exit. Drive east 1.5 miles on the gravel Shell Creek Road. Proceed carefully past the stop sign, as vision is limited. Follow the dirt track down the hill to your left after crossing the cattle guard. If it is wet, don't try it.

10C. Piney Creek Access

Description: This dam is at the inlet of the reservoir. It has adequate parking and foot access, but no boat ramp.

Directions: From Buffalo, take I-90 west 12 miles to exit 44, the Piney Creek Road exit. After exiting, turn right onto gravel Lower Piney Creek Road and drive 0.6 mile to the Lake DeSmet access.

⑪ North and South Fork Sayles Creek Ponds

Key species: brook trout, rainbow trout

Description: Willows and cottonwoods line the creek while pine and fir trees dominate the higher country.

Tips: In the early spring, both the rainbow trout and the mosquitoes will bite anything.

The fishing: These five manmade ponds are stocked yearly with trout averaging 6 to 10 inches. Worms work fairly well during the day until late summer. Dry flies are productive in the early morning or late evening with a little more success in the heat of the summer. Grasshoppers and their imitations improve chances in late fall. Brook trout range from 6 to 8 inches. Worms work well in the spring, and grasshoppers are even more productive when available.

Directions: Follow US 16 west in Buffalo to Fort Street in the central-west portion of the town. Look for the Bud Love Wildlife Habitat Management Area sign on the north side of Fort Street and follow directions. The Bud Love Wildlife Habitat Management Area is northwest of Buffalo on a paved road that becomes improved dirt road.

Additional information: Both North and South Fork Sayles Creek flow through the Bud Love Wildlife Habitat Management Area and is closed from November 16 to April 30. Camping is available in the management area, which has three parking areas.

Contact: Wyoming Game and Fish Department, Sheridan.

⑫ North Fork Clear Creek

Key species: brook trout, rainbow trout

Description: The water in this mountain creek can be ice cold all year. Lodgepole pine and aspen surround it and provide cool shade on hot summer days. Large boulders are strewn along the bottom and sides of the creek.

Tips: Look for the cutbanks and hidden holes under rocks or logs.

The fishing: Brook trout are well represented in the upper parts of this creek. They average 4 to 8 inches and seem to always be hungry. Rainbow trout are found farther downstream and range from 8 to 10 inches. Worms and grasshoppers are productive for rainbow. Fly fishing can also create some action.

9–21 Healy Reservoir, Lake Desmet, North and South Fork Sayles Creek Ponds, North Fork Clear Creek, Middle Fork Clear Creek, Sherd Lake, Willow Lake, South Fork Clear Creek, North Fork Crazy Woman Creek, North Fork Powder River, Doyle Creek, Dull Knife Reservoir, Beartrap Creek

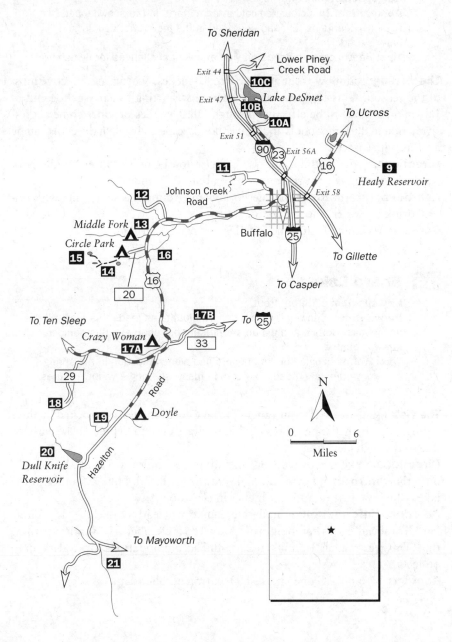

To Sheridan

Lower Piney
Creek Road

Exit 44

10C

Exit 47
10B *Lake DeSmet*

10A

To Ucross

Exit 51

90 **23** *Exit 56A*

11

16

9

Healy Reservoir

12

Johnson Creek
Road

Exit 58

Middle Fork **13**

Circle Park

15

14

16

Buffalo

25

To Gillette

16

20

To Casper

17B To **25**

To Ten Sleep

Crazy Woman **17A**

33

29

18

19 *Doyle*

Road

N

0   6
Miles

20

*Dull Knife
Reservoir*

Hazelton

To Mayoworth

★

21

Directions: Take US 16 west out of Buffalo for 13 miles. Turn right onto FR 19 and travel 1.5 miles to the North Fork Picnic Ground.
Additional information: A picnic area is available.
Contact: Wyoming Game and Fish Department, Sheridan.

13 Middle Fork Clear Creek

See map on page 35

Key species: rainbow trout
Description: This clear, ice-cold stream starts in the snowcapped Bighorn Mountains. Elk and deer feed in the meadows, usually just before sundown.
Tips: Beaver-created ponds provide excellent challenges for fly fishers.

The fishing: Rainbow trout average 8 to 10 inches. Worms are effective most of the season. Grasshoppers top the menu list starting as early as the end of July and continue to be effective through fall. Dry flies produce some aggressive action in the larger pools and beaver ponds, especially when the cool evening air fills with insects.
Directions: From Buffalo, take US 16 west for 14 miles to the Middle Fork Campground sign. Turn right and drive about 0.25 mile.
Additional information: Middle Fork Campground has nine units with toilets, drinking water, and spaces for trailers.
Contact: Wyoming Game and Fish Department, Sheridan.

14 Sherd Lake

See map on page 35

Key species: cutthroat trout
Description: Snowmelt in the Bighorn Mountains feeds this 4-acre alpine lake. Spruce and aspen are present but sparse in this boulder-strewn country.
Tips: Worms dangled under bobbers find plenty of action in the spring and early summer. These trout can be fussy, so bring a variety of lures, flies, and bait.

The fishing: Cutthroat trout ranging from 6 to 14 inches are stocked in alternating years by helicopter. Fishing doesn't start until mid-June at the earliest, due to the high elevation.
Directions: Take US 16 west out of Buffalo, 15 miles to FR 20. Turn right onto this dirt road and drive 2.5 miles to the trailhead. Hike 1.5 miles to the lake, which is close to 500 feet higher in elevation.
Additional information: A moderate, 1-mile trail leads to the lake. The Circle Park Trailhead offers camping from May 15 to October 31, weather permitting. This fee area has 10 units, toilets, and accommodations for trailers up to 16 feet.
Contact: Wyoming Game and Fish Department, Sheridan.

15 Willow Lake

See map on page 35

Key species: grayling, splake

Description: The trees are sparse in this rocky mountain country. Over 9,000 feet, the air can get a little thin and cold, even on a summer day. Depending on the time of year, vibrant wildflowers add color to the ground in the harsh terrain surrounding these 10 surface acres of melted ice.

Tips: Try small, standard dry flies just before the sun goes down.

The fishing: Grayling average 7 to 12 inches. These teaser fish tend to strike at artificial flies and run to deep water without taking the hook.

Directions: Take US 16 west out of Buffalo, 15 miles to FR 20. Turn right onto the dirt road and drive 2.5 miles to the trailhead. Hike the mildly difficult trail past Sherd Lake, about 2.5 miles, to the Willow Lake Trail, which is near Rainy Lake. Follow this difficult trail to the right about 1 mile. The elevation gain from the parking area at Circle Park is about 1,000 feet.

Additional information: Willow Lake is in the Cloud Peak Wilderness, where no motors or mountain bikes are allowed. If you want to fish until dark, plan to stay overnight.

Contact: Wyoming Game and Fish Department, Sheridan.

16 South Fork Clear Creek

See map on page 35

Key species: brook trout, brown trout, rainbow trout

Description: This clear, cold stream cuts through some steep, forested canyons on its way north.

Tips: Look for the eddies where the large boulders break the current.

The fishing: Brook trout average 3 to 8 inches and dominate the upper creek. Worms are the most effective bait, but small spinners also produce some response. Rainbow trout average 6 to 10 inches. They have an appetite for worms, but fly fishing is the most popular method. Wet flies and worms produce rainbow trout effectively in the spring. The less numerous browns can get up to 12 inches and prefer the clear pools. Small streamers and grasshopper imitations work well from late August through September.

Directions: Take US 16 west out of Buffalo, 15 miles to the South Fork Campground.

Additional information: The South Fork Campground offers 18 camping units, drinking water, toilets, and trailer accommodations.

Contact: Wyoming Game and Fish Department, Sheridan.

17 North Fork Crazy Woman Creek

See map on page 35

Key species: brook trout

Description: Lodgepole pine, spruce, and aspen line both banks of this crystal-clear snowmelt that crashes through Crazy Woman Canyon. The creek can be 5 feet wide and equally deep. Entire cliff walls have

Use care when fishing in Crazy Woman Canyon. The rocks are sharp and the current is fast.

tumbled down into the canyon bottom. The creek winds its way through this rubble, disappearing here and there and creating pools.
Tips: Look for hidden undercuts under the boulders.

The fishing: Brook trout average 4 to 8 inches. Worms are the most productive bait, although placing the worm in a promising hole may involve minor acrobatics. Take plenty of extra hooks; there are many snags. Wading is helpful but can be very dangerous on the sharp, slippery rocks along the banks. Short rods and lightweight fishing gear is the easiest to use, especially when you are moving from one spot to another.
Additional information: Camping is allowed in the canyon, but the areas fill quickly. Cars may enter the canyon, but don't attempt it if you are unfamiliar with mountain driving. It is steep, narrow, and unsuitable for trailers.
Contact: Wyoming Game and Fish Department, Sheridan.

17A. Crazy Woman Campground

Description: Crazy Woman Campground has 6 units and toilets. There are no trailer accommodations here.
Directions: Take US 16 west of Buffalo for 25 miles. The campground will be on your right.

17B. Crazy Woman Canyon

Description: The gravel road here is mostly single lane for 5 miles, with some pullouts. There are some steep grades with limited vision.
Directions: Take US 16 west of Buffalo for 25.5 miles to FR 33. Turn left on FR 33 and travel about 5 miles.

18 North Fork Powder River

See map on page 35

Key species: brown trout, rainbow trout
Description: This bubbling brook winds through alpine meadows lined with sagebrush and grass. Lodgepole pines border the upper meadows. The rocky bottom invites waders, but the creek is rarely wider than 5 feet.
Tips: Be patient; the big fish know how to position themselves to observe incoming anglers.

The fishing: Brown and rainbow trout range from 8 to 10 inches. Fresh worms are the most effective. Grasshoppers are also a favorite when available, but worms are tougher for the trout to "steal."
Directions: From Buffalo, take US 16 west about 36 miles. Turn left onto gravel FR 29 and travel 5 miles.
Additional information: There are no facilities here, but camping is allowed within certain guidelines. Most of the regulations are related to the level of fire danger. Check current conditions with the Forest Service.
Contact: Wyoming Game and Fish Department, Sheridan.

North Fork of the Powder River winds through grassy meadows.

19 Doyle Creek

See map on page 35

Key species: brook trout, brown trout
Description: This clear, lazy creek is rarely wider than 6 feet. Aspen groves are interspersed with pine and spruce forest, which line the mountain meadows. Near the campground, Doyle Creek leaves the meadow and flows directly into the forest, offering plenty of shade and log jam pools for the angler. This area's 8,000-foot elevation can make it very cold after sunset.
Tips: Find the hidden undercuts, especially near log jams.

The fishing: Brook trout average 4 to 8 inches. Worms are productive almost all season, and grasshoppers provide a lot of action. Farther away from the campground, the fish will be less spooky. Brown trout average 6 to 8 inches. Dry flies are productive but difficult in the better fishing areas. Long rods are useful in the meadows when you are trying to avoid detection.

Directions: From Buffalo, take US 16 west for 26 miles. Turn left onto FR 32/Hazelton Road/CR 3 and travel 6 miles southwest to the Doyle Campground. This road becomes gravel about 3.5 miles after leaving the highway. Turn left at the Doyle Campground sign and travel 0.25 mile.

Additional information: Doyle Campground has 18 units, toilets, and trailer spots. This fee area is open from mid-May to the end of October.

Contact: Wyoming Game and Fish Department, Sheridan.

20 Dull Knife Reservoir

See map on page 35

Key species: brown trout, rainbow trout
Description: The North Fork Powder River feeds this 38-acre, manmade reservoir. Pine, spruce, and aspen line the steep, grassy ridges. The shoreline dives steeply and has sparse grass and plenty of boulders near the access point. Numerous houses and barbed wire fences make the area somewhat unappealing, so it gets less use than nearby picturesque mountain lakes.
Tips: Worms or Power Bait work well when you are bottom-fishing in the spring.

The fishing: Brown trout average 8 to 12 inches. Worms are effective for catching these trout in the deep waters near the dam. Later in the fall, spoons give more action in the shallows. Rainbow trout average 8 to 12 inches. Worms and Power Bait attract these fish in the spring and early summer. Mepps spinners and colorful spoons take the lead when the fish move into deep water later in the season.

Directions: Take US 16 west out of Buffalo 26 miles. Turn left onto the Hazelton Road/FR 32/CR3 and travel about 10 miles to the public access parking on your right.

Additional information: Most of the lakeshore is privately owned. Launching boats is difficult, and the hike to the lake is steep. Floating devices could become a dangerous handicap on one of the many windy days.

Contact: Wyoming Game and Fish Department, Sheridan.

Doyle Creek provides a pleasant day of trout fishing.

21 Beartrap Creek

See map on page 35

Key species: brook trout

Description: This creek is just wide enough to make crossing it a wet affair. The grassy banks have been improved for better trout habitat. Spruce and lodgepole pine stand out along the distant ridgetops with a windy, grassland meadow below.

Tips: Look for the deep backwaters created when the stream surges over a log or large rock.

The fishing: Low fishing pressure in this area gives anglers an advantage. Brook trout range from 4 to 8 inches in length. Worms work well most of the season. Grasshoppers and their imitations do very well. Both dry and wet flies offer action, though no casting is required because of the creek's small size.

Directions: From Buffalo, take US 16 west 26 miles. Turn left onto the Hazelton Road/FR 32/CR3 and travel about 15 miles. Bear left at the intersection for Slip Road/Mayoworth Road/RD 67. Shortly after you cross a cattle guard, about 0.5 mile past this intersection, Beartrap Creek briefly parallels the road on the right.

Additional information: There are no services at this location. This distant creek is unlikely to be crowded.

Contact: Wyoming Game and Fish Department, Sheridan.

You'll find the brook trout in Beartrap Creek hiding in the deep backwaters.

22 East Tensleep Lake

Key species: cutthroat trout, rainbow trout
Description: Pine, spruce, and aspen trees are abundant along the route to this 45-acre mountain lake, which is near the timberline.
Tips: Worms produce well, but a selection of spinners is easier to pack in.

The fishing: Rainbow trout range from 10 to 18 inches. Early in the summer, worms produce the most action. Closer to fall, spinners and small spoons create the best action. Cutthroat range from 6 to 12 inches. The bubble-and-fly technique offers greater access on the lake surface. A clear, slender bobber or "bubble" is tied to the casting line well in front of the fly; this way an angler can cast and retrieve the fly much the same as an artificial lure. Dry flies tend to be the most effective. Glassy waters of late evening offer the best results.

Directions: Take US 16 west out of Buffalo 42 miles to FR 430. Turn right onto this four-wheel-drive trail and travel about 6 miles to the lake. After 4 or 5 miles, this trail will become extremely rough. Some drive on, but most walk or ride mountain bikes.

Additional information: Reaching this lake is difficult, requiring four-wheel-drive and some footwork. Walking may be faster. Camping is allowed, but there are no developed sites or amenities.

Contact: Wyoming Game and Fish Department, Sheridan.

23 Meadowlark Lake

Key species: brook trout, rainbow trout
Description: Lodgepole pine and spruce fill the forest around these 182 acres of icy water. The 8,000-foot elevation makes the days cool and the nights cold, even in the summer.
Tips: Early spring offers the best fishing with worms and Power Bait.

The fishing: Brook trout range from 4 to 9 inches. Worms work well when drifted into the lake from the stream inlet early in the year. As the summer warms up, these little fish become inactive. Late in August, Panther Martins and other spinners attract attention; results drop off during midday. Small mosquito and black gnat imitations work well in the evenings.

Rainbow trout average 10 to 14 inches. Bottom fishing worms, Power Bait, and salmon eggs does well near the points. Activity drops off severely during the hotter summer months. As fall cools off and mosquitoes disappear, spinners and colorful spoons produce some action in the deeper waters.

Directions: Take US 16 west out of Buffalo 43 miles to the Lakepoint Picnic Ground on FR 437. The lake will be on the south side of the highway.

Additional information: Camping, picnicking, a boat ramp, and a nearby convenience store are available. This popular area fills early, especially on weekends and holidays.

Contact: Wyoming Game and Fish Department, Sheridan.

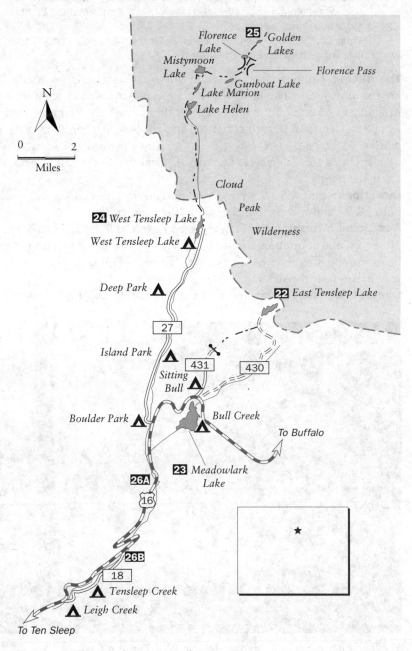

N

0   2
Miles

Florence Lake
25 Golden Lakes
Mistymoon Lake
Florence Pass
Gunboat Lake
Lake Marion
Lake Helen

Cloud Peak Wilderness

24 West Tensleep Lake
West Tensleep Lake

Deep Park

22 East Tensleep Lake

27

Island Park

431   430

Sitting Bull

Boulder Park

Bull Creek

To Buffalo

23 Meadowlark Lake

26A

16

26B

18

Tensleep Creek

Leigh Creek

To Ten Sleep

★

24 West Tensleep Lake

See map on page 45

Key species: brook trout, rainbow trout

Description: This 42-acre mountain lake lies above 9,000 feet. Spruce and lodgepole pine surround the lake while the snowcapped Bighorn Mountains loom above.

Tips: Dry flies work best in the early evening with bubble-and-fly tackle offering greater surface coverage.

The fishing: Brook trout range from 4 to 6 inches and spook easily. Worms are the most productive bait in spring, especially near the stream inlet. Later, in summer and into fall, small, black dry flies work well. Rainbow trout range from 8 to 10 inches. In spring, bottom anglers do well when shore fishing with worms. As the sun goes down, the trout move toward the surface, offering opportunities for fly fishers. By August, bright spinners can stir up a strike along the points.

Directions: Take US 16 west out of Buffalo 45 miles to FR 27. Turn right onto FR 27 and travel 7 miles north to the campground.

Additional information: West Tensleep Lake Campground provides toilets, 10 spaces, and accommodations for trailers up to 16 feet. Only non-motorized boats and floating devices are allowed. There is no boat ramp, but the roadway passes near the shore.

Contact: Wyoming Game and Fish Department, Sheridan.

The Bighorn Mountains loom over 42-acre West Tensleep Lake.

25 Golden Lakes

See map on page 45

Key species: golden trout
Description: The nearly vertical cliffs of Bomber Mountain embrace these two small, isolated lakes near the summit.
Tips: This difficult hike requires overnight camping.

The fishing: Golden trout range from 8 to 9 inches. At this 11,000- to 12,000-foot elevation, ice remains longer than in the lower country. Don't plan to put a line in here before June, at the earliest.

Directions: Take US 16 west out of Buffalo 45 miles to FR 27. Turn right onto FR 27 and travel 7 miles north past the campground to the Mistymoon Trailhead. Follow West Tensleep Creek on this moderate-to-difficult trail about 6 miles, past Lake Helen, to Mistymoon Lake. Take the difficult Florence Pass Trail east, past the Fortress Lakes and Gunboat Lake, through Florence Pass for 2.5 miles to Florence Lake. From Florence Lake there is no designated trail for the steep, difficult climb to the Golden Lakes about one mile to the northeast.

Additional information: These lakes are in the Cloud Peak Wilderness Area and have no designated trail.

Contact: Wyoming Game and Fish Department, Sheridan.

26 Tensleep Creek

See map on page 45

Key species: brook trout, rainbow trout
Description: The contrasting colors of the massive limestone cliffs make an unforgettable backdrop for this swift stream, especially when the aspens turn gold in the fall.
Tips: Don't overlook the small holes created by the abundant boulders in the stream. A carefully guided hook can find an otherwise hidden trout.

The fishing: Rainbow trout range from 7 to 9 inches. Worms are the most effective bait here, but wet flies can produce some action as well. Brook trout average 3 to 6 inches and are less common in the more accessible areas. The boulders provide plenty of snags, so be sure to take extra hooks, flies, and leader.

Directions: Take US 16 west out of Buffalo 50 to 57 miles. There are pullouts along the highway, as well as access at Tensleep Campground near Ten Sleep.

Additional information: Tensleep Creek Campground has 5 spaces and toilets. The campground is open from May 15 to October 31.

Contact: Wyoming Game and Fish Department, Sheridan.

27 Paintrock Creek

See map on page 49

Key species: brown trout, rainbow trout
Description: This coldwater stream cuts a spectacular path through colorful, rugged Paintrock Canyon.
Tips: Pack lightweight gear and lunches.

The fishing: Brown trout average 12 to 16 inches. You can find them in the fast water later in fall. The larger ones usually feed in early morning or late evening. Grasshoppers or their imitations are effective in hooking brown trout. Rainbow trout range from 12 to 16 inches and are usually in the faster water. April through May is the most productive time with worms or artificial flies.

Directions: From Manderson, drive east on WY 31 for 15 miles to Hyattville. The highway turns right into Hyattville near Cold Springs Road. Turn left onto Cold Springs Road and follow the signs to the Medicine Lodge State Archaeological Site, which will include another right turn in 1 mile. Continue 6 miles to the fork of Hyatt Drive and Cold Springs Road. Stay to your left on the now-gravel Cold Springs Road for 1 mile to the Paintrock Canyon Trailhead.

Additional information: The trail down to and along the canyon is moderate to slightly difficult. Trespassing over private ground to the public lands is allowed for a little less than 1 mile, but from October 1 to May 10 you need permission from the landowner.

Contact: Wyoming Game and Fish Department, Sheridan.

28 (Lower) Medicine Lodge Creek

Key species: brown trout, rainbow trout

Description: This river slows after crashing down out of the mountains. Cottonwood and willow brush line the banks as it enters the broad high desert near Hyattville.

Tips: Long poles and dry flies offer a challenge in the many glassy pools.

A sign provides anglers with additional information along the access road to Paint Rock Creek.

27–29 Paintrock Creek, (Lower) Medicine Lodge Creek, Renner Reservoir

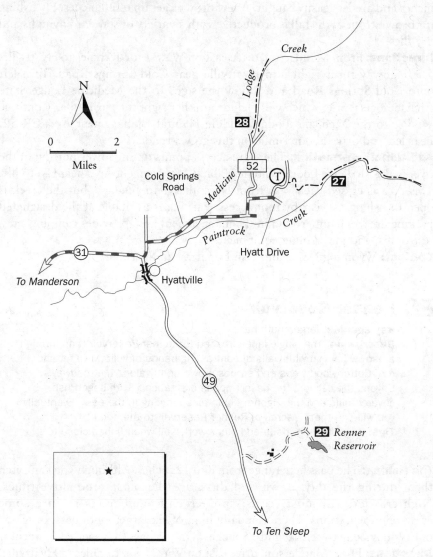

Creek

Lodge

28

N

0   2

Miles

Medicine

52

Cold Springs
Road

Ⓣ

27

Paintrock

Creek

Hyatt Drive

31

To Manderson

Hyattville

49

29 Renner
Reservoir

★

To Ten Sleep

The fishing: Rainbow trout average 8 to 14 inches. Worms are the most productive for rainbows in early spring. Grasshoppers and their imitations create more action from late summer through early fall. Brown trout average 8 to 14 inches and are less easily caught. A few browns get up to 20 inches. Fly fishing for brown trout in the fall is productive with a variety of standard nymphs and dry flies.

Directions: From Manderson, drive east on WY 31 for 15 miles to Hyattville. The highway turns right into Hyattville near Cold Springs Road. Turn left onto Cold Springs Road and follow the signs to the Medicine Lodge State Archaeological Site, which will include another right turn in 1 mile. Continue 4 miles to the Medicine Lodge Wildlife Habitat Management Area/CR 52. Bear left and drive about 1 mile on this gravel road.

Additional information: There are access points on the lower portion of the river in the Medicine Lodge Wildlife Habitat Management Area near Hyattville. This area is closed each year from December 1 to June 30, but the creek is open to fishing all year by foot access. Parking is available at the designated parking area. A campground in the management area provides camping sites, restrooms, and playground equipment.

Contact: Wyoming Game and Fish Department, Sheridan.

29 Renner Reservoir

See map on page 49

Key species: largemouth bass

Description: The single-lane dirt road to Renner Reservoir runs through a narrow canyon with walls of contrasting bands of yellow, white, and red. Cottonwood trees and shrubs crowd tightly along the roadway. Beyond the canyon, the desert opens dramatically with sagebrush-covered hills and the Bighorn Mountains looming in the east. Eventually you will see the 72 acres of Renner Reservoir to the south.

Tips: Bright spinner baits and plugs work well when fished close to shady weedlines.

The fishing: The bass here range from 8 to 12 inches. Although you can catch them during the day, dawn and dusk are the most productive times. Nightcrawlers fill most creels; spinner baits and plugs require some creative presentations. There is a daily limit of six largemouth bass, of which only 2 may be between 10 and 15 inches. Only 1 bass may exceed 15 inches.

Directions: From Manderson, drive east on WY 31 for 15 miles to Hyattville. The highway turns right into Hyattville. Drive south through Hyattville across both Medicine Lodge Creek and Paintrock Creek. The Hyattville Road turns into gravel and becomes County Road 49 just outside of town. Drive down this gravel road for 6 miles to the Renner Wildlife Management Access Road. There is a cattle guard with a boundary sign about 4 miles south of Hyattville. Turn left 2 miles past the cattle guard onto the single lane dirt road and travel 2.5 miles. Bear right at the fork and drive another 0.5 mile.

Additional information: Renner Reservoir has a boat ramp, but motors cannot

The Renner Reservoir access road takes you through colorful country.

exceed 15 horsepower. Toilets and camping are available, but the camping services are limited.

Contact: Wyoming Game and Fish Department, Sheridan.

30 East Fork Big Goose Creek

See map on page 53

Key species: brook trout, rainbow trout
Description: This cold, clear water is 10 feet wide in spots as it glides through grassy meadows while willow brush clings tightly to its banks. Lodgepole pine and spruce line the outer edges of the meadows.
Tips: Fly fishing for rainbows warms up about mid-June.

The fishing: Rainbow trout average 6 to 10 inches. When the water level drops in late spring, wet flies can be productive. Worms are the most effective, but aren't the best for catch-and-release. Brook trout average 4 to 8 inches. Worms are usually the most productive. Later in the fall when these trout start to spawn, just about anything will work. Grasshopper and mosquito imitations are both productive and challenging.

Additional information: Camping is available at various locations along the creek.
Contact: Wyoming Game and Fish Department, Sheridan.

30A. East Fork Campground

Description: This fee area has 12 units with drinking water, toilets, a picnic area, and accommodations for trailers up to 22 feet long. The campground is open from June 1 to October 31, weather permitting.

Directions: From Burgess Junction, head south on US 14 about 7 miles to FR 26. Turn left onto FR 26 and drive 20 miles.

30B. Coffeen Park Campground

Description: There is no fee at this wilderness access area, but it has only five units with primitive facilities. A four-wheel-drive vehicle is recommended for the last 2 miles of access.

Directions: From Burgess Junction, go south on US 14 about 7 miles to FR 26. Turn left onto FR 26 and drive 20 miles to Park Reservoir Road/FR 293. Turn right onto this gravel road. Follow the signs past the Spear O Wigwam Guest Ranch and drive a total of 12 miles.

31 Weston Reservoir

Key species: grayling
Description: This 33-acre lake is near timberline.
Tips: Pack light gear and a heavy lunch for the steep climb.

The fishing: Grayling range from 8 to 10 inches. Fly fishing is the best method. The fish often nip at a fly several times then retreat into deeper water without taking it. Grayling will school to feed and can be very fussy. Take a variety of small dark flies. Try fishing Babione Creek upstream on the journey to the lake. Grayling may be in the creek, though brook trout dominate.

Directions: From Burgess Junction, take US 14 west about 7 miles. Turn left onto FR 26 and drive 19 miles to FR 299 across from the Big Goose Ranger Station. Turn right onto this four-wheel-drive road and drive 2 miles to a large meadow. Don't drive through it, even though it looks dry. This meadow is actually a swampy bog. Hike the next 3 miles up the mountainside.

Additional information: Access to the reservoir requires a four-wheel-drive vehicle and a 3-mile hike uphill.

Contact: Wyoming Game and Fish Department, Sheridan.

32 West Fork Big Goose Creek

Key species: brook trout, cutthroat trout
Description: This twisting stream offers slow rapids and deep, wide pools. Lodgepole pines share the banks with tall grass and large boulders.
Tips: Fly fishing is most productive from mid-June through late fall.

The fishing: Brook trout average 6 to 8 inches. Cutthroat average 8 to 10 inches. The same methods work well for both. Worms do well in the early part of the summer. In the fall, grasshoppers provide the most action. Fly fishing with grasshopper and mosquito imitations create some explosive action in the deep pools. Wading can be inviting, but you might get cold quickly at this high elevation of 6,000 to 7,000 feet.

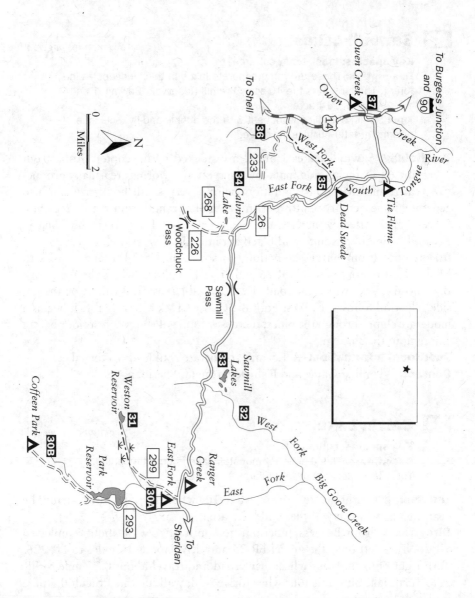

Directions: From Burgess Junction, go south on US 14 about 7 miles to FR 26. Turn left onto FR 26 and drive 17 miles.

Additional information: There are campgrounds nearby, Owen Creek and Tie Flume are the closest, but none are within walking distance.

Contact: Wyoming Game and Fish Department, Sheridan.

33 Sawmill Lakes

See map on page 53

Key species: brook trout, cutthroat trout

Description: These are three separate lakes in thick lodgepole-pine forest. The largest is the 40-acre Sawmill Reservoir. Sawmill 1 and 2 are each about 14 acres.

Tips: Small, dark flies work best with the bubble-and-fly technique offering greater surface coverage.

The fishing: Sawmill Lakes 1 and 2 are stocked by helicopter. Brook trout averaging 6 to 8 inches dominate the reservoir and worms are usually productive year-round. Mosquito imitations with a very small hook size can also generate some activity. Cutthroat in Sawmill 1 range from 8 to 12 inches. Power Bait is effective here. Cutthroat range from 10 to 16 inches long in Sawmill 2. Small mosquito and black ant imitations work well here.

Directions: From Burgess Junction, go south on US 14 about 7 miles to FR 26. Turn left onto gravel FR 26 and drive 17 miles to where the West Fork Big Goose Creek crosses the road. The Sawmill Lakes Trail will be on the left side. The trail follows the West Fork Big Goose Creek briefly before it begins a moderate climb through the pines. It crosses 1 mile of rocky forest floor before climbing to the shoreline.

Additional information: A 1.5-mile, moderate trail leads to the lakes.

Contact: Wyoming Game and Fish Department, Sheridan.

34 Calvin Lake

See map on page 53

Key species: cutthroat trout

Description: This 4-acre, icy mountain lake is near timberline.

Tips: Take plenty of different lures and flies.

The fishing: Cutthroat trout average 8 to 10 inches. They get fussy later in the year, so a good variety of flies and lures are necessary.

Directions: From Burgess Junction, go south on US 14 about 7 miles to FR 26. Turn left onto the gravel FR 26 and drive about 10 miles to FR 226. Turn right onto this four-wheel-drive road and travel about 0.75 mile to FR 268. Turn right onto this four-wheel-drive trail; walking the difficult 0.5 mile trail may be quicker.

Additional information: Reaching this little lake is not easy; vehicles need to ford the East Fork South Tongue River. In early spring this may not be possible.

Contact: Wyoming Game and Fish Department, Cody.

35 East Fork South Tongue River

See map on page 53

Key species: brook trout, rainbow trout
Description: This classic trout stream with deep pools up to 12 feet wide has slow but strong rapids, cut banks, and corners with deep hideouts. Plenty of spruce and lodgepole pines line the stream, offering cool and shady fishing holes.
Tips: Fish the ripples as they enter one of the many pools.

The fishing: Brook trout average 4 to 9 inches. These little trout usually prefer worms. The clear water and heavy fishing pressure make these trout hard to catch. If you see them, they have probably seen you. Rainbow trout average 8 to 12 inches. Worms are productive in the early part of summer. Flies can be productive, but these fussy fish often jump madly with no interest in what you offer. Spinners can create explosive behavior in the pools later in fall.

Directions: From Burgess Junction, go south on US 14 about 7 miles to FR 26. Turn left onto gravel FR 26 and travel 4 miles to the Dead Swede Campground.

Additional information: The Dead Swede Campground has drinking water, 22 sites, toilets, a picnic area, and accommodations for trailers up to 22 feet. This fee area is open from the middle of June to the end of October, depending on weather.

Contact: Wyoming Game and Fish Department, Cody.

36 West Fork South Tongue River

See map on page 53

Key species: brook trout, rainbow trout
Description: This little stream resembles East Fork South Tongue River but has slightly less water. The pools average 6 to 8 feet wide. Open meadows run along the course of this stream with a pine forest nearby.
Tips: Look for hidden cutbanks near the rapids.

The fishing: Rainbow trout average 6 to 10 inches. Worms are the most productive in the spring and are effective through summer, though spinners offer more aggressive action. Brook trout average 4 to 8 inches. Worms are productive for brook trout all summer long with more action in fall.

Directions: From Burgess Junction, go south on US 14 about 11 miles to FR 233. Turn left onto the dirt FR 233 and travel about 0.5 mile to where the stream crosses the road.

Additional information: You can also reach the West Fork South Tongue River on foot from the Dead Swede Campground, but the distance is considerable, about 1.5 to 2 miles one way.

Contact: Wyoming Game and Fish Department, Cody.

37 Owen Creek

See map on page 53

Key species: brook trout
Description: This little mountain meadow brook reaches widths of

The East Fork South Tongue River is a classic western trout stream.

almost 6 feet. Willow brush lines its grassy banks.
Tips: Look for the eddies and deep undercuts where you will be less visible to the fish.

The fishing: Brook trout range from 6 to 10 inches. Worms are the most productive bait and easiest to use in this brushy area. Take plenty of hooks along.

Directions: From Burgess Junction, go south on US 14 about 7 miles to FR 26. Turn right at the Owen Creek Campground sign and drive 0.5 mile.

Additional information: Owen Creek Campground has seven units, drinking water, toilets and accommodations for trailers up to 22 feet long. This fee area is open from the middle of June to the end of October depending on weather. Young anglers from a nearby 4-H Camp fish here during the course of the summer.

Contact: Wyoming Game and Fish Department, Cody.

38 Tongue River

See map on page 60

Key species: brown trout, rainbow trout, whitefish
Description: Vertical limestone cliffs form countless shapes along the cottonwood-shaded, boulder-strewn Tongue River. Lodgepole pines cling to every available space along the cliffs.
Tips: Fish the water directly below where large boulders break the current.

The fishing: Both brown and rainbow trout average 10 to 12 inches. A variety of both wet and dry flies produce trout here. The best time to fly fish is when the high water drops in late June or July. Grasshoppers and spinners are

The vertical limestone canyon cliffs provide a spectacular backdrop while fishing the Tongue River.

The banks of Owen Creek are lined with grass.

very productive for both browns and rainbows. The wily browns show up in creels more often in the fall. Whitefish range from 8 to 12 inches. Worms usually produce these fish.

Additional information: Primitive camping is available along the river. More camping facilities are available near Ranchester.

Contact: Wyoming Game and Fish Department, Cody.

38A. Tongue Canyon Campground

Description: This is a primitive campground with toilets and fire rings. This narrow, single-lane trail is unsuitable for trailers and large RVs.

Directions: From Sheridan, head west on I-90 about 10 miles to exit 9. Drive west on US 14 for 6 miles to Dayton. Just before entering central Dayton, turn right at the Amsden Creek Wildlife Habitat Management Area access sign. Follow this gravel road 4 miles, staying to the left.

38B. Connor Battlefield

Description: This historic site offers camping for a fee and has accommodations for trailers, toilets, group picnic facilities, and playground equipment.

Directions: From Sheridan, head west on I-90 about 10 miles to exit 9. Drive west on US 14 for 1 mile to Ranchester. In Ranchester turn left onto Gillette Street/CR 67 and drive 1 mile. After crossing the river, turn left into the historic site.

Contact: Wyoming Game and Fish Department, Sheridan, Wyoming.

39 Sibley Lake

See map on page 60

Key species: brook trout, cutthroat trout, rainbow trout

Description: Spruce trees mingled with lodgepole forest surround this 33-acre mountain lake.

Tips: Avoid the crowded weekends by fishing here during the week.

The fishing: The best fishing is in the early morning or late evening, although trout are caught throughout the day. Rainbow trout averaging 8 to 12 inches are stocked here. Brook trout range from 4 to 10 inches and are only occasionally hooked. Cutthroat trout can reach lengths of 12 inches, but are rarely caught. Almost anything produces fish here, so take a variety of lures and flies when you go.

Directions: From Burgess Junction, take US 14 east to Sibley Lake. Both the lake and the campground are on the right about 10 miles away.

Additional information: Wheelchair-accessible fishing is available, with plenty of room, along the dock. A boat ramp is present, but boats with motors are not allowed. Sibley Lake Campground has 16 units with drinking water, toilets, and accommodations for trailers up to 32 feet. Some of the units have electricity for an additional cost. This fee area is open from the middle of June to the end of October, weather permitting.

Contact: Wyoming Game and Fish Department, Cody.

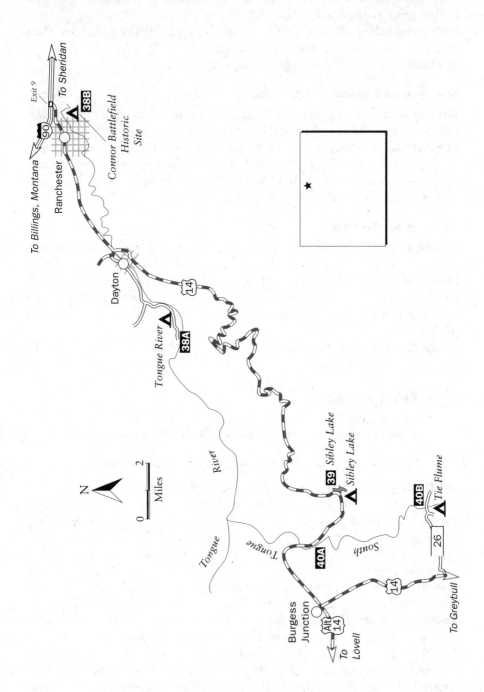

Sibley Lake has campgrounds, a boat ramp, and other facilities useful to anglers.

40 South Tongue River

Key species: brook trout, brown trout, rainbow trout
Description: Deep pools with 3- to 4-foot banks wind along grassy meadows and through a pine forest. Large boulders are strewn along the streambed. The bottom is easily visible in this clear creek, even in depths of up to 6 feet.
Tips: Fish the ripples at the entrances to the larger pools.

The fishing: Brook trout range from 4 to 10 inches. These little fish are most common in the upper areas. Worms and grasshoppers are effective when you can approach the trout without being detected. Brown and rainbow trout range from 8 to 14 inches. Worms and grasshoppers are productive, although fly fishing with dry flies is the most appealing method. Look for rainbows in the faster waters during the early spring. Later in fall, small spinners provide action in the slower pools.

Additional information: Camping and picnic facilities are available at various locations.

Contact: Wyoming Game and Fish Department, Cody.

40A. Pine Island Picnic Ground

Description: This day-use area has group facilities, a playground, a group shelter, drinking water, and toilets. Group size determines reservations and fees. This area is open from June 15 to October 31, depending on the weather.

Directions: From Burgess Junction, take US 14 east. The picnic ground will be on the right side about 2 miles away.

40B. Tie Flume Campground

Description: This fee area has 25 units with drinking water, toilets, and accommodations for trailers up to 22 feet. The campground is open from June 15 to October 31 depending on the weather.

Directions: From Burgess Junction, go south on US 14, 7 miles to FR 26. Turn left onto this gravel road and drive 2 miles.

41 Shell Creek

Key species: brook trout, brown trout, rainbow trout
Description: This mountain stream cascades over boulders between limestone cliffs as it leaves the Bighorn Mountains. The cliffs close in near its exit, just east of Shell, with a spectacular waterfall display.
Tips: Fish the eddies directly below the rock barriers in the streambed.

The fishing: Brook trout range from 4 to 8 inches. Worms are the most productive and commonly used bait. The swift pace of the creek tends to make other baits difficult to use. Brown trout range from 10 to 12 inches and are not usually found upstream. Wet flies are effective during the fall. Rainbow trout average 8 to 12 inches. Worms are the most productive in the rapids where large boulders break the current.

Additional information: Camping is available at several points.

Contact: Wyoming Game and Fish Department, Cody.

41A. Shell Creek Campground

Description: This fee area has 11 units with drinking water, toilets, and accommodations for trailers up to 22 feet. The campground is open from May 30 to October 31, weather permitting.

Directions: From Burgess Junction, go south on US 14 for 17.3 miles to FR 17. Turn left onto FR 17 and drive 1.2 miles to the campground. Fishing access is also available along US 14 from this point for about 4 miles.

41B. Ranger Creek Campground

Description: This fee area has 10 units with drinking water, toilets, and accommodations for trailers up to 22 feet long. The campground is open from May 30 to October 31, weather permitting.

Directions: From Burgess Junction, go south on US 14, 17.3 miles to FR 17. Turn left and drive 2 miles on FR 17 to the campground.

42 Shell Creek Reservoir

Key species: brook trout
Description: Stunted pine trees and huge rocks dot the mountainsides surrounding this 85-acre, manmade lake. Be prepared for a temperature drop after sunset in this high country.
Tips: Take a variety of lures along with a big lunch.

41–47 Shell Creek, Shell Creek Reservoir, (Upper) Medicine Lodge Creek, Upper Medicine Lodge Lake, Lower Medicine Lodge Lake, Upper Paint Rock Lake, Lower Paint Rock Lake

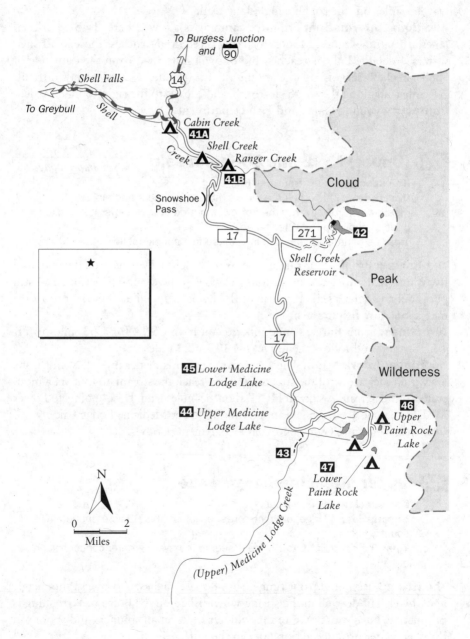

The fishing: Brook trout range from 8 to 10 inches. These trout usually take anything until later in the summer, when they get fussy until spawning starts in the fall. The hungrier fish will be in the stream at that time. A canoe or small boat is useful for access to the upper stream areas.

Directions: From Burgess Junction, go south on US 14 for 17.3 miles to FR 17. Turn left and follow gravel FR 17 for 10 miles to FR 271. Bear left and travel 3 miles on this rough, single-lane trail.

Additional information: Primitive camping is allowed here. Two additional lakes are within 4 miles. Moderate hiking is required to access these less-fished waters. Adelaide Lake is reached by following the road from the dam side of Shell Creek Reservoir up the mountain for 1 mile. A moderately difficult 2.5-mile trail along the south side of this lake leads to the right to Lake Arden.

Contact: Wyoming Game and Fish Department, Cody.

43 (Upper) Medicine Lodge Creek

See map on page 63

Key species: brook trout, rainbow trout
Description: This creek meanders through boulders and alpine meadows on its way into the narrow, forested canyon cliffs. It has plenty of deep pools up to 10 feet wide.
Tips: Be mindful of your shadow; these fish spook easily.

The fishing: Brook trout range from 6 to 8 inches. Worms are effective, and fly fishing with mosquito imitations provides some explosive action. The still pools tax an angler's skill. A worm or fly that is dropped on the water too hard may spook any fish in the area.

Directions: From Burgess Junction, go south on US 14 for 17.3 miles to FR 17. Turn left and follow the gravel FR 17 for 23 miles.

Additional information: There are campgrounds at nearby lakes, but none are within easy access of the stream. You can reach the stream on foot via a moderately difficult trail. A sign on FR 17 about 19 miles from US 14 points to Lower Medicine Lodge Trail, which is not a trail to Lower Medicine Lodge Lake.

Contact: Wyoming Game and Fish Department, Cody.

44 Upper Medicine Lodge Lake

See map on page 63

Key species: rainbow trout
Description: A lodgepole pine forest envelops this 65-acre, mountain-country lake.
Tips: The deep water to the west seems to have a greater concentration of fish.

The fishing: Rainbow trout range from 8 to 12 inches. Worms, salmon eggs, and Power Bait do well in the spring when fished on the bottom. Fly fishing is productive, but slows down in the summer heat. Small spinners and spoons in the deep water produce action later in the fall.

Directions: From Burgess Junction, go south on US 14 for 17.3 miles to FR 17. Turn left and follow gravel FR 17 for 25 miles.

Additional information: A makeshift boat ramp is available at this lake. Be prepared to dodge some large boulders. Medicine Lodge Lake Campground offers 8 units with drinking water, toilets, and accommodations for trailers up to 22 feet long. This fee area is open from the end of May to the end of October.

Contact: Wyoming Game and Fish Department, Cody.

45 Lower Medicine Lodge Lake

See map on page 63

Key species: rainbow trout
Description: This 43-acre lake is in the same forest as Upper Medicine Lodge Lake.
Tips: If you plan a trip in the fall, take a variety of lures and bait.

The fishing: Rainbow trout range from 8 to 12 inches. The fishing pressure is lighter here than at the Upper Medicine Lodge Lake, but these trout can still be fussy. Worms are best in early spring. Shore fishing is the most practical method. Any floating device will have to be packed in and out. Both flies and spinners create some action, but the fish get picky. Early morning and late evening are the best times during the hot part of summer.

Directions: A moderate 0.5-mile hike to this lake starts at Medicine Lodge Lake Campground, site 46. (Note: A sign on FR 17 about 19 miles from US 14 points to Lower Medicine Lodge Trail. This is a trail to Medicine Lodge Canyon, not the lake.)

Contact: Wyoming Game and Fish Department, Cody.

46 Upper Paint Rock Lake

See map on page 63

Key species: brook trout, rainbow trout
Description: Spruce and pine line the banks of this 15-acre lake.
Tips: The bubble-and-fly method is productive when you cast toward the middle of the lake.

The fishing: Brook trout range from 6 to 8 inches. Worms work well in spring and summer, but in late August flies tend to be more effective. Rainbow trout range from 8 to 10 inches and are caught mostly in the spring.

Directions: From Burgess Junction, go south on US 14 for 17.3 miles to FR 17. Turn left and follow gravel FR 17 for 25.7 miles to the Upper Paint Rock Campground. Take the foot trail from the campground for 0.25 mile.

Additional information: Upper and Lower Paint Rock campgrounds are separated by 0.5 mile. Both fee areas have 4 units, toilets, and accommodations for trailers up to 22 feet. These campgrounds are open from the end of May to the end of October, weather permitting. A dry season with extreme fire danger can also cause early closure.

Contact: Wyoming Game and Fish Department, Cody.

47 Lower Paint Rock Lake

See map on page 63

Key species: brook trout
Description: A large alpine meadow stands between the forest and this 24-acre, wind-swept lake.
Tips: Floating devices can be helpful later in the year when weeds engulf the banks.

The fishing: Brook trout range from 6 to 10 inches. Worms fished with bobbers produce some action early in the season. Later in the fall, try fishing flies with either a fly rod or a casting rod with a bubble.

Directions: From Burgess Junction, go south on US 14 for 17.3 miles to FR 17. Turn left and follow gravel FR 17 for 26 miles to Lower Paint Rock Campground.

Additional information: The lake is a short distance from Lower Paint Rock Campground, which is covered in site description 48.

Contact: Wyoming Game and Fish Department, Cody.

48 North Fork Tongue River

Key species: brook trout, cutthroat trout
Description: This snowmelt-fed river passes through alpine meadows and mountain grasslands on its way to the Tongue River Canyon. Various barriers, from beaver dams to log jams, create deep pools along the way.
Tips: Be prepared to wade.

The fishing: Brook trout range from 4 to 10 inches. Cutthroat trout range from 7 to 15 inches. Check the current regulations for restrictions; as of this writing all trout other than brook trout must be immediately released. Only artificial flies and lures are allowed here. Wading is the most appealing and effective way of accessing the majority of the river. The thick willow brush does not allow easy foot travel.

Additional information: Camping is available at nearby fee areas. There are additional fishing opportunities in other nearby streams where 10- to 15-inch cutthroat trout have been reported. Check current regulations for Bull Creek and Big Willow Creek.

Contact: Wyoming Game and Fish Department, Cody.

48A. US Alternate 14

Directions: From Burgess Junction, take US Alternate 14 west about 5 miles. The North Fork Tongue River is accessible from numerous points along the road.

48B. National Forest Access

Directions: From Burgess Junction, take FR 15 north about 2 miles. The river crosses the road within sight of the North Fork Campground.

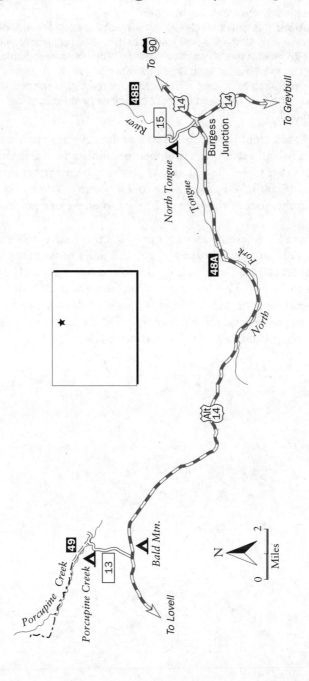

49 Porcupine Creek

See map on page 67

Key species: brook trout, rainbow trout

Description: This creek starts out as a 4-foot-wide brook in a wide, forested canyon. As the ice-cold water crashes over progressively bigger rocks, it gains width as the canyon narrows. There is a spectacular waterfall on the Bucking Mule Creek tributary and plenty of rapids.

Tips: Be prepared for a long, difficult hike for the bigger rainbow trout. The Devil's Canyon Trailhead is about 1.5 miles past Porcupine Campground.

The fishing: Brook trout range from 4 to 6 inches. Worms are used the most and will attract fish all season. Grasshoppers are more effective in the late fall. Rainbow trout range from 10 to 16 inches. These fish are farther downstream and require a difficult hike in some very rough country. Worms are the most effective bait in this part of the stream. Be sure to take extra hooks and a big lunch.

Directions: Take US Alternate 14 west out of Burgess Junction 27 miles to FR 13. Turn right onto this gravel road and travel 2 miles to the campground.

Additional information: Porcupine Campground offers 16 units and spaces for trailers up to 32 feet. This fee area is open from the middle of June to the end of October. From the campground, a short, moderate hike leads to the creek where you should find the big fish after 3 to 4 miles.

Contact: Wyoming Game and Fish Department, Cody.

Northwest

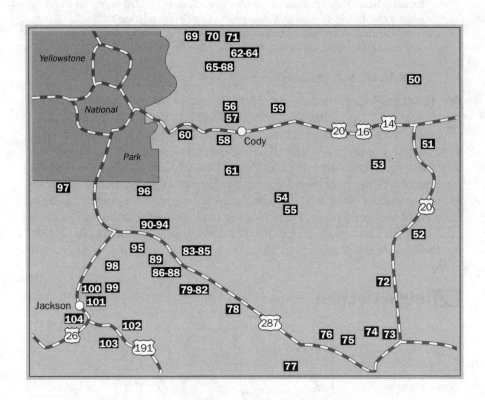

50 Bighorn Lake

Key species: catfish, sauger, walleye

Description: This spectacular desert lake covers 17,300 acres on the west slope of the Bighorn Mountains. The northern portion of this reservoir is surrounded by brilliantly colored cliffs. The southern side has rolling hills and sandy beaches. The Bighorn Mountains rise to the east.

Tips: Trolling with nightcrawlers is the most successful method.

The fishing: Walleye range from 12 to 30 inches and are most frequently caught from early spring through June. Trolling with nightcrawlers and worm-tipped jigs can be especially effective in the Horseshoe Bend area. Catfish weigh up to 10 pounds and respond well to nightcrawlers, minnows, and stink bait. The most productive area for these fish is toward the southern end of the reservoir where the river enters. Sauger range from 10 to 22 inches. The techniques for walleye work well on these fish. The best times to catch them are in early April and September. There is some bank fishing, but boating is more productive and is the only way to reach the best fishing areas. Special ice fishing regulations allow anglers to use up to 6 poles at one time within certain guidelines.

50 Bighorn Lake

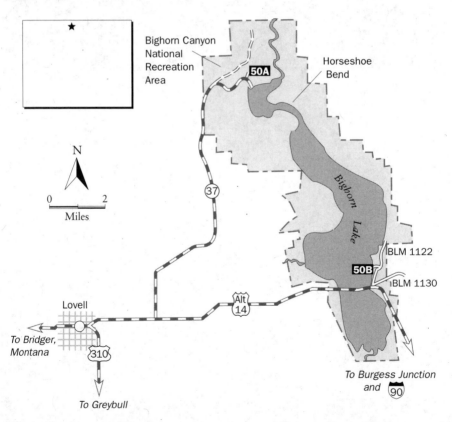

Additional information: Camping, a marina, a store, toilets, and a boat ramp are available on the west side of Horseshoe Bend. The Old Kane Boat Ramp is on the east shore just north of US Alternate 14, but there are no other amenities. Boaters should watch for driftwood while on the reservoir.
Contact: Bighorn Canyon Recreation Area.

50A. Horseshoe Bend

Directions: From Lovell, take US Alternate 14 east 2 miles. Turn left onto WY 37 and drive north about 9 miles to the Bighorn Canyon National Recreation Area.

50B. Old Kane Boat Ramp

Directions: From Lovell, take US Alternate 14 east about 10 miles. After crossing the lake turn left onto a gravel road and drive 1.5 miles to the shoreline access.

51 Lower Bighorn River

Key species: catfish, ling, sauger
Description: This part of the Bighorn River is classified as a warm-water fishery.
Tips: Floating is the best way to reach this part of the river.

The fishing: Sauger average about 1 pound and are generally caught in the area between Thermopolis and Manderson. Jigs with pieces of worm attached are effective, especially in areas just below irrigation diversions. Catfish weighing up to 10 pounds are generally caught from Manderson downstream to Bighorn Lake. Worms, minnows, and stink bait all work well. Ling weighing up to 5 pounds are found all along the river, although backwater areas and big holes produce the most action. Nightcrawlers are preferred by ling. Night is the best fishing time for catfish and ling, but floating in the dark can be extremely hazardous.
Additional information: An annual sauger derby is held in Worland in April or May. Weather and water conditions set the date, so check with area authorities.
Contact: Wyoming Game and Fish Department, Cody.

51A. Worland Riverside Park

Description: Picnicking and a boat ramp are available.
The fishing: Sauger fishing is generally the best from here to Manderson, although there are other species present such as Catfish, Ling, and some trout.
Directions: From Worland, head north a short distance on 2nd Street. Turn left onto Robertson Avenue and drive west one block to Riverside Park.

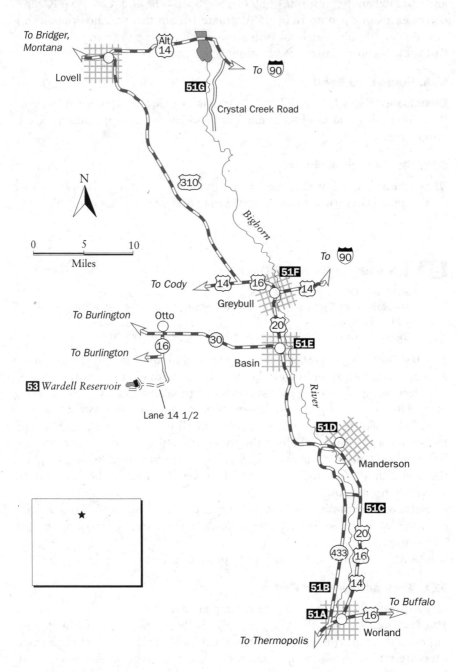

To Bridger, Montana

Alt 14

To 90

Lovell

51G

Crystal Creek Road

N

310

Bighorn

0   5   10
Miles

To Cody

14   16

51F

To 90

14

Greybull

To Burlington

Otto

20

To Burlington

16   30

51E

Basin

53 Wardell Reservoir

Lane 14 1/2

River

51D

Manderson

51C

20

433   16

51B

14

To Buffalo

51A   16

To Thermopolis   Worland

51B. Duck Swamp

Description: A footpath is the only access.
The fishing: Sauger and other warm-water species, namely Catfish, are found here.
Directions: From Worland, take WY 433 north for 2.5 miles.

51C. Rairden Bridge

Description: Shoreline access is available.
Directions: From Worland, head north on US 16/20 for 7.2 miles. Turn left onto Rairden Lane, near mile marker 178. Follow Rairden Lane west 1 mile. Access is on the west bank of the river on the south side of the road.

51D. Manderson Highway Bridge

Description: A boat ramp is available.
The fishing: Sauger are present, but catfish dominate from here downstream, including Bighorn Lake.
Directions: From Greybull, drive south on US 16/20 for 20 miles to Manderson. Access is on the east side of the river and the north side of the bridge.

51E. Basin Bridge

Description: A boat ramp is available here.
Directions: From Greybull, drive south on US 16/US 20 for 8 miles to Basin. At Basin turn left onto B Street and cross the railroad tracks. Follow the signs to the access on the west side of the river.

51F. Greybull Bridge

Description: A boat ramp is available here.
Directions: In Greybull, drive 0.5 mile east after the stoplight at the intersection of US 14 and US 16/20. The boat ramp is east of the river and north of the highway after you cross the bridge.

51G. ML Dike Boat Ramp

Description: A boat ramp is available for lighter craft.
Directions: From Lovell, take US Alternate 14 east about 13 miles. After crossing Bighorn Lake, turn right onto Crystal Creek Road and drive 3.2 miles. Turn right again. Be careful; this area is marshy during high-water seasons and you could easily get stuck.

52 Upper Bighorn River

Key species: brown trout, cutthroat trout, rainbow trout
Description: This section of river flows from the "Wedding of the Waters" just outside Wind River Canyon to Worland, 33 miles north of Thermopolis. This wide river winds its way past farms and large cottonwoods. Mountains and other formations offer a shifting backdrop.
Tips: Wet flies are best when allowed to drift with the current.

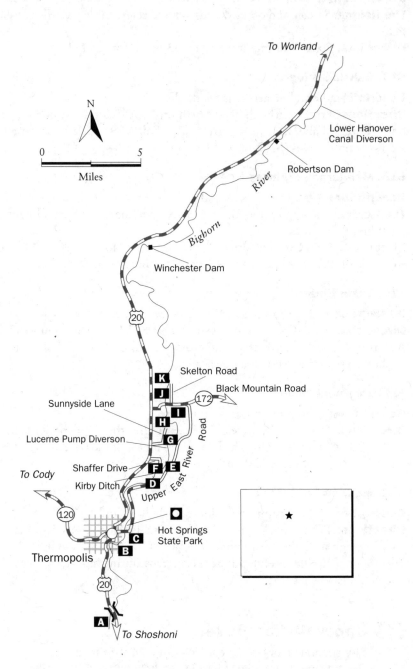

To Worland

Lower Hanover
Canal Diverson

Robertson Dam

N

0   5
Miles

Bighorn River

Winchester Dam

20

Skelton Road

K
J   Black Mountain Road
I   172
Sunnyside Lane
H
G
Lucerne Pump Diverson

Upper East River Road

Shaffer Drive   **F** **E**
Kirby Ditch   **D**

To Cody

120

O

C   Hot Springs
B   State Park

Thermopolis

20

A
To Shoshoni

★

The fishing: Trout range from 1 to 5 pounds. There are special regulations along parts of the river. From Wedding of the Waters, downstream to the Black Mountain Road Bridge, there is a limit of 3 trout per day, only one of which may be over 18 inches. Check the current regulations—only artificial flies and lures have been allowed in certain areas in the past. Weeds pose a problem for the angler. Drifting flies or bait is productive, while recovering a spinner across the current may produce only slimy seaweed. Ling respond well to nightcrawlers. In late summer when the water gets low, wading is quite productive.

Additional information: The Bighorn River changes its name at the Wedding of the Waters and becomes the Wind River upstream. Floating any river exposes anglers to potential hazards. Be aware of the hazards listed below and note them on the map:

Contact: Wyoming Game and Fish Department, Cody.

1. Kirby Ditch

A portage may be necessary around this diversion. Check the conditions before proceeding.

2. Lucerne Pump Diversion

A Portage may be necessary around this diversion. Check the conditions before proceeding.

3. Winchester Dam or Upper Hanover Canal

A high drop with powerful wave action and undercurrent makes a portage necessary here.

4. Robertson Dam

A high drop with powerful wave action and undercurrent makes a portage necessary here.

5. Lower Hanover Canal Diversion

A high drop with powerful wave action and undercurrent makes a portage necessary here.

Estimated float times:

Wedding of the Waters to Hot Springs State Park: 3 to 5.5 hours
Hot Springs State Park to Wakely: 4 hours
Wakely to Skelton: 4.5 hours
Winchester Dam to Robertson Dam: 6 hours
Robertson Dam to Worland Riverside Park: 5 hours
Worland Riverside Park to Rairden Bridge: 8 hours

52A. Wedding of the Waters

Description: Parking, a boat ramp, toilets, and wheelchair-accessible fishing access are available, as well as 0.25 mile of shoreline for bank fishing.

Directions: Take US 20 south out of Thermopolis for 4 miles to the Wedding of the Waters public access on the west side of the highway.

52B. Thermopolis Bridge

The fishing: Parking is available here with foot access for fishing on both sides of the bridge.

Directions: In Thermopolis, drive east of the junction of US 20 and Broadway 0.5 mile.

52C. Hot Springs State Park

Description: A boat ramp, picnic and swimming areas, and stone flows (unique mineral formations still in the forming process) created by the hot spring are present, along with motels and restaurants.

Directions: In Thermopolis, go north on US 20 to Hot Springs State Park.

Contact: Thermpolis Chamber of Commerce.

52D. Kirby Ditch

Description: Shore fishing is the only option here; there is no boat ramp.

The fishing: Ling and trout inhabit this stretch of water. Wading is popular when the water is low.

Directions: From Thermopolis, head north on US 20 and drive to Hot Springs State Park on the right hand side. Drive east on the Hot Springs access road about 0.5 mile. Turn left onto Upper East River Road/CR 8 and drive 2.7 miles.

52E. McCarthy

Description: A boat launch is available for small, light craft.

Directions: From Thermopolis, drive north on US 20 to the Hot Springs State Park on the right hand side. Drive east on the Hot Springs access road about 0.5 mile. Turn left onto Upper East River Road/CR 8 and drive 3.5 miles.

52F. Wakely

Description: A boat ramp is available.

Directions: From Thermopolis, drive north on US 20 about 5 miles to mile marker 137. Turn right onto Shaffer Drive and drive 0.6 mile to the Wakley Ranch. Turn right and travel 0.4 mile south.

52G. Shaffer

Description: Shoreline access is limited to a foothpath from the designated parking area or by boat.

Directions: From Thermopolis, head north on US 20 about 6 miles to mile marker 138. Turn right onto Sunnyside Lane/CR 27 and travel 1 mile.

52H. Longwell

Description: A boat ramp is available.

The fishing: Trout and ling are caught here, but the trout are less dominant than they are upstream.

Directions: From Thermopolis, head north on US 20 and drive about 6 miles to mile marker 138. Turn right onto Sunnyside Lane/CR 27 and travel 1.7 miles through the Longwell Ranch.

52I. Marino

Description: A boat ramp is available for lighter craft.
Directions: From Thermopolis, head north on US 20 about 7 miles to Black Mountain Road/WY 172. Turn right and drive 0.6 mile. Turn right onto the dirt road and drive 0.2 mile.

52J. Skelton

Description: A boat ramp is available.
Directions: From Thermopolis, drive north on US 20 about 7 miles to Black Mountain Road/WY 172. Turn right and drive 1 mile, crossing the river. At mile marker 1, turn left onto Skelton Road/CR 21 and drive 1.1 miles.

52K. Sorenson

Description: Shoreline access is available.
Directions: Follow the directions to site 54J, and drive 0.1 mile further.

53 Wardell Reservoir

See map on page 72

Key species: crappie, perch, walleye
Description: This 107-acre, warm-water reservoir is in desert prairie just south of the cottonwood-lined Greybull River.
Tips: All the fish here respond to nightcrawlers. The walleye are found in the deep water.

The fishing: Wardell Reservoir is one of the best walleye producers in this region. These fish range from 10 to 13 inches. Nightcrawlers, minnows, and jigs produce walleye almost all year long. Perch range from 4 to 8 inches and respond well to small jigs, salmon eggs, and worms. Crappie range from 4 to 10 inches. Worms tend to be the bait of choice for these aggressive little fish. Both perch and crappie are usually found in the weedy sections near the shore. Special regulations for ice fishing allow anglers to use up to 6 lines within certain guidelines.
Directions: From Basin, drive west on WY 30 for 12 miles to Otto. Take CR 16 south out of Otto for 2 miles. The paved road turns left here. Go straight ahead onto the improved dirt road, which is still Road 16. Follow this rapidly worsening roadway for 2 miles south. When this dirt road turns west, it will be Lane 14 1/2. Travel another 2 miles to the reservoir.
Additional information: There is no boat ramp. The gumbo road near the lake becomes extremely difficult, if not impassable, in wet weather. When dry, the road is not a problem, although low-profile vehicles might not clear the ruts.
Contact: Wyoming Game and Fish Department, Cody.

54, 55 Lower Sunshine Reservoir, Upper Sunshine Reservoir

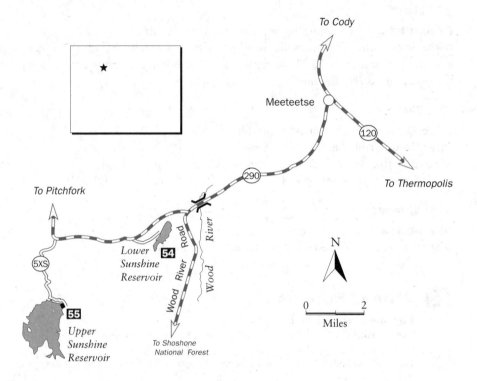

54 Lower Sunshine Reservoir

Key species: brown trout, cutthroat trout
Description: The Absaroka Mountains are the backdrop for this 250-acre manmade lake.
Tips: Trolling generally produces the largest fish.

The fishing: Brown trout range from 10 to 20 inches. Trollers take a few of these fish from deep water in the summer, but the best time is late fall. An assortment of dry flies and spinners will find action in the early morning in shallower waters. Cutthroat range from 10 to 13 inches. Red and white Dardevle spoons, and bucktail Mepps spinners find action in the shallower waters during June and late September. Some anglers successfully catch trout from the bank, but trolling is more productive. The action slows on hot days when the fish stay in deep water.

Directions: From Cody, head south on WY 120 for 31 miles to Meeteetse. At Meeteetse take WY 290 southwest for 7 miles. The reservoir is to the left of the road.

Additional information: A boat ramp and camping are available, but there are no facilities.
Contact: Wyoming Game and Fish Department, Cody.

55 Upper Sunshine Reservoir

Key species: cutthroat trout, splake
Description: This 600-acre, manmade reservoir is in the grassy foothills of the Absaroka Mountains.
Tips: Some trout are caught off the bank early in the season with spinners and colorful spoons.

The fishing: Cutthroat average 10 to 13 inches. Trollers are the most successful, even when fishing drops off during the hot months. Small, colorful spinners and spoons work well. Splake range from 10 to 20 inches.
Directions: From Cody, head south on WY 120 for 31 miles to Meeteetse. At Meeteetse, take WY 290 southwest for 11.5 miles. Turn left onto the gravel FR 208/CR 5XS and drive 3 miles.
Additional information: Camping and a boat ramp are available, but there are no facilities.
Contact: Wyoming Game and Fish Department, Cody.

56 East Newton Lake

Key species: rainbow trout
Description: This 51-acre mountain lake is in the eastern foothills of the Absaroka Mountains.
Tips: Large streamers produce some very explosive action later in the day.

The fishing: Rainbow trout range from 10 to 20 inches. Early spring is the most active time, with less success later in the summer. Small bright spinners will give limited results in the fall. There is a one trout limit, and your trout may not exceed 20 inches in length. Only artificial flies and lures are allowed.
Directions: From Cody, take WY 120 north 3 miles. Turn left onto Cottonwood Drive/CR 7WC and travel 1.5 miles to the lake.
Additional information: A boat ramp is available, but motors may not exceed 15 horsepower.
Contact: Wyoming Game and Fish Department, Cody.

57 West Newton Lake

Key species: cutthroat trout, yellow perch
Description: This 30-acre lake is a short distance from East Newton Lake.
Tips: Flies fished with bubbles produce action for shore anglers.

56, 57, 59 East Newton Lake, West Newton Lake, Shonshone River

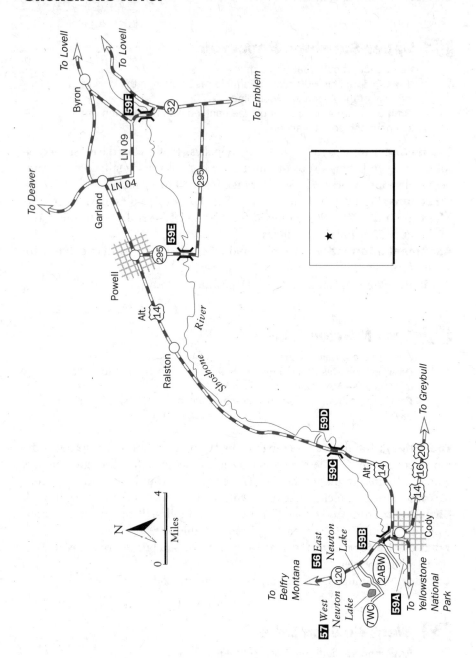

The fishing: Cutthroat range from 10 to 16 inches. Worms, Power Bait, and salmon eggs produce well in the early spring, becoming less effective toward the end of June. Bright spinners and colorful spoons create a little more action when the fish do not respond to the bait. The time between strikes steadily increases as the weather grows warmer. Perch range from 4 to 10 inches. Salmon eggs, worms, jigs, and small lures work well on these aggressive eaters.

Directions: From Cody, take WY 120 north 3 miles. Turn left onto Cottonwood Drive/CR 7WC and travel 1.7 miles to the lake.

Additional information: Boats with motors exceeding 15 horsepower are not permitted.

Contact: Wyoming Game and Fish Department, Cody.

58 Buffalo Bill Reservoir

See map on page 83

Key species: brown trout, cutthroat trout, rainbow trout, mackinaw, whitefish

Description: Colorful mountain badlands contain this 4,900-acre reservoir.

Tips: Trolling with pop gear can result in some very explosive action. Be sure to check current regulations.

The fishing: Brown, cutthroat, and rainbow trout average 12 to 18 inches. In early spring, fishing from shore with salmon eggs, Power Bait, cheese, and worms is best. Mackinaw weigh up to 15 pounds and are usually caught from boats in deep water. Large Flatfish and Rapalas work well. Whitefish range from 8 to 14 inches. Worms fished on the bottom do well for shore anglers. There is a daily limit of four trout, of which only one may be over 20 inches. The western portion of the reservoir from Rattlesnake Creek, to the north, and Sheep Creek, to the south, upstream to Gibbs Bridge is closed to fishing from April 1 through July 14.

Additional information: Camping and boat ramps are available. The reservoir is in Buffalo Bill State Park, which is open from May 1 to September 30 with limited access in the winter. Shreve Lodge has indoor facilities available by reservation only.

Contact: Cody Chamber of Commerce.

58A. Low water ramps

Description: Boat ramps at different levels are available to allow access at fluctuating water levels.

Directions: Take US 14/16/20 west out of Cody for 6.5 miles. Just beyond the tunnel look for the access on your left.

58B. North Shore Bay

Description: This fee area has camping units, drinking water, a telephone, toilets, a picnic area, and a boat ramp.

Directions: Take US 14/16/20 west out of Cody for 7 miles.

58C. North Fork

Description: This fee area has camping units, a picnic area, toilets, drinking water, a telephone, and a trailer dumpsite.
Directions: Take US 14/16/20 west out of Cody for 13 miles to CR 6KV. Turn left onto this paved road. The campground access is to the right.

58D. South Shore

Description: A boat ramp and toilets are available here.
Directions: Take US 14/16/20 west out of Cody for 13 miles to CR 6KV. Turn left onto this paved road and cross the river. Turn left onto gravel CR 6FU and drive 1.5 miles.

58E. Bartlett Lane

Description: This day use area has group picnic shelters, a picnic area, toilets, drinking water, and a boat ramp.
Directions: Take WY 291 southwest out of Cody 6.5 miles to Bartlett Lane. Turn right and drive 2.25 miles on this road, which will turn into gravel.

59 Shoshone River

See map on page 80

Key species: brown trout, cutthroat trout, rainbow trout, whitefish
Description: This river rushes out of the mountains west of Cody, maintaining its momentum to just south of Powell.
Tips: Floating is the best option; consult a local guide, as there are a lot of hazards and private stretches.

The fishing: Brown trout range from 10 to 20 inches. Large streamers and colorful spinners produce fish mostly in the fall. Some browns make it up to the waters below Buffalo Bill Reservoir, but most of these trout stay downstream. Rainbow trout average 10 to 16 inches. Early April and May offer the best opportunity with Yuk Bugs, Woolly Worms, and Woolly Buggers. In September and October, switch to spinners and spoons. Between May and September fishing is generally not good. Whitefish range from 8 to 14 inches. Worms work well when drifted along the bottom of deep holes and slower waters.
Additional information: This is a long stretch of river with numerous access areas, but no campgrounds are available.
Contact: Wyoming Game and Fish Department, Cody.

59A. Shoshone Canyon

Description: The river here flows from below Buffalo Bill Reservoir though a narrow canyon with high, colorful cliffs.
Directions: In Cody, take WY 120 north from the US Alternate 14 intersection. After crossing the bridge to the north side of the river, take CR 2ABW to

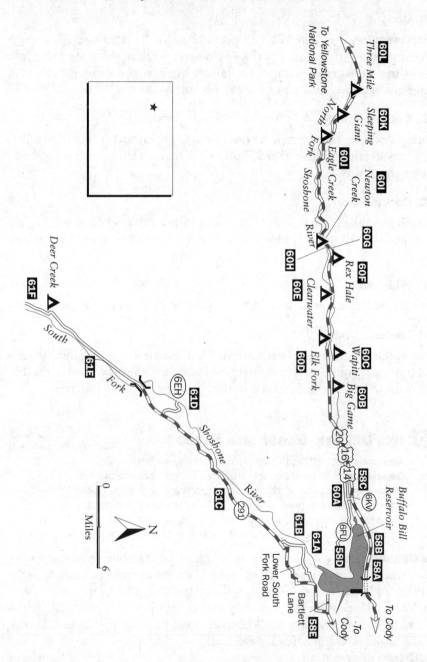

the west. At the river, turn right onto the gravel road. Foot access to the upper portions of the river can be difficult. There are multiple undesignated access points for several miles.

59B. Cody

Directions: In Cody, take WY 120 north from the US Alternate 14 intersection. At the next street, just before going down the hill to the bridge, turn left. Follow this paved road about 0.2 mile past a gravel plant to a gravel road. Turn right onto this road and follow it 0.3 mile to the riverbank.

59C. Corbett Bridge

Directions: Take US Alternate 14 east out of Cody toward Powell for 4 miles. After crossing the bridge over the Shoshone River turn left onto "the old highway" right of way.

59D. Corbett Dam

Directions: Take US Alternate 14 east out of Cody toward Powell for 5 miles. Turn right onto the gravel public access road and drive 0.5 mile to the parking area.

59E. Willwood

Directions: From Powell, take WY 295 south 2.75 miles to the river.

59F. Penrose Dam

Directions: From Powell, head east on US Alternate 14 to Garland. At Garland turn right onto Lane 4 and drive 2 miles. Follow the main road to the left, as it turns to Lane 9, for 3.5 miles to the parking area along the river.

60 North Fork Shoshone River

See map on page 83

Key species: cutthroat trout, rainbow trout, whitefish
Description: This river courses down from the mountains near Yellowstone National Park. The upper portions of this river pass through a forest of spruce, pine, and aspen. Along the way, large cottonwood trees increase in number as the mountains become badlands.
Tips: Wet flies produce some lively action in the numerous pools.

The fishing: Cutthroat, which are stocked here, and rainbow trout range from 6 to 10 inches. Worms work well for most of the season with best results in the spring. Caddis patterns and other dry flies claim some of the larger fish. There is a limit of three trout per day, only one of which may be over 20 inches. Check the current regulations. Whitefish range from 8 to 10 inches. Worms are the most successful bait with these fish.

Additional information: Camping is available for several miles at numerous campgrounds on a first-come, first-served basis. This is the main route to Yellowstone National Park, so camping units fill fast.

Contact: Wyoming Game and Fish Department, Cody.

60A. Sheep Mountain

Description: Toilets, picnic tables, and parking are available here.

Directions: Take US 14/16/20 west out of Cody for 13 miles. Pass the Buffalo Bill Reservoir and turn left on CR 6KV to the public access parking area south of the river.

60B. Wapiti Public Access

Description: Toilets and parking are available here.

Directions: Take US 14/16/20 west out of Cody for 18 miles. The parking area and river are south of the highway.

60C. Livermore Public Access

Description: Toilets and parking are available here.

Directions: Take US 14/16/20 west out of Cody, 21 miles to CR 6CU. Turn right and travel about 0.5 mile to the parking area.

60D. Big Game Campground access

Description: This fee area has 16 units and accommodations for trailers up to 32 feet. It is open from May 15 to September 30.

Directions: Take US 14/16/20 west out of Cody for 28.6 miles.

60E. Wapiti Campground

Description: This fee area has 41 units and accommodations for trailers up to 22 feet and is open from May 15 to October 30.

Directions: Take US 14/16/20 west out of Cody, 29 miles.

60F. Elk Fork Campground access

Description: This fee area has 13 units and accommodations for trailers up to 22 feet and is open from May 15 to October 30.

Directions: Take US 14/16/20 west out of Cody for 29.2 miles.

60G. Clearwater Campground access

Description: This fee area has 32 units and accommodations for trailers up to 32 feet and is open from May 15 to September 30.

Directions: Take US 14/16/20 west out of Cody for 31.8 miles.

60H. Rex Hale Campground

Description: This fee area has 8 units and accommodations for trailers up to 16 feet and is open from May 15 to September 30.

Directions: Take US 14/16/20 west out of Cody for 35.9 miles.

60I. Blackwater Pond Picnic Area

Description: This day use area has 4 units with wheelchair-accessible facilities and fishing access. It is open from June 1 to September 30.
Directions: Take US 14/16/20 west out of Cody for 36 miles.

60J. Newton Spring Picnic Area

Description: This day-use area has 4 units with tables and toilets. It is open from June 1 to September 30.
Directions: Take US 14/16/20 west out of Cody for 37 miles.

60K. Newton Creek Campground

Description: This fee area has 31 units and accommodations for trailers up to 22 feet long. It is open from May 15 to September 30.
Directions: Take US 14/16/20 west out of Cody for 37.3 miles.

60L. Eagle Creek Campground

Description: This fee area with 20 units is open from May 15 to October 30. It has accommodations for trailers up to 22 feet.
Directions: Take US 14/16/20 west out of Cody for 44.7 miles.

60M. Sleeping Giant Campground

Description: This fee area has 6 units and can accommodate trailers up to 22 feet. It is open from May 15 to October 30.
Directions: Take US 14/16/20 west out of Cody for 48 miles.

60N. Three Mile Campground

Description: This fee area has 33 units and accommodations for trailers up to 22 feet. It is open from May 15 to October 30.
Directions: Take US 14/16/20 west out of Cody for 48.6 miles.

61 South Fork Shoshone River

See map on page 83

Key species: Brook trout, brown trout, cutthroat trout, rainbow trout, whitefish
Description: This mountain river cuts through some remote country. WY 291 follows the river and dead ends after 35 miles.
Tips: Undercuts and large boulders provide hiding spots for the bigger brown trout.

The fishing: This is about a 50-mile stretch of water with varying numbers of trout. Brook trout range from 6 to 10 inches, although it is a long hike (up to 25 miles) to get to these fish. Brown trout range from 12 to 16 inches and are more common in the lower portions of the river. Worms and wet flies are productive in the eddies and cutbanks. Cutthroat can get up to 16 inches, but they are rarely caught. Whitefish are found anywhere in the river and average 10 inches. Worms are the best producer for both. Wet flies and spinners take a good number of rainbows in the early spring while whitefish are more active later in the summer.

Additional information: Camping is available at Deer Creek Campground, but river access involves travel by foot only, about 1 mile away to the east. The campground is a no-fee area with 7 units and accommodations for trailers up to 16 feet. There is no water or trash collection.

Contact: Wyoming Game and Fish Department, Cody.

61A. Cody Canal access

Directions: Take WY 291 southwest out of Cody about 8 miles. Turn right onto the Lower South Fork Road and drive about 4 miles. Follow the public access signs to the parking area.

61B. Andy Martin access

Directions: Take WY 291 southwest out of Cody for about 13.5 miles. Turn right onto the Lower South Fork Road and follow the public access signs to the parking area.

61C. Ishawooa Guard Station access

Directions: Take WY 291 southwest out of Cody about 22 miles. Parking is on the west side of the road.

61D. Houlihan access

Description: Small craft can be launched here.

Directions: Take WY 291 southwest out of Cody about 27 miles. Turn right onto the gravel CR 6EH and follow the public access signs to the parking area about 2.5 miles away.

61E. Shoshone National Forest

Directions: Take WY 291 southwest out of Cody for about 30 miles. The paved road will become gravel shortly before reaching the access areas. Private land is intermingled with public land along the river, with the exception of the more distant upstream portions. Watch for small Forest Service signs along the road that announce public access.

61F. Cabin Creek

Description: The Cabin Creek Trailhead just past Deer Creek Campground offers foot access to the river. There are 25 miles of river upstream from here, of which the upper portions are the best. The hike is fair-to-moderate, but long.

Directions: Take WY 291 southwest out of Cody for 35 miles to the end of the road.

62   Luce Reservoir

Key species: rainbow trout
Description: This 30-acre lake is on the windy eastern edge of the Absaroka Mountains. Trees line the distant mountains, but sagebrush dominates the lake area.
Tips: Dry flies are most productive late in the evening, just before dark.

The fishing: The rainbow trout here are commonly over 20 inches long. This reservoir is managed as a trophy fishery. The regulations and continued growth of the resident fish make the action excellent. All trout must be released immediately. Fishing is allowed with artificial flies and lures only.
Directions: Take WY 120 north out of Cody for 18 miles. Turn left onto CR 7RP and drive 4.5 miles to the Hogan Reservoir. Go south of Hogan Reservoir 1 mile to the parking area.
Additional information: This area has parking and toilets. A short hike leads to the lake.
Contact: Wyoming Game and Fish Department, Cody.

63   Hogan Reservoir

Key species: Snake River cutthroat trout
Description: Sagebrush surrounds this 35-acre reservoir in desert prairie. The Absaroka mountains loom into the sky to the west, but they offer no protection from the relentless wind.
Tips: Spoons and spinners can provide anglers with some aggressive strikes when worms are unproductive.

The fishing: Cutthroats average 8 to 14 inches. Early spring offers plenty of activity with worms and dry flies. Worms work best when fished from the bottom and can produce at any time of day. The flies show more action in the late evening. The fishing drops off and becomes marginal in midsummer. Early spring and late fall are the best times to fish.
Directions: Take WY 120 north out of Cody for 18 miles. Turn to the left onto CR 7RP and drive 4.5 miles to the reservoir.
Additional information: This area has parking and toilets.
Contact: Wyoming Game and Fish Department, Cody.

64   Lower Clarks Fork River

Key species: brown trout, cutthroat trout, rainbow trout, grayling, whitefish
Description: As the river leaves the mountains it fans out into a wider flat-bottomed stream. The water is still swift, but relatively unhindered in the high prairie desert it courses through.
Tips: Look for large boulders and pull a spinner through the deep eddies they create.

62–64 Luce Reservoir, Hogan Reservoir, Lower Clarks Fork River

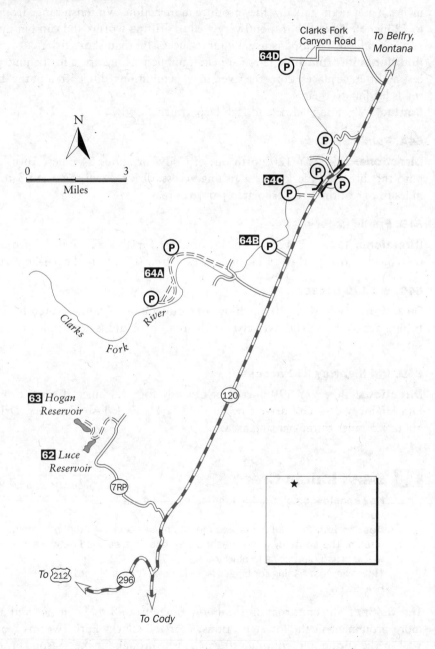

Clarks Fork Canyon Road

To Belfry, Montana

64D Ⓟ

Ⓟ

64C Ⓟ

Ⓟ

Ⓟ

N

0   3

Miles

Ⓟ

64B Ⓟ

Ⓟ

64A Ⓟ

Clarks Fork River

120

63 Hogan Reservoir

62 Luce Reservoir

7RP

★

To 212

296

To Cody

The fishing: Brown, cutthroat, and rainbow trout range from 10 to 14 inches. Cutthroats are caught more frequently than the others. Early in the spring, small spinners and large streamers are productive. Grayling range from 8 to 14 inches. Later in the fall, dry flies produce more action. Whitefish range from 8 to 12 inches. Whitefish respond very well to drifting worms and can put up a very good fight. Floating is usually more successful than shore fishing.

Additional information: There are eight public parking areas for fishing access at different places along the river. In wet conditions, don't attempt the dirt roads leading to them.

Contact: Wyoming Game and Fish Department, Cody.

64A. Public access

Directions: Take WY 120 north out of Cody for about 24 miles. Turn left onto the dirt road marked as a fishing access. Drive down this road 3 to 4 miles to one of the two designated parking areas.

64B. Public access

Directions: Take WY 120 north out of Cody for about 25 miles. Turn left onto the dirt road marked as a fishing access. Drive 0.5 mile to the parking area.

64C. WY 120 access

Directions: Take WY 120 north out of Cody about 27 miles. Watch for the fishing access signs. The river crosses the road here and is accessible on both sides.

64D. Old Highway 292 access

Directions: Take WY 120 north out of Cody for 29.3 miles. Turn left onto Old Highway 292 and drive toward the Clark's Fork Fish Hatchery. Drive about 2.5 miles to the parking area.

65 Dead Indian Creek

See map on page 92

Key species: brook trout, cutthroat trout, rainbow trout

Description: Colorful and steep mountainsides surround this mountain stream. The swift, icy water crashes over boulders stacked between willow brush, spruce, and pine trees.

Tips: The best fishing for bigger trout is downstream toward the Clarks Fork River.

The fishing: The cutthroat and rainbow range from 8 to 12 inches and are more prominent in the lower portions, near the Clarks Fork. Worms work well in the spring and continue to catch fish throughout the season. Brook trout range from 4 to 6 inches; worms work the best. The farther you are from the highway access, the better the fishing will be.

Directions: Take US 120 north out of Cody for 17 miles. Turn left onto WY 296/Chief Joseph Highway and drive 20 miles.

Additional information: Dead Indian Campground is a no-fee area with 12 units that can accommodate trailers up to 32 feet. The campground is open all year, weather permitting.

Contact: Wyoming Game and Fish Department, Cody.

66 Sunlight Creek

Key species: brook trout, cutthroat trout, rainbow trout

Description: This mountain stream cuts through some rough country on its way to the Clarks Fork River. There are steep, vertical rock cliffs in the lower portion. WY 296 is a bridge between these cliffs. A nearby parking area gives site-seers access to the walkway located on the bridge.

Tips: Small colorful spinners provide some explosive action in the pools.

The fishing: Cutthroat and rainbow trout range from 8 to 14 inches and populate the lower portions of the creek. Worms produce varying success almost all season. Nymphs and small spinners work well in the early spring until the middle of June, depending on weather. The best fishing involves a fairly difficult hike to the less-fished waters. Brook trout range from 4 to 6 inches and dominate the upper parts of the creek. Worms are the most effective bait for these aggressive little trout. Spinners can produce fish, but the brush and foliage make using them difficult.

Additional information: Little Sunlight Campground is a no-fee area with 4 units that can accommodate trailers up to 32 feet. The campground is open from May 1 to November 30. A picnic area is also available near the highway.

Contact: Wyoming Game and Fish Department, Cody.

66A. Shoshone National Forest

Description: There are undesignated pullouts that allow safe parking and relatively easy access to the creek here with no other services provided.

Directions: Take WY 120 north out of Cody for 17 miles. Turn left onto the Chief Joseph Highway/WY 296 and drive about 21 miles to the Sunlight Basin Road/FR 101. Turn left onto this gravel road and drive 13 miles, past the ranger headquarters, to the access areas.

66B. Sunlight Picnic Area

Description: This day-use fee area has fire rings, tables, and toilets. Don't use the road when it's wet. The river here crashes through a steep canyon with cottonwoods and spruce trees clinging to the bottom. Boulders and cliff walls create deep, inviting channels between rapids.

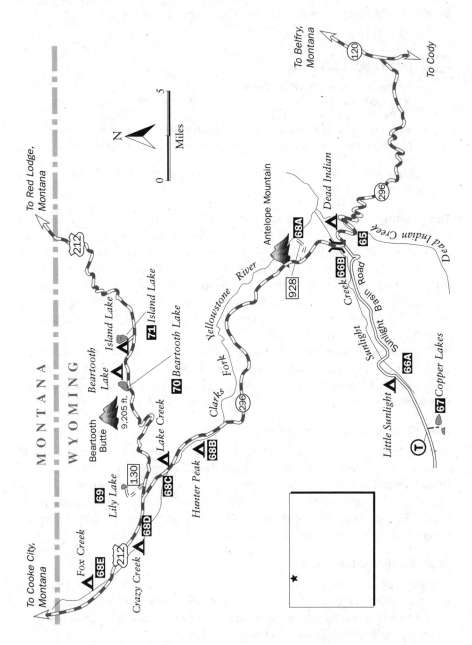

To Belfry, Montana

120

To Cody

To Red Lodge, Montana

N

5

Miles

0

Dead Indian

296

MONTANA

WYOMING

212

Antelope Mountain

Island Lake

71 Island Lake

Beartooth Lake

70 Beartooth Lake

9,205 ft.

Beartooth Butte

Yellowstone River

68A

928

66B

65

Dead Indian Creek

Sunlight Creek

Sunlight Basin Road

Clarks Fork

296

130

Lily Lake

69

68C

68D

68B

Lake Creek

Hunter Peak

Little Sunlight

66A

67 Copper Lakes

T

Fox Creek

68E

212

Crazy Creek

To Cooke City, Montana

Directions: Take WY 120 north out of Cody for 17 miles. Turn left onto the Chief Joseph Highway/WY 296 and drive about 23 miles, crossing the Sunlight Bridge. Turn left onto unimproved CR 7GR and travel 1 mile.

67 Copper Lakes

Key species: Yellowstone cutthroat trout, golden trout
Description: Copper Lake 1 is the largest with 35 acres of snowmelt nestled in the mountaintop above timberline. Copper Lake 2 holds 5 surface acres; Copper Lake 3 has 8 acres.
Tips: Mepps spinners are productive; a variety will maximize success. Keep the steep climb in mind when choosing rods and equipment.

The fishing: Copper Lake 1 holds Yellowstone cutthroat, ranging from 9 to 15 inches. The smaller Copper lakes 2 and 3 hold golden trout that range from 8 to 14 inches. An assortment of spinners and dry flies will produce action. Bottom fishing can be costly due to hook loss caused by snags. Flies are more productive toward dark.

Directions: Take WY 120 north out of Cody for 17 miles. Turn left onto Chief Joseph Highway/WY 296 and drive about 21 miles to the Sunlight Basin Road/FR 101. Turn left onto this gravel road and drive about 21 miles to the trailhead.

Additional information: There are no services at this location. Camping is available nearby, but not within easy walking distance. This is grizzly country, so take the necessary precautions. A difficult hike of about 1.75 miles leads to this area. Depending upon your physical condition, the climb can take up to 4 hours.

Contact: Wyoming Game and Fish Department, Cody.

68 Upper Clarks Fork River

Key species: cutthroat trout, rainbow trout
Description: This swift river starts in the mountains near Yellowstone National Park and cascades its way to the desert below. The Clarks Fork Canyon stretches 16 miles with steep, rocky cliffs up to 1,200 feet high on both sides.
Tips: Streamers can be very effective in the summer and late fall.

The fishing: Cutthroat average 6 to 14 inches. The farther one goes upstream, the smaller the fish become. The less accessible area of the canyon has fewer fish, although the "big ones" dominate this stretch. Rainbow trout average 6 to 12 inches. Small spinners and larger streamers work well in the spring but taper off during the summer. Dry flies take over as the major producer in the late fall. Fishing is allowed with artificial flies and lures only. From Reef Creek, upstream to the Montana state line, there is a limit of six trout per day or six in possession. All trout over 8 inches must be released.

Additional information: Camping is available at different locations along this river.

Contact: Wyoming Game and Fish Department, Cody.

68A. Clark Canyon

Description: There is a designated trail with two access points for this area. One leaves the Dead Indian Campground area, described in site 68, and follows Dead Indian Creek to the river. The other follows Reef Creek to the river. This description covers a more commonly used, unofficial trail. The trail is difficult, but it is the most direct route.

The fishing: From Reef Creek, downstream to the national forest boundary, there is a limit of three trout, of which only one may be over 12 inches.

Directions: Take WY 120 north out of Cody for 17 miles. Turn left onto the Chief Joseph Highway/WY 296 and drive about 26 miles. Turn right onto the dirt FR 928. As you approach this area, a limestone cliff formation is on the right. FR 928 heads toward the river before passing this landmark, known as Antelope Mountain. Drive as close as safely possible to the canyon edge. Then the adventure starts. It is all downhill, or down-cliff, until your return.

68B. Hunter Peak Campground access

Description: This fee area with 9 units is open all year and has accommodations for trailers up to 32 feet.

Directions: Take WY 120 north out of Cody for 17 miles. Turn left onto the Chief Joseph Highway/WY 296 and drive 42 miles.

68C. Lake Creek Campground access

Description: This fee area with 6 units is open from June 1 to September 30. It has accommodations for trailers up to 22 feet.

Directions: Take US 120 north out of Cody for 17 miles. Turn left onto the Chief Joseph Highway/WY 296 and drive 46 miles.

68D. Crazy Creek Campground access

Description: This fee area has 19 units and accommodations for trailers up to 32 feet. It is open from June 1 to October 20.

Directions: Take US 120 north out of Cody for 17 miles. Turn left onto the Chief Joseph Highway/WY 296 and drive 47 miles. Turn left onto US 212 and drive 5 miles.

68E. Fox Creek Campground

Description: This fee area with 27 units is open from June 1 to September 30. It can accommodate trailers up to 32 feet.

Directions: Take US 120 north out of Cody for 17 miles. Turn left onto Chief Joseph Highway/WY 296 and drive 47 miles. Turn left onto US 212 and drive 10 miles.

69 Lily Lake

See map on page 92

Key species: brook trout, rainbow trout, grayling
Description: This 40-acre lake is tucked away just north of the highway. Spruce, fir, and lodgepole pine surround alpine meadows studded with large boulders. Snowcapped mountains are in the background.
Tips: Small mosquito and black ant flies work well in the early morning.

The fishing: Brook trout range from 4 to 12 inches. Worms are productive all summer. Rainbow trout range from 8 to 14 inches. These fish can be touchy; take a variety of bait and lures. Grayling range from 7 to 14 inches. Small black dry flies work well in the early morning or late evening.

Directions: Take US 120 north out of Cody for 17 miles. Turn onto the Chief Joseph Highway/WY 296 and drive 47 miles. Turn right onto US 212 and drive 0.75 mile. Turn left onto the Lily Lake Road/FR 130 and travel 1.6 miles. The road condition deteriorates.

Additional information: Boats are the most effective way to fish this lake, but launching one requires a good deal of effort; the boat launch is not well developed or maintained.

Contact: Wyoming Game and Fish Department, Cody.

70 Beartooth Lake

See map on page 92

Key species: brook trout, cutthroat trout, rainbow trout, mackinaw, grayling
Description: This 110-acre lake sits in majestic mountain country. Dense fir and pine border the alpine meadows and shoreline. Wildlife can often be spotted in the area.
Tips: Mackinaw fishing is best in early spring with a variety of baits including worms, salmon eggs, and Power Bait.

The fishing: Brook trout get up to 11 inches and respond well to just about anything. Rainbow and cutthroat get up to 12 inches. Worms, salmon eggs, and Power Bait produce well in the early spring. Later in the summer, fishing is less productive. Grayling average 13 inches. Small black flies find some action in the early morning near the deepwater dropoffs. Mackinaw can get up to 22 pounds here and tend to stay in deep water, except in early spring. A deep dropoff on the northeast shore, opposite the campground, produces the majority of mackinaw.

Directions: Take US 120 north out of Cody for 17 miles. Turn left onto Chief Joseph Highway/WY 296 and drive 47 miles. Turn right onto US 212 and drive 13 miles. Beartooth Lake is north of the highway.

Additional information: Beartooth Lake Campground is a fee area with 21 units, a boat ramp, and accommodations for trailers up to 32 feet. The campground is open from July 1 to September 7, weather permitting.

Contact: Wyoming Game and Fish Department, Cody.

71 Island Lake

See map on page 92

Key species: brook trout
Description: This is a beautiful, 146-acre alpine lake.
Tips: Look for the deep drop-offs and shadows in the lake.

The fishing: Brook trout get up to 12 inches, but average 6 to 9 inches. Boating is the best option for reaching the larger fish. Worms are effective from boat or shore most of the day. Late evenings offer fly fishers an opportunity as the trout feed on insects.

Directions: Take US 120 north out of Cody for 17 miles. Turn left onto the Chief Joseph Highway/WY 296 and drive 47 miles. Turn right onto US 212 and drive 16 miles. Turn left onto the Island Lake Road and travel this gravel road for 0.5 mile.

Additional information: Island Lake Campground is a fee area with 20 units, a boat ramp, and accommodations for trailers up to 32 feet. The campground is open from July 1 to September 7, weather permitting.

Contact: Wyoming Game and Fish Department, Cody.

72 Wind River Canyon

Key species: brown trout, cutthroat trout, rainbow trout, walleye, ling
Description: The controlled water flow of this portion offers some challenging conditions. The weeds and moss are very healthy and thick from the Boysen Reservoir to the Wedding of the Waters, where Wind River becomes Bighorn River. The river passes through the colorful Wind River Canyon.
Tips: Wet flies drifting with the current can produce some explosive action.

The fishing: Rainbow trout range from 12 to 20 inches while brown trout are a bit larger. Worms are the most productive bait for trout, but wet flies provide some very good action. This portion of the river is swift, making bank fishing and wading the most effective methods to work the water. If you choose to float the river, consider an outfitter. Rainbow and cutthroat trout are stocked in the spring. The best time for trout fishing is from early spring to mid-May. Walleye between 12 to 30 inches are caught with nightcrawlers and jigs in the deep pools and backwater near Boysen Dam. The best time for walleye fishing is early spring to June. Ling range from 16 to 30 inches; all year long, nightcrawlers produce the most fish in the deep pools at night.

Additional information: Avoid the private land along this stretch of river; if you are unsure whether or not an area is public, don't try it. Also, a good portion of this river is on the Wind River Indian Reservation, which requires anglers to have a reservation permit.

Contact: Wyoming Game and Fish Department, Cody.

72-74 Wind River Canyon, Boysen Reservoir, Lake Cameahwait

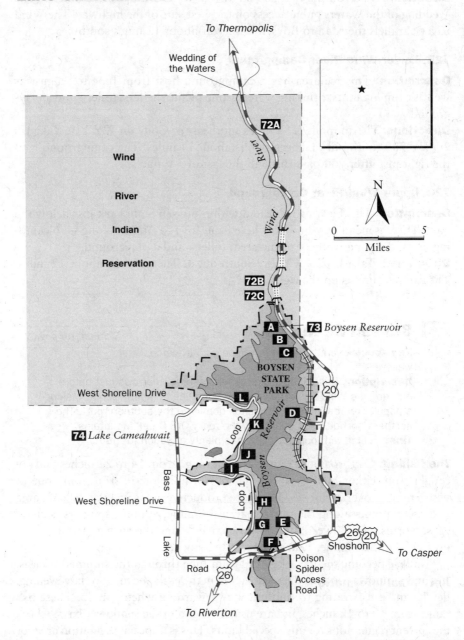

To Thermopolis

Wedding of
the Waters

72A

Wind

River

Indian

Reservation

Wind

River

River

Wind

N

0   5
       Miles

72B
72C

A   73 Boysen Reservoir
B
C

BOYSEN
STATE
PARK

West Shoreline Drive   L

20

74 Lake Cameahwait   K

Loop 2   D

Boysen Reservoir

J

I

Loop 1

West Shoreline Drive   H

G   E

Bass   F

Lake   26 20
                        Shoshoni   To Casper

Road   26
                              Poison
                              Spider
                              Access
To Riverton   Road

72A. Highway access

Description: Numerous pullouts allow foot access along US 20/WY 789.
Directions: Take US 20/WY 789 south out of Thermopolis, 2 miles to the Wedding of the Waters pubic access on the west side of the highway. The Wind River parallels the road to Boysen Reservoir about 12 miles south.

72B. Lower Wind River Campground

Description: This fee area has a campground host from June to August as well as camping units, drinking water, group picnic shelters, toilets, and a playground.
Directions: Thermopolis is 84 miles southeast of Cody on WY 120. Take US 20/WY 789 south out of Thermopolis about 11 miles. The campground is to the right just after you pass through the last of 3 tunnels.

72C. Upper Wind River Campground

Description: This fee area is located within Boysen State Park just below the dam. There is a campground host here from June to August along with camping units, drinking water, a picnic area, toilets, and a playground.
Directions: Take US 20/WY 789 south out of Thermopolis about 12 miles. The campground is on the right.

73 Boysen Reservoir

See map on page 97

Key species: cutthroat trout, rainbow trout, perch, walleye
Description: This 19,000-acre desert reservoir narrows just before entering the Wind River Canyon. The shoreline is mostly sandy, making it a popular recreation site. Badlands dominate the southern part. The northern portion rises sharply to the rocky Owl Creek Mountains.
Tips: Trolling with pop gear provides plenty of action for trout.

The fishing: Cutthroat and rainbow trout range from 14 to 22 inches and are caught from either boat or shore. There is a limit of six trout, only one of which may be over 20 inches. The more productive areas include the dam area and rocky points along the northeastern shoreline. Spoons, spinners, salmon eggs, worms, and Power Bait are productive during the spring. Trout fishing drops off in the summer heat. Rainbow are stocked every year.

Walleye become the fish of choice from June through the summer months. Jigs and minnows produce the most action in the early morning or late evening. Perch can be frustrating to find but very rewarding when you do. These fish range from 10 to 12 inches and are usually found in the shallower bays. Check the current regulations for any special limits. This is a special regulation area for ice fishing, which allows anglers to use up to 6 poles within certain guidelines.
Additional information: Boysen State Park offers camping, a marina, a boat ramp, and related water sports.
Contact: Wind River Indian Reservation.

73A. Brandon Campground

Description: This fee area has camping units, drinking water, a picnic area, toilets, a telephone, a playground, and a boat ramp.

Directions: From Shoshoni, take US 20/WY 789 north 10 miles. The campground is on the left side.

73B. Marina

Description: The marina offers food, supplies, permits, and licenses. Camping is also available with drinking water, a picnic area and toilets.

Directions: From Shoshoni, take US 20/WY 789 north for 10 miles. Turn left onto the paved access road and travel 0.25 mile.

73C. Tamarask Campground

Description: This fee area has camping units, a picnic area, drinking water, a playground, and toilets.

Directions: From Shoshoni, take US 20/WY 789 north for 10 miles. Turn left onto the paved access road and travel 0.75 mile.

73D. Tough Creek Campground

Description: This fee area has camping units with drinking water, a picnic area, toilets, and a boat ramp.

Directions: From Shoshoni, take US 20/WY 789 north for 6 miles. Turn left onto the paved road marked as the Tough Creek Campground access and drive about 1 mile.

73E. Poison Creek Campground

Description: This fee area has camping units, a picnic area, toilets, and a boat ramp.

Directions: From Shoshoni, head west on US 26/WY 789 for about 1 mile to the Poison Spider access road. Turn right onto this gravel road and drive about 1.25 miles.

73F. Lakeside Picnic Area

Description: This day-use area has toilets and a boat ramp.

Directions: From Shoshoni, head west on US 26/WY 789 for 2 miles. The picnic area is on the right side.

73G. North Five Mile

Description: There are no facilities here.

Directions: From Shoshoni, head west on US 26/WY 789 about 5.5 miles to the Bass Lake Road/CR 540. Turn right onto this paved road and bear right in order to access the West Shoreline Drive Loop 1. Drive about 2.5 miles on this road, which becomes gravel.

73H. Fremont Bay Campground

Description: This fee area has camping units, a picnic area, group picnic shelters, a playground, toilets, and a boat ramp.
Directions: Follow the directions to site 75G, and drive 2.5 miles farther north.

73I. South Muddy Campground

Description: This fee area has camping units, a picnic area, and toilets.
Directions: Follow the directions to site 75G, and drive about 4.5 miles farther north.

73J. North Muddy Campground

Description: This fee area has camping units and toilets.
Directions: From Shoshoni, head west on US 26/WY 789 about 5.5 miles to the Bass Lake Road/CR 540. Turn right and follow it as it goes west and then north about 9 miles to the Lake Cameahwait access. Turn right and drive about 3.75 miles on this road, which becomes gravel.

73K. Sand Mesa Campground

Description: This fee area has camping units, a picnic area, and toilets.
Directions: From Shoshoni, head west on US 26/WY 789 about 5.5 miles to the Bass Lake Road/CR 540. Turn right and follow it as it goes west and then north about 7 miles to the Lake Cameahwait access. Turn right and travel down this paved road, which will become gravel, for about 3.75 miles. Bear left and follow the shoreline about 4 miles north.

73L. Cottonwood Campground

Description: This fee area has camping units, a picnic area, group picnic shelters, toilets, and a boat ramp.
Directions: From Shoshoni, head west on US 26/WY 789 about 5.5 miles to the Bass Lake Road/CR 540. Turn right onto this road, which becomes gravel, and follow it west and then north past the Lake Cameahwait access for a total of about 15.5 miles.

74 Lake Cameahwait

See map on page 97

Key species: rainbow trout, largemouth bass, perch
Description: A variety of waterfowl visits this wetland seasonally. Cattails and rushes are abundant along the shore.
Tips: Plastic worms provide some explosive action during June when fished close to the cattails.

The fishing: Rainbow trout range from 6 to 8 inches. Worms, salmon eggs, and Power Bait produce fish throughout the summer. Early morning and late evening are the best times. Perch range from 2 to 6 inches and will hit almost

100

anything. Largemouth bass are the fish of choice for most anglers. There is a limit of two bass per day or two in possession, of which only one may be over 15 inches. You must release all bass between 10 and 15 inches. Some of these feisty fish reach 6 pounds. The best time to fish is early spring, from a boat near the shore. Cast into the weedline as closely as possible; the bass will be in the shadows.

Directions: From Shoshoni, head west on US 26/WY 789 about 5.5 miles to the Bass Lake Road/CR 430. Turn right and drive about 7 miles to the access road. Turn right onto this road, which becomes gravel, and drive about 2.5 miles.

Additional information: Camping, a boat ramp, and restrooms are available. This area is open all year.

Contact: Wind River Indian Reservation.

75 Ocean Lake

See map on page 103

Key species: largemouth bass, black crappie, walleye, perch
Description: This wetland lake is home to a multitude of waterfowl. The shoreline is shallow and weedy.
Tips: Walleye respond well to minnows early in the spring through mid-June.

The fishing: Largemouth bass range from 5 to 8 inches. From May through June almost anything attracts these fighters. Later in the summer they will move into deep water and show more interest in spinner baits. Crappie range from 3 to 7 inches. Fishing from a boat with worms and jigs produces many of these fish. Walleye average 8 to 10 inches; early spring is usually the only good time for catching them. Jigs and nightcrawlers offer the greatest success. Boating is the best way to fish here. Special restrictions for ice fishing allow anglers to use up to 6 lines within certain guidelines.

Additional information: Three boat ramps, picnic areas, and camping are available, Six parking areas have restroom and trash facilities. Ocean Lake is open all year.

Contact: Boysen State Park.

75A. Ocean Lake Road

Directions: From Riverton, take US 26 northwest about 15 miles. Turn right onto Ocean Lake Road/CR 476 and drive about 1.75 miles.

75B. WY 134

Description: A designated parking area is provided with access to a boat ramp.
Directions: From Riverton, take US 26 for 6 miles northwest to Eight Mile Road. Turn right and drive about 9 miles to the Missouri Valley Road/WY 134. Turn left onto this paved road and drive 2.5 miles. Turn left onto the dirt access road and travel 0.75 mile.

75C. Shady Lane

Description: There are 7 designated parking areas and 2 boat ramps here.
Directions: From Riverton, take US 26 for 6 miles northwest of Riverton to Eight Mile Road. Turn right onto this paved road and drive about 9 miles to Missouri Valley Road/WY 134. Turn left and drive about 11.5 miles to Shady Lane. Turn left onto this gravel road. There are several access areas along Shady Lane.

76 Pilot Butte Reservoir

Key species: rainbow trout, ling
Description: This 921-acre, manmade lake sits in windy, sage-covered prairie.
Tips: Try drifting while dragging a minnow along the bottom.

The fishing: Trout average from 8 to 12 inches; large ones get up to 4 pounds. Worms, cheese, Power Bait, and salmon eggs work well for the smaller fish, either from shore or by boat. Ling can get up to 10 pounds. Minnows produce the bigger ling, and night fishing is the most productive. Special ice fishing regulations allow anglers to use up to 6 poles within certain guidelines.
Directions: From Riverton, take US 26 northwest for 25 miles.
Additional information: Camping and picnic facilities are available, as well as a boat ramp and toilets.
Contact: Wyoming Game and Fish Department, Lander.

77 Ray Lake

Key species: rainbow trout
Description: This dam-created prairie lake just east of the Wind River Mountains holds 575 surface acres of water.
Tips: Worms work well when fished on the bottom near the dam.

The fishing: Rainbow trout range from 8 to 14 inches. Early in the spring, rainbow trout are caught from shore along the dam with worms, Power Bait, and salmon eggs. Fishing drops off during the summer and trollers have limited success. Irrigation causes the water level to fluctuate; when the water level is not too low, Mepps and Panther Martin spinners can produce some strikes.
Directions: From Lander, take US 287 northwest about 10 miles. Ray Lake is to the left of the road and is accessible from the old highway; the dam is visible from this road.
Additional information: This manmade lake is on the Wind River Indian Reservation. A reservation permit is required and can be obtained from any of the reservation vendors listed in Appendix A. Ray Lake is open year-round with a boat ramp available.
Contact: Wyoming Game and Fish Department, Lander.

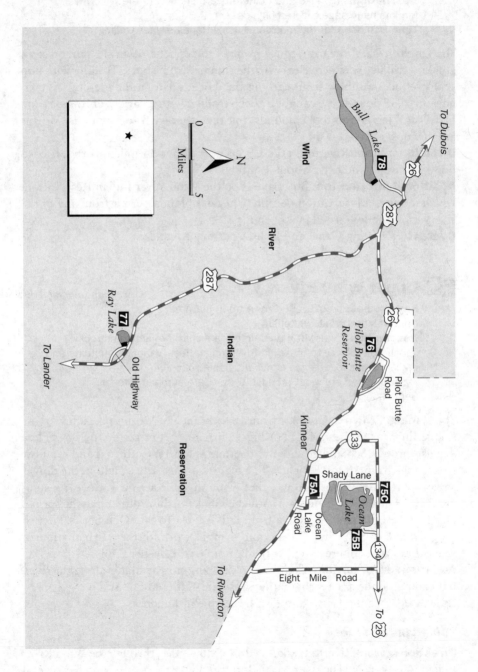

78 Bull Lake

See map on page 103

Key species: rainbow trout, mackinaw, ling
Description: This lake sits in the eastern shadow of the Wind River Mountains in sage-covered high desert.
Tips: Fish deep for the mackinaw using Rapalas when trolling.

The fishing: Rainbow trout range from 14 to 20 inches. Worms, salmon eggs, and Power Bait are effective early in the summer from shore. Trolling with pop gear produces rainbow trout early in the day and late in the evening. Mackinaw up to 35 pounds are caught by deep trolling with a variety of Rapalas and Flat Fish. Ling get up to 17 pounds, but they average 3 to 5 pounds. Worms are the most effective bait.

Directions: From Riverton, take US 26 west about 36 miles. Turn left onto Bull Lake Road and drive about 1.5 miles.

Additional information: Bull Lake is on the Wind River Indian Reservation, which requires a reservation permit. You can obtain a permit from any of the reservation vendors listed in Appendix A.

Contact: Wyoming Game and Fish Department, Lander.

79 Upper Wind River

See map on page 106

Key species: brook trout, brown trout, cutthroat trout, rainbow trout, whitefish
Description: This swift mountain stream cuts through some rocky country on its way to the Wind River Indian Reservation. Mountains and badlands mix together in a brilliant display of color.
Tips: Dry flies are most productive from late summer through September.

The fishing: Brown trout range from 10 to 18 inches. Worms take a few of the smaller browns in the spring. For bigger fish and better action, fish from late August through September with dry flies and spinners. Cutthroat and rainbow trout range from 10 to 16 inches. The big fish are usually caught in the downstream portions. Worms and wet flies result in some action in the early summer. High runoff from mountain snowmelt makes fishing difficult in the spring. Dry flies become more effective from late August to late October. Whitefish range from 8 to 16 inches. Worms and nymphs work for these fish anytime of year. They often congregate near the bottom of the deeper pools.

Additional information: There are no camping sites available along the river, but campgrounds are nearby in the Shoshone National Forest.

Contact: Wyoming Game and Fish Department, Lander.

79A. Highway access

Directions: From Riverton, take US 26 west 67 miles, through the Wind River Indian Reservation. The river parallels the highway to the west and has several public access sites in the next 7 miles.

79B. Jakeys Fork/Dubois Hatchery

Directions: From Riverton, take US 26 west 67 miles, through the Wind River Indian Reservation. Continue on US 26 from the reservation boundary for 8 miles to the pubic access parking.

79C. Dunoir

Directions: From Dubois, take US 26 west for 6 miles to the designated public access parking.

80 Torrey Lake

Key species: brown trout, rainbow trout, ling, mackinaw, splake

Description: This 231-acre lake is at the mouth of a rugged mountain canyon. The Wind River Mountains are to the west and south.

Tips: Troll the deep waters with pop gear for mackinaw.

The fishing: Mackinaw range from 13 to 30 inches. Trolling with pop gear is the most effective method of fishing for them. Salmon eggs fished from shore occasionally take a few smaller mackinaw in early June. Brown trout average 12 to 16 inches. Boaters find these fish in deep water during the summer. Late in the fall, worms and salmon eggs do well on the bottom. Spinners and spoons take fish both from shore and by boat. Trollers do well in the fall when passing near points and along the shoreline. Rainbow trout range from 8 to 12 inches. Worms, salmon eggs, and Power Bait create the best action in the early spring through June. The fishing picks up again in the fall; try using dry flies in the late evening. Splake range from 12 to 16 inches. Trollers do the best, but anglers using spinners from shore should also be successful. Ling range from 18 to 24 inches and respond well all season to worms fished at night.

Directions: From Dubois, head east on US 26 about 3.5 miles. At the road sign for the Dubois Fish Hatchery and the Whiskey Basin Wildlife Habitat Management Area, turn right and drive a short distance to FR 411. Turn left onto gravel FR 411 and drive about 4 miles.

Additional information: Primitive camping is available at nearby Ring and Trail lakes. There is no designated camping area at this site, but a boat ramp is available. This area contains a lot of private ground, so be aware of the signs.

Contact: Wyoming Game and Fish Department, Lander.

81 Ring Lake

Key species: brown trout, rainbow trout, splake

Description: The Wind River Mountains shoot skyward south and west of this 108-acre mountain lake. To the north and east, vast badlands display vivid contrasts of reddish hues. In between, grass and sagebrush mingle with cottonwood, pine, and willow brush.

Tips: Fishing is best in early spring or late fall.

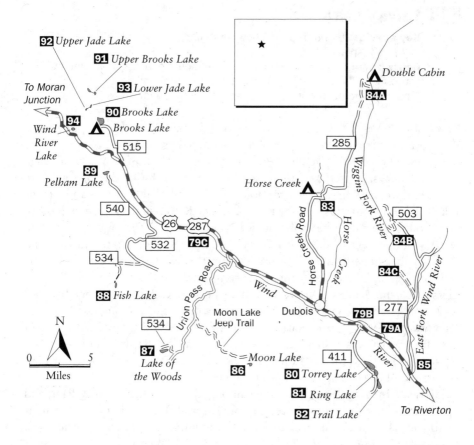

92 Upper Jade Lake

91 Upper Brooks Lake

93 Lower Jade Lake

To Moran Junction

94 Wind River Lake

90 Brooks Lake
Brooks Lake

515

89 Pelham Lake

540

26 287

532 **79C**

534

88 Fish Lake

N

0 — 5
Miles

534

87 Lake of the Woods

Union Pass Road

Moon Lake Jeep Trail

86 Moon Lake

Wind

Double Cabin

84A

285

Wiggins Fork River

Horse Creek **83**

Horse Creek Road

Horse Creek

503

84B

84C

East Fork Wind River

411

Dubois

79B 277

79A

River

80 Torrey Lake

81 Ring Lake

82 Trail Lake

85

To Riverton

The fishing: Brown trout range from 10 to 18 inches. The better fishing begins in late August. Red and white Dardevle spoons, Bucktail Mepps, and large streamers can get the attention of these fish. Browns will take worms, though they do not seem to hit bait with the same impact that they do lures. Rainbow trout range from 12 to 16 inches. Worms and salmon eggs work best fished on the bottom in the early summer. The fishing drops off severely during the summer months, though spinners and dry flies take a few in the evenings. Splake range from 12 to 16 inches. Trollers do well. Shore anglers get some action with spoons and spinners.

Directions: Follow the directions to site 82 and drive 1 mile further south on FR 411.

Additional information: Primitive camping is available nearby in designated areas operated by the state. Be aware of private land and respect the desires of the owners.

Contact: Wyoming Game and Fish Department, Lander.

82 Trail Lake

Key species: brown trout, rainbow trout, splake
Description: This 120-acre mountain lake has the Wind River
Mountains as a scenic backdrop. This lake is nestled into the steeper
part of the canyon above the previously mentioned sites.
Tips: Early spring and late fall are best.

The fishing: The trout here range from 12 to 16 inches. Shore fishing is best with worms and salmon eggs. Early mornings and late evenings in early spring and late fall are the most productive times. Splake range from 12 to 16 inches.

Directions: Follow the directions to site 82, and drive about 2 miles farther south on FR 411. This gravel road will turn to improved dirt, so be mindful of weather conditions.

Additional information: Primitive camping is available in designated state-operated areas.

Contact: Wyoming Game and Fish Department, Lander.

83 Horse Creek

Key species: brook trout, cutthroat trout, rainbow trout
Description: This creek meanders through mountain meadows with
lodgepole pine and aspen. There are wide pools up to 10 inches and
narrow places.
Tips: Fish the ripples and undercuts.

The fishing: Trout range from 7 to 12 inches here. Catchable fish are stocked yearly to maintain population levels. Worms are productive in the early spring, while flies create more action in the fall.

Directions: From Dubois, head north on the Horse Creek Road/FR 508 and drive about 12 miles on this asphalt-to-gravel-to-improved dirt road.

Additional information: Horse Creek Campground is a fee area with 9 units that can accommodate trailers up to 16 feet. The campground is open from June 1 to October 30, weather permitting. This is grizzly bear country, so take the necessary precautions.

Contact: Wyoming Game and Fish Department, Lander.

84 Wiggins Fork River

See map on page 106

Key species: brook trout, brown trout, cutthroat trout, whitefish

Description: The Wiggins Fork River passes through cottonwood and sagebrush on its way out of the Absaroka Mountains. This rocky river covers 31.5 miles on its way to the East Fork Wind River.

Tips: Fish the shadows, under logs, overhanging branches, and undercuts.

The fishing: This river is stocked with fingerlings. Trout range from 8 to 14 inches. Worms produce trout in the early summer, but whitefish are the most commonly caught fish with this type of bait. Flies and spinners can create some explosive action later in the fall.

Additional information: This is grizzly country so be sure to take the necessary precautions.

Contact: Wyoming Game and Fish Department, Lander.

84A. Double Cabin Campground

Description: This fee area has 15 units and can accommodate trailers up to 16 feet long. It is open from June 1 to September 30. Weather conditions may change the opening and closing dates of the campground.

Directions: From Dubois, head 12 miles north on Horse Creek Road/FR 508, which becomes gravel then improved dirt. Continue north on improved dirt FR 285 for 16 miles.

84B. Spence/Moriarity

Description: There is camping available with toilets.

Directions: From Dubois, take US 26 east 10 miles. Turn left onto the East Fork Road/CR 277 and drive about 5 miles. The Wiggins Fork River crosses the road on its way to the East Fork Wind River.

84C. Kirk Inberg/Kevin Roy Wildlife Management Area

Description: Camping and toilets are available in this elk winter range. The area is closed from December 1 to April 30.

Directions: From Dubois, take US 26 east for 10 miles. Turn left onto gravel East Fork Road/CR 277 and drive about 8 miles. At the intersection, bear left and drive another 2 miles to FR 503. A four-wheel-drive road heads left to the river.

85 East Fork Wind River

See map on page 106

Key species: brown trout, cutthroat trout, rainbow trout, whitefish
Description: The river runs through sage-covered grasslands in the midst of some beautiful mountain scenery. This is grizzly bear country, so take the necessary precautions.
Tips: Dry flies offer the best fishing for trout in the fall.

The fishing: Brown trout range from 12 to 18 inches. These fish migrate from downstream in late August and respond well to spinners and dry flies. Worms take a few, but whitefish more often grab the hook first. Cutthroat and rainbow trout range from 10 to 16 inches, although larger ones have been reported. Early spring is a good time to use nymphs and worms. Results drop off drastically in the heat of the summer with limited success using spinners and spoons. Dry flies fished in the shadows will produce in the fall. Whitefish range from 10 to 14 inches. These fish like worms and wet flies and are usually in the deep, slow currents. Fishing quality can change drastically when storms cloud the water; most area storms occur in June.
Directions: From Dubois, take US 26 east for 10 miles. Turn left onto the East Fork Road/CR 277. The river parallels the road on the east side.
Additional information: The Spence/Moriarity Wildlife Management Area has camping and toilets available. Portions of the area are closed from December 1 to April 30.
Contact: Wyoming Game and Fish Department, Lander.

86 Moon Lake

See map on page 106

Key species: rainbow trout, mackinaw
Description: This is a 60-acre alpine lake.
Tips: Worms offer the best results just after the ice melts in the early spring.

The fishing: Rainbow trout range from 8 to 12 inches; worms provide the most action. Mackinaw can get up to 16 inches. Early spring, just after the ice melts, is the best time to fish for them. Salmon eggs work well for mackinaw. Fingerlings are stocked here as needed.
Directions: From Dubois, drive west on US 26 for 9.5 miles to Union Pass Road/CR 240. Turn left onto this gravel road and drive about 10 miles to the Moon Lake jeep trail. Turn left onto this four-wheel-drive trail and travel about 7 miles.
Additional information: This lake is in a remote area that requires some effort and a four-wheel-drive vehicle.
Contact: Wyoming Game and Fish Department, Lander.

87 Lake of the Woods

See map on page 106

Key species: cutthroat trout, grayling
Description: This 98-acre mountain lake sits in the historic Union Pass.
Tips: The bubble-and-fly technique works well for both trout and grayling.

109

The fishing: The cutthroat range from 10 to 14 inches. Worms, salmon eggs, small spinners, and flies can be productive just about anytime. Later in the summer the best results come during the early morning or late evening. Bring a variety of lures and bait to satisfy the fussy ones. Grayling range from 6 to 9 inches. Small, black dry flies tend to be the choice for these challenging fish. There is a limit of three trout or grayling, of which only one may be over 20 inches long.

Directions: From Dubois, head west on US 26 for 9.5 miles to Union Pass Road/CR 240. Turn left onto this gravel road and drive 15 miles.

Additional information: No motorized boats are allowed.

Contact: Wyoming Game and Fish Department, Lander.

88 Fish Lake

See map on page 106

Key species: cutthroat trout
Description: This mountain lake holds 28 ice-cold surface acres.
Tips: Colorful spinners may work when the fish are ignoring worms.

The fishing: Cutthroat range from 8 to 10 inches. Worms, salmon eggs, and Power Bait work well in early spring. As the water warms up in the summer, the fish tend to be less hungry. Spinners can sometimes aggravate them enough to produce a strike. Using dry flies in shady areas in the late evening creates some activity later in the fall.

Directions: From Dubois, head west on US 26 for about 17.5 miles to the Sheridan Creek Road/ FR 540. Turn left onto this gravel road and drive about 0.5 mile to FR 532. Travel down this gravel road for about 6 miles to FR 544. Turn right onto this four-wheel-drive road and go about 2.25 miles to FR 234. The last 1.5 miles of the road requires a four-wheel-drive vehicle.

Additional information: Consider walking this rough four-wheel-drive trail for the last 1.5 miles to the lake.

Contact: Wyoming Game and Fish Department, Lander.

89 Pelham Lake

See map on page 106

Key species: cutthroat trout
Description: Snowcapped mountains break the horizon beyond this 33-acre, natural alpine lake.
Tips: The bubble-and-fly method offers the greatest coverage.

The fishing: Cutthroat average 10 to 16 inches. Dry flies work best in early spring and fall. Later in the summer, small, colorful spinners catch fish in the deep, shaded waters. Fishing is allowed only with artificial flies or lures, and there is a limit of 2 trout, which must be over 14 inches. All trout under this length must be immediately released. This lake is stocked with fingerlings.

Directions: From Dubois, head west on US 26 about 17.5 miles to the Sheridan Creek Road/ FR 540. Turn left onto this gravel road and drive 0.25 mile to the first road on your right. This improved dirt road, which becomes a four-wheel-drive trail, is the Pelham Lake Road. Turn right onto this road and travel 4.5 miles.

Additional information: No motorized boats are allowed.

Contact: Wyoming Game and Fish Department, Lander.

90 Brooks Lake

See map on page 106

Key species: mackinaw, rainbow trout
Description: This 234-acre, natural alpine lake is tucked away in a majestic mountain canyon. Layers of rock are stacked like cake with snow for icing, overshadowing the fir, spruce, and pine forest encompassing the lake area.
Tips: Worms work best when fished from the bottom in the early spring.

The fishing: Rainbow trout range from 9 to 13 inches. Natural baits work best either from shore or by boat. This lake is stocked with fish raised to catchable size. Mackinaw up to 20 pounds are caught occasionally just after the ice melts. Salmon eggs and worms provide the most action from shore. Trolling with Rapalas and Flatfish in deep waters will produce mackinaw later in the summer.

Directions: From Dubois, head west on US 26 for 23 miles to FR 515. Turn right onto this gravel road and drive 5 miles.

Additional information: Brooks Lake Campground is a fee area with 14 units, accommodations for trailers up to 22 feet, and a boat ramp. It is open from June 20 to September 30, weather permitting. This is grizzly bear country, so take the necessary precautions.

Contact: Wyoming Game and Fish Department, Lander.

91 Upper Brooks Lake

See map on page 106

Key species: brook trout, rainbow trout
Description: This 25-acre lake is even more isolated than its larger counterpart.
Tips: Bobbers and bubbles with either worms or flies are very effective.

The fishing: Brook trout range from 4 to 6 inches. Worms work well when fished with bobbers. Bottom fishing produces limited results with these fish. Small imitation mosquito flies find action late in the evening. Later in the fall, just about anything works in the shallow waters when the brook trout start spawning. Rainbow trout range from 7 to 10 inches. Worms, salmon eggs, and Power Bait are effective from shore. Flies and grasshoppers are more productive in the fall.

Directions: From Dubois, head west on US 26 for 23 miles to FR 515. Turn right onto this gravel road and drive 6 miles. The trail is about 3 miles long.

Additional information: A moderate hike leads to the lake. Camping is available at nearby campgrounds. This is grizzly bear country so take the necessary precautions.

Contact: Wyoming Game and Fish Department, Lander.

92 Upper Jade Lake

See map on page 106

Key species: cutthroat trout
Description: This 15-acre lake is in the same canyon that holds the Brooks Lakes. No motorized boats are allowed.
Tips: Take a variety of small colorful spinners.

The fishing: Cutthroat trout range from 7 to 10 inches. Worms work well in the spring. A variety of small spinners with a light spinning rod could find more action, but adds to packing weight. Fishing is not the best during the summer, but the scenery is.

Directions: From Dubois, head west on US 26 for 23 miles to FR 515. Turn right onto this gravel road and drive 6 miles. The foot trail is about 1.5 miles long.

Additional information: A moderate hike leads to the lake. This is grizzly bear country, so take the necessary precautions.

Contact: Wyoming Game and Fish Department, Lander.

93 Lower Jade Lake

See map on page 106

Key species: cutthroat trout, mackinaw
Description: This 23-acre lake is a little larger than Upper Jade Lake.
Tips: Mackinaw with appetites visit the rocky shallows in early spring.

The fishing: Cutthroat trout range from 6 to 10 inches. Spinners are the most convenient means of catching them; bait works well for both cutthroat and mackinaw. Mackinaw range from 8 to 12 inches. Early in the spring, these fish respond well to bottom fishing with worms, salmon eggs, and Power Bait. Spinners will create some limited action.

Directions: From Dubois, head west on US 26 for 23 miles to FR 515. Turn right onto this gravel road and drive 6 miles. The foot trail is about 1.75 miles long.

Additional information: A moderate hike leads to the lake. No motorized boats are allowed. This is grizzly bear country, so take the necessary precautions.

Contact: Wyoming Game and Fish Department, Lander.

94 Wind River Lake

See map on page 106

Key species: brook trout, rainbow trout
Description: This small mountain lake sits beside the highway near Togwotee Pass and is easily missed. Tall spruce, fir, and some lodgepole pines crowd in along the banks from the gently rising ridges. This is grizzly bear country, so take the necessary precautions.
Tips: Patience and a picnic lunch work well while you smell the mountain air and watch the pole tip.

The fishing: Brook trout range from 4 to 6 inches. Worms work the best. The majority of trout are near the rocky shallows. Fall offers better fishing when spawning gives the fish large appetites. Rainbow trout range from 6 to 8 inches. Worms, salmon eggs, and Power Bait are effectively fished on bottom. Fishing drops off dramatically during the summer, then improves slightly in the fall.

Directions: From Dubois, head west on US 26 for about 30 miles. The lake is on the right side of the highway.

Additional information: The Wind River Lake Picnic Area has 3 units and toilets. No motorized boats are allowed.

Contact: Wyoming Game and Fish Department, Lander.

95 Leidy Lake

See map on page 117

Key species: cutthroat trout

Description: This little-visited, 9-acre lake is tucked away deep in a mountain forest within sight of the Tetons.

Tips: Worms fished on the bottom are the best bet in the early spring.

The fishing: Cutthroat trout range from 8 to 13 inches. Worms and salmon eggs are effective in the early spring when fished on the bottom. Spring may not begin until early June in this high country. These trout get fussy during the hot parts of the summer, and you will find little action before nightfall. Dry flies used just before dark can persuade a few to tickle a line. If winter doesn't set in too early, late August and September will see some action with flies and spinners.

Directions: From Moran Junction take US 26/287 east for 6 miles to FR 30160. Turn right onto this improved dirt road and travel about 7 miles to FR 30100. Turn right onto this improved dirt road and drive about 3 miles to FR 30250. Turn right onto this improved dirt road and travel about 4.5 miles. The road will become a four-wheel-drive trail. You can also reach this lake from FR 30100 just east of Togwotee Lodge on US 26/287.

Additional information: Camping is available along US 26/287 at the Hatchet Campground, although this is some distance away, 12 to 15 miles from the lake. Be sure to have plenty of bug repellent if you plan a trip in the spring.

Contact: Wyoming Game and Fish Department, Jackson.

96 Bridger Lake

Key species: cutthroat trout

Description: This cold, 104-acre lake is in the Teton Wilderness and has plenty of mountain scenery and wildlife. Yellowstone National Park is a short distance north of the lake. The trails do not open up before the middle of June in this high country.

Tips: Worms are the most productive just after ice melt, which can be fairly late in the spring.

The fishing: The cutthroat range from 14 to 18 inches. Early in spring, worms are very productive. Later in the summer, grasshoppers, flies, and small spinners provide the best action.

Directions: Take US 89/287 north out of Moran Junction for about 1 mile to the Pacific Creek Road. Turn right onto this gravel road and travel about

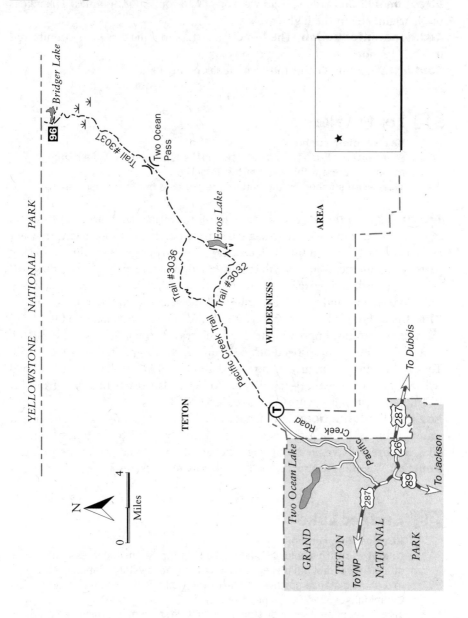

8 miles to the Pacific Creek Trailhead, which is at the end of the road. This 25-mile trail into the Teton Wilderness ranges from moderate to difficult. Overnight camping and additional research are necessary for a trip to this lake.

Additional information: There are 25 miles of wilderness to trek through to access this lake. Footwork is required, either a horse's or your own. Mountain bikes are not allowed. Camping is permitted; check current conditions for fire regulations.

Contact: Wyoming Game and Fish Department, Jackson.

97 Grassy Lake

Key species: cutthroat trout, mackinaw
Description: This 346-acre, manmade lake sits in some wild and little-visited country. Lodgepole pine and spruce trees provide shade and scenery along the shore and blanket the ridges in all directions.
Tips: Mackinaw are usually close to shore just after ice melt and respond well to salmon eggs.

The fishing: Cutthroat range from 14 to 18 inches. Early spring is the most productive time of year for bait. Mackinaw range from 9 to 20 inches with some larger ones caught from time to time.

Directions: From Moran Junction, take US 287/89/191 north about 23 miles to the Flagg Ranch. Turn left off the highway and proceed toward the Flagg Ranch. Almost immediately after turning left, turn right onto Reclamation Road/FR 3261, which will become dirt. Travel down this road about 25 miles. If the road is dry, a conventional vehicle can make it, but high clearance or four-wheel-drive vehicles are advised.

Additional information: This lake is in grizzly country and will be closed at certain times of the year to minimize impact.

Contact: Wyoming Game and Fish Department, Jackson.

98 Toppings Lake

Key species: grayling
Description: The snow and ice melt slowly in this high country. Winter can hang on until the middle of June at this 5-acre mountain lake.
Tips: Set the hook carefully, as these fish have a small jawbone. A hard jerk can pull the hook right through the bone.

The fishing: Grayling range from 8 to 13 inches. Small black flies and mosquito imitations are productive, especially in the early evening. The bubble-and-fly method works well.

Directions: Drive north from Jackson on US 26/89/191 about 24.5 miles. Turn right onto FR 30310 across from the Cunningham Cabin Historical Site. Travel down this gravel road, which eventually becomes an improved dirt road, about 5 miles to the trailhead.

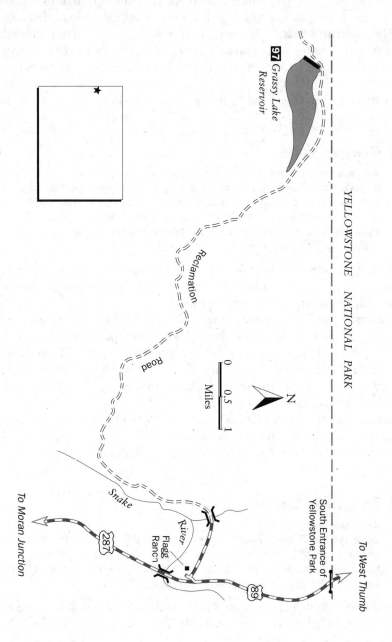

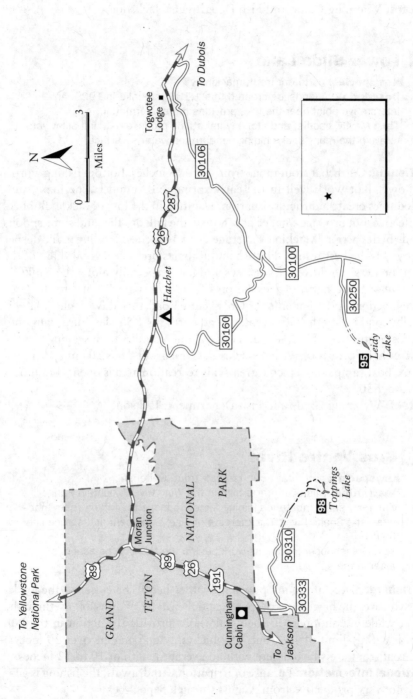

To Dubois

Togwotee
Lodge

30106

287

26

Hatchet

30100

30160

30250

95 Leidy Lake

Miles

N

0   3

NATIONAL   PARK

TETON

GRAND

Moran
Junction

89

89

26

191

Cunningham
Cabin

To Jackson

To Yellowstone
National Park

98 Toppings Lake

30310

30333

Additional information: A 2-mile hike on a moderately difficult trail leads to the lake.

Contact: Wyoming Game and Fish Department, Jackson.

99 Lower Slide Lake

Key species: cutthroat trout, mackinaw

Description: A landslide created this 1,133-acre lake in 1925. An interpretive point near the lake provides more information.

Tips: Mayfly, caddis, and stonefly imitations produce fish and allow you to avoid the many snags hiding beneath the water's surface.

The fishing: Cutthroat trout range from 14 to 18 inches. Bottom fishing worms and Power Bait work well in the early spring and summer. The many submerged trees create a difficult situation, resulting in the loss of tackle. Bobbers are effective, but produce smaller fish. Late in the fall, dry flies and some spoons provide better action. Mackinaw average 10 to 14 inches. Trolling in the deeper water yields the best results. Flatfish and Rapalas produce a good share of the action. Boaters should watch for trees and logs, especially along the banks.

Directions: Drive north of Jackson on US 26/89/191 for 7 miles to the Gros Ventre Junction. Turn right onto the Gros Ventre Road, then drive 7 miles to Kelly. At Kelly, continue on the Gros Ventre Road north for 1.5 miles. Turn right onto the Gros Ventre Road/FR 30400 and drive about 5.5 miles to the campground.

Additional information: Atherton Creek Campground has 20 units, drinking water, a boat ramp, and a picnic area. This recreation area is open from June 5 to October 30.

Contact: Wyoming Game and Fish Department, Jackson.

100 Gros Ventre River

Key species: cutthroat trout, rainbow trout, whitefish

Description: This river starts high in the Wind River Mountain Range with many small tributaries joining forces to make the wide stream that enters the Snake River. Thick forests of pine, fir, aspen, and spruce line the river.

Tips: Grasshopper imitations work best in the fall, but the action is faster in the spring.

The fishing: There are many pools and riffles here. The closer to the Snake River you are, the bigger and deeper the pools will be. Worms are useful in the spring, while grasshoppers or their imitations provide the action in the fall. There is a daily limit of six trout, of which only one may be over 20 inches. Cutthroat trout are stocked here with an average length of 10 to 12 inches.

Additional information: Because of irrigation withdrawals, the fishing is generally not very productive from August through September.

Contact: Wyoming Game and Fish Department, Jackson.

99–103 Lower Slide Lake, Gros Ventre River, Flat Creek, Granite Creek, Hoback River

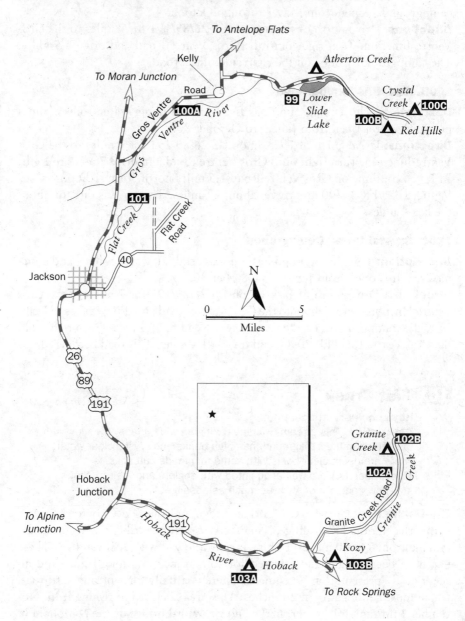

To Antelope Flats

Kelly

Atherton Creek

To Moran Junction

Road

Gros Ventre Road

Gros Ventre

100A River

Gros

Crystal Creek

99 Lower Slide Lake

100B

100C

Red Hills

Flat Creek

101

Flat Creek Road

40

Jackson

N

0   5
Miles

26

89

191

★

Granite Creek

102B

102A

Granite Creek

Hoback Junction

To Alpine Junction

Hoback

191

Granite Creek Road

Kozy

103B

River

Hoback

103A

To Rock Springs

119

100A. Gros Ventre Campground

Description: This fee area has 360 units, modern comfort stations, and a trailer dumping station. There are accommodations for trailers and RVs. The campground is open from May 1 through October 4.

Directions: Drive north of Jackson on US 26/89/191 for 7 miles to the Gros Ventre Junction. Turn right onto the Gros Ventre Road and drive 4.5 miles. The campground will be on the right side of the road.

100B. Red Hills Campground

Description: This campground has five units, drinking water, toilets, and a picnic area. It is open from June 5 to October 30.

Directions: Drive north of Jackson on US 26/89/191 for 7 miles to the Gros Ventre Junction. Turn right onto Gros Ventre Road and drive 7 miles to Kelly. At Kelly, continue on Gros Ventre Road 1.5 miles north. Turn right onto Gros Ventre Road/FR 30400 and travel about 11 miles. This road is dirt for about the last 4 miles.

100C. Crystal Creek Campground

Description: This campground has 6 units, drinking water, toilets, and a picnic area. It is open from June 5 to October 30.

Directions: Drive north of Jackson on US 26/89/191 for 7 miles to the Gros Ventre Junction. Turn right onto the Gros Ventre Road and drive 7 miles to Kelly. At Kelly, continue north on the Gros Ventre Road for 1.5 miles. Turn right onto the Gros Ventre Road/FR 30400 and travel 11.5 miles. This road becomes dirt.

101 Flat Creek

See map on page 119

Key species: cutthroat trout

Description: This stream, winding through a wide, grassy meadow with the Tetons in the background, has high banks and crystal-clear water. There are deep, clear pools with some manmade cutbanks.

Tips: These fish are well acquainted with anglers and their methods; stay down and out of sight as much as possible.

The fishing: The area from McBride Bridge and the Old Crawford Bridge, within the National Elk Refuge, is managed as a trophy fishery with cutthroats ranging from 8 to 20 inches. Fishing is only allowed with artificial flies. These fish have been caught and released for some time, so a long leader and an accurate fly presentation is required. There is a daily limit of one cutthroat, which must be longer than 20 inches. This area is closed to fishing from November 1 through July 31. From the Old Crawford Bridge on the National Elk Refuge, downstream to the western boundary of the elk refuge, the area is closed to fishing. Downstream from the National Elk Refuge to US 191, adjacent to the Sagebrush Motel, general regulations apply but are restricted to anglers under 14 years of age.

Directions: Flat Creek is accessed from Jackson. The National Elk Refuge provides fishing for the adults while children can access the creek from town. Follow the signs in Jackson to the refuge, which borders the northeastern part of town.

Additional information: Flat Creek flows through the National Elk Refuge just north of Jackson. Motels, restaurants, and stores are available in town.

Contact: Wyoming Game and Fish Department, Jackson.

102 Granite Creek

See map on page 119

Key species: cutthroat trout, whitefish
Description: Granite Creek starts in the rugged Gros Ventre Wilderness and cascades its way to the Hoback River.
Tips: Fall fishing with grasshopper imitations produces the most action.

The fishing: Trout and whitefish range from 8 to 12 inches. Early spring is not very productive; the rainy season produces cloudy, turbid water fairly constantly. Late in the summer fishing improves with grasshoppers or their imitations. Worms will take more whitefish when fished along bottom.

Additional information: Camping is available along the creek.

Contact: Wyoming Game and Fish Department, Jackson.

102A. Granite Creek Campground

Description: There are 52 units, a picnic area, drinking water, and toilets. This area is open from June 15 to September 15.

Directions: From Hoback Junction, take US 189/191 southeast 10 miles to FR 30500. Turn left onto this gravel road and drive about 9 miles.

102B. Granite Hot Springs

Description: A natural hot spring here has been converted into a swimming pool. This fee area is open year-round, unless the road is closed due to snow. Camping is allowed and toilets are available.

Directions: From Hoback Junction, take US 189/191 south 10 miles to FR 30500. Turn left onto this gravel road and drive about 9.5 miles.

103 Hoback River

See map on page 119

Key species: cutthroat trout, whitefish
Description: This mountain stream, surrounded by thickly-forested ridges and intermittent meadows, gathers water and depth as it approaches the Snake River.
Tips: Panther Martins work well in the deep, shaded waters in late summer.

The fishing: Cutthroat trout range from 8 to 10 inches. The big ones tend to come from the waters closer to the Snake River, but much of this area is on private ground. The water quality changes quickly, making fishing rather poor

121

in the spring. Late in the summer, fly fishing is good with Adams and Wulff patterns. Panther Martins and Mepps spinners are also effective late in the summer. Whitefish range from 8 to 12 inches. Nymphs and worms work well on whitefish in the deep pools.

Additional information: Camping is available along the river.

Contact: Wyoming Game and Fish Department, Jackson.

103A. Hoback Campground

Description: This area has 26 units, a picnic area, drinking water, and toilets. The campground is open from June 1 to September 30.

Directions: From Hoback Junction, take US 189/191 southeast 6 miles.

103B. Kozy Campground

Description: This area has 8 units, a picnic area, and toilets. The campground is open from June 1 to September 30.

Directions: From Hoback Junction, take US 189/191 southeast 11 miles. The campground is on the right side of the road.

104 Snake River

Key species: brown trout, cutthroat trout, whitefish

Description: The terrain along this 100-mile stretch of river changes from rugged rocky mountains to flat valleys. Alpine meadows graced with lodgepole pines, spruce, and fir give way to willows, cottonwoods, and aspen increasing in number on the way to the canyon. South of Jackson, the mountains close in on this widening river to form a whitewater canyon before it plunges into the Palisades Reservoir.

Tips: Waders find the best action and conditions from July through October.

The fishing: From Yellowstone National Park to Jackson Lake, the trout range from 8 to 16 inches. Wading is the most effective method, but floating is also popular. This section of river is closed to trout fishing from November 1 through March 31. There is a daily limit of three trout, of which only one my be over 20 inches. Whitefish can be caught year-round and range from 8 to 12 inches. Both trout and whitefish respond well to nightcrawlers, grasshoppers, and minnow rigs. Spinners, spoons, dry flies, and wet flies are also very effective for trout, but the nymphs tend to produce more whitefish.

From the gauging station, 1,000 feet below Jackson Lake Dam, to the WY 22 bridge/Wilson Bridge, cutthroat range from 8 to 18 inches. Floating is the most effective method, but there are some wading opportunities. This stretch is closed to trout fishing from November 1 through March 31. There is a limit of three trout per day or 3 in possession, of which only 1 may be over 18 inches. All trout 12 to 18 inches must be released. Fishing is allowed with artificial flies or lures only.

Fly fishing for cutthroat trout is good in late summer in the waters of the scenic Hoback River.

From the Wilson Bridge to the West Table Boat Ramp, trout average 8 to 12 inches. This stretch of river is closed to trout fishing from November 1 to March 31. There is a limit of 3 trout per day or 3 in possession, of which only 1 may be over 12 inches.

The Snake River, from the West Table Boat Ramp to Palisades Reservoir, is not subject to special regulations, but it is closed to trout fishing from November 1 through March 31.

Additional information: The Snake River covers about 100 miles before entering southern Idaho. Portions of the river are in Yellowstone National Park and Grand Teton National Park. These sections are covered in this book under separate headings. Numerous access areas are available, as well as highway pullouts at many points that are not listed here.

Contact: Wyoming Game and Fish Department, Jackson.

104A. Snake River Picnic Area

Description: This is a former campground across the river from the old Flagg Ranch. Picnic tables, fire rings, and toilets are available.

Directions: Take US 26/89/191 north out of Jackson for 30 miles to Moran Junction. Take US 89/191/287 north of Moran Junction toward Yellowstone National Park for 22 miles.

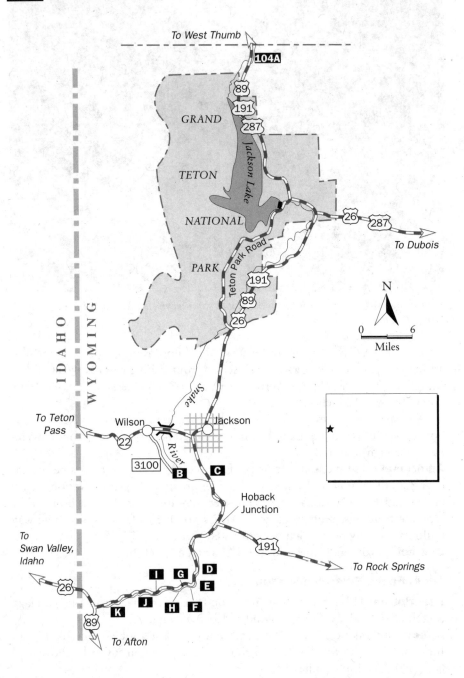

To West Thumb

104A

89

191

287

Jackson Lake

GRAND

TETON

NATIONAL

PARK

26   287

To Dubois

Teton Park Road

191

89

26

N

0   6
Miles

IDAHO

WYOMING

Snake

To Teton
Pass

Wilson

22

3100

B   C

Jackson

River

Hoback
Junction

To
Swan Valley,
Idaho

191

To Rock Springs

I G D

E

26

J H F

K

89

To Afton

104B. Public access

Directions: Take WY 22 west out of Jackson for about 5 miles to the Wilson Bridge. After crossing the bridge, turn left onto FR 31000 and drive south on this gravel road about 6.5 miles. Access and parking will be on the left side of the road.

104C. South Park Wildlife Habitat Management Area

Description: A short distance by foot that ranges from easy to difficult is required to reach certain areas. Small boats can be launched with a little effort. This area is closed from November 16 to April 30.
Directions: Take WY 26/89/191 south out of Jackson for 8 miles. The access parking will be on the right side of the highway.

104D. Cabin Creek Campground

Description: This area has 10 campsites, a picnic area, drinking water, and toilets.
Directions: Take US 26/89/191 south out of Jackson for 12 miles to Hoback Junction. Take US 26/89 south out of Hoback Junction for about 6.75 miles.

104E. East Elbow Campground

Description: This area has 9 units, a picnic area, drinking water, toilets, and a boat ramp. It is open from May 25 through September 5.
Directions: Take US 26/89/191 south out of Jackson 12 miles to Hoback Junction. Take US 26/89 south out of Hoback Junction for about 9.25 miles.

104F. West Elbow Campground

Description: This area has 8 units, a picnic area, drinking water, and toilets. Group reservations can be arranged for this location as well. It is open from May 25 through September 5.
Directions: Take US 26/89/191 south out of Jackson 12 miles to Hoback Junction. Take US 26/89 south out of Hoback Junction for about 9.5 miles.

104G. East Table Creek Campground

Description: This area has 18 units, a picnic area, drinking water, toilets, and a boat ramp. It is open from May 25 through September 5.
Directions: Take US 26/89/191 south out of Jackson 12 miles to Hoback Junction. Take US 26/89 south out of Hoback Junction about 10 miles.

104H. West Table Creek Boat Ramp

Description: Toilets and a boat ramp are available here. This area is open from April through October.
Directions: Take US 26/89/191 south out of Jackson for 12 miles to Hoback Junction. Take US 26/89 south out of Hoback Junction for about 10.75 miles.

104I. Station Creek Campground

Description: This area has 14 units, a picnic area, drinking water, and toilets. It is open from May 25 through September 5.

Directions: Take US 26/89/191 south out of Jackson for 12 miles to Hoback Junction. Take US 26/89 south out of Hoback Junction for about 11.5 miles.

104J. Wolf Creek Campground

Description: This area has 10 units, a picnic area, and toilets. It is open from May 25 through September 5.

Directions: Take US 26/89/191 south out of Jackson for 12 miles to Hoback Junction. Take US 26/89 south out of Hoback Junction for about 13 miles.

104K. Sheep Gulch Boat Ramp

Description: Toilets and a boat ramp are available here. This area is open from April through October.

Directions: Take US 26/89/191 south out of Jackson for 12 miles to Hoback Junction. Take US 26/89 south out of Hoback Junction for about 17.5 miles.

Southwest

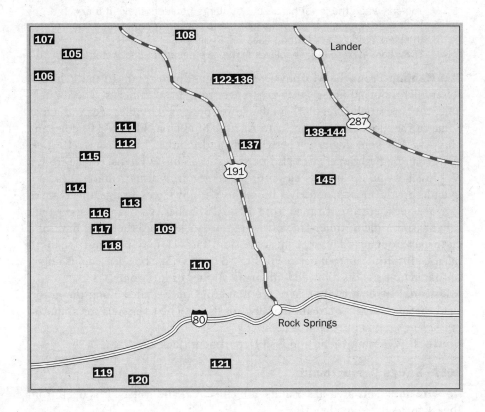

105 Greys River

Key species: cutthroat trout, whitefish

Description: This clear, ice-cold stream starts small but gets big fast. You can wade the lower parts, but the large boulders make it tricky. The swift water bounces over rocks in a steep canyon. Willow brush lines the banks as it flows to the Palisades Reservoir.

Tips: Look next to large boulders in the streambed for backwater eddies.

The fishing: From the Murphy Creek Bridge, downstream to the Palisades Reservoir, about 20 miles, cutthroat range from 8 to 12 inches. These catchable trout are stocked regularly in this lower portion. Dry flies are productive. Some of the more popular ones are Adams, Blue Dun, Elk Hair Caddis, and Hoppers. For spin anglers, Rooster Tails and Panther Martins are effective. Worms and grasshoppers can also be very successful. Whitefish range from 8 to 14 inches and are usually closer to the reservoir. Worms, salmon eggs, and nymphs are the most productive. From the Murphy Creek Bridge, upstream to Corral Creek, cutthroat range from 10 to 16 inches, with a few larger ones caught from time to time. These fish are not stocked and there is a limit of 2 cutthroat trout per day or 2 in possession. Only 1 may be longer than 16 inches; all cutthroat trout between 11 to 16 inches must be released. Fishing in this stretch of river is allowed with artificial flies or lures only.

Additional information: There are numerous access sites along the gravel road that parallels the stream that are not listed. The river runs for about 60 miles, leaving lots of room for company.

Contact: Wyoming Game and Fish Department, Jackson.

105A. Bridge Campground

Description: This area has 5 units, a picnic area, and toilets. It is open from June 1 through September 10.

Directions: Alpine Junction is 35 miles south of Jackson on US 26/89. Take US 89 for 0.5 mile south to Alpine. Turn left onto the gravel FR 10138 and drive 2.25 miles.

105B. Lynx Creek Campground

Description: This area has 14 units, a picnic area, and toilets. It is open from June 1 through September 10.

Directions: From Alpine, head east on FR 10138 and drive about 10.5 miles.

105C. Murphy Creek Campground

Description: This area has 10 units, a picnic area, and toilets. It is open from June 1 through September 10.

Directions: From Alpine head, east on FR 10138 and drive about 12.5 miles.

105D. Moose Flat

Description: This area has 10 units, a picnic area, and toilets. It is open from June 1 through September 10.

105 Greys River

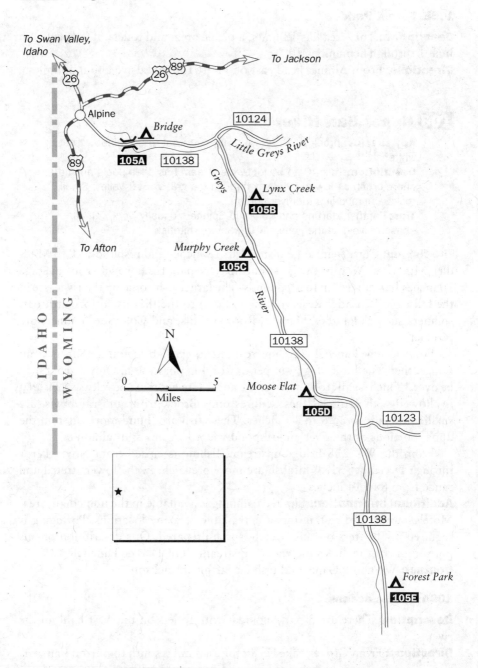

To Swan Valley, Idaho

26

26 89

To Jackson

Alpine

Bridge

10124

Little Greys River

105A 10138

Greys

89

Lynx Creek

105B

To Afton

Murphy Creek

105C

River

IDAHO   WYOMING

10138

N

0   5
Miles

Moose Flat

105D

10123

★

10138

Forest Park

105E

Directions: From Alpine, head east on FR 10138 and drive about 21 miles.

105E. Forest Park

Description: This area has 13 units, a picnic area, and toilets. It is open from June 1 through September 10.
Directions: From Alpine, head east on FR 10138 and drive about 35 miles.

106 Upper Salt River

Key species: brook trout, brown trout, cutthroat trout, rainbow trout, whitefish
Description: This 40- to 50-foot-wide stream has deep pools and little shore brush as it works its way through the grassy Star Valley. Small rocks and mud line the river bottom.
Tips: Panther Martins and Colorado Spinners usually work well all season, avoiding the generally unwanted whitefish.

The fishing: Cutthroat range from 11 to 18 inches and respond well to Muddler Minnows, Woolly Buggers, and mayfly patterns. Brown trout average 10 inches but can get up to 10 pounds. The larger fish come up the river late in the fall from Palisades Reservoir. In addition to the flies listed for cutthroat, spinners such as Panther Martins, Rooster Tails, and Colorado Spinners are productive.

From Thayne Lane/CR 125, upstream to the US 89 bridge at the Silverstream Lodge, there is a limit of 4 trout per day or 4 in possession. Only 1 trout may be over 18 inches; all trout between 11 and 18 inches must be released. Fishing is allowed with artificial flies or lures only. Brook trout and rainbows, are smaller, ranging from 6 to 10 inches. These fish are found more often in the upper portions of the river and respond well to worms and salmon eggs.

From the WY 238 bridge upstream, fishing is closed from November 1 through December 31. Whitefish are more prevalent in the lower stretch and range from 8 to 14 inches.
Additional information: Limited camping is available in the immediate area. Motels, stores, and restaurants are available at many locations. Portaging is required for floaters on this stretch, so be prepared. Our description of this portion of river includes the waters upstream from Thayne Lane/CR 125.
Contact: Wyoming Game and Fish Department, Jackson.

106A. Public access

Description: There are 3 parking areas with toilets on the west bank of the river.
Directions: From Grover, take US 89 for 2.75 miles south to Burton Lane/CR 136. Turn right onto this paved road and drive 2.25 miles to the access parking areas.

106 Upper Salt River

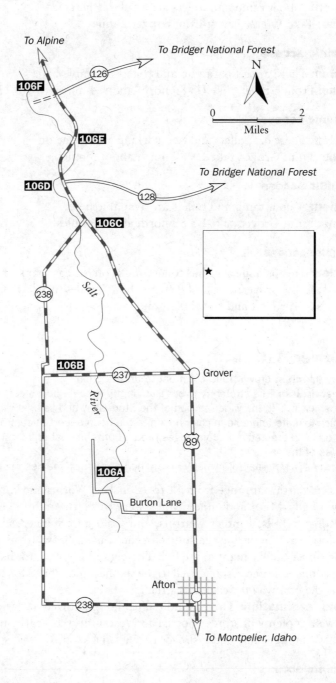

106B. Public access

Description: A boat ramp and toilets are available here.
Directions: Take WY 237 west from Grover 2 miles.

106C. Public access

Description: There are a boat ramp and toilets available here.
Directions: From Grover, take US 89 north about 4 miles to WY 238.

106D. Public access

Description: There are toilets and two parking areas, one on each bank.
Directions: From Grover, take US 89 north about 5 miles.

106E. Public access

Description: A boat ramp and toilets are available here.
Directions: From Grover, take US 89 north about 6 miles.

106F. Public access

Description: This parking area has toilets and is on the east bank of the river.
Directions: From Grover, take US 89 north about 7 miles to Strawberry Creek Road/CR 126. Turn left and travel 0.25 mile.

107 Lower Salt River

Key species: brown trout, cutthroat trout, whitefish
Description: This stretch of river gains depth while its banks get brushier. It is in the wider portion of the Star Valley and can get windy, which is quite tolerable in comparison to the open desert of central Wyoming. Forested mountain ridges are on both the east and west sides of the valley.
Tips: Allow your bait or nymph to drag the bottom into the deep pools.

The fishing: Cutthroat range from 11 to 18 inches. Worms and wet flies are productive. Lady Mites and Sandy Mites seem to be the fly of choice here. Mepps, Rooster Tails, Panther Martins, and Colorado Spinners also create some explosive action during the course of the season. Brown trout up to 10 pounds are most often caught in the fall. The big ones move into the river for spawning at this time and respond well to the spinners mentioned for cutthroat. Floating is the best way to reach this stretch of river.
Additional information: There is limited camping allowed at various locations, as well as plenty of stores, motels, and restaurants at nearby towns.
Contact: Wyoming Game and Fish Department, Jackson.

107A. Public access

Description: There are 2 parking areas with toilets on the east bank of the river.

107 Lower Salt River

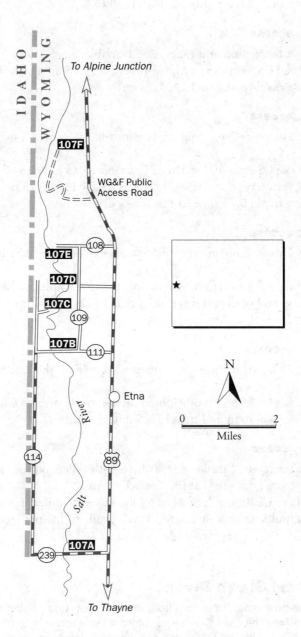

Directions: Take US 89 south of Alpine Junction for 14 miles to WY 239. Turn right onto this paved road and drive 0.75 mile.

107B. Public access

Description: A boat ramp and toilets are available.
Directions: Take US 89 south of Alpine Junction 10.25 miles to CR 111. Turn right onto this gravel road and drive 1.25 miles.

107C. Public access

Description: There are 2 parking areas with toilets on the west bank of the river.
Directions: Take US 89 south of Alpine Junction 10.25 miles to CR 111. Turn right onto this gravel road and drive 1.5 miles to CR 114. Turn right onto this gravel road and travel 0.75 mile to the access drive.

107D. Public access

Description: This parking area has toilets available on the east bank of the river.
Directions: Take US 89 south of Alpine Junction for 9 miles to CR 108. Turn right onto this gravel road and travel 0.75 mile to CR 109. Turn left onto this gravel road and travel 0.75 mile.

107E. Public access

Description: This parking area has toilets available on the east bank of the river.
Directions: Take US 89 south of Alpine Junction for 9 miles to CR 108. Turn right onto this gravel road and travel 1.25 miles.

107F. Public access

Description: There are 2 parking areas here with toilets on the east bank of the river. There is a boat ramp at the last access area.
Directions: Take US 89 south of Alpine Junction for 8 miles. Turn right onto this improved, public access dirt road, travel 1 mile to the first access and an additional mile to the access with a boat ramp.

108 (Upper) Green River

Key species: brown trout, cutthroat trout, rainbow trout, whitefish
Description: The clear Green River winds its way across sagebrush flats between forested ridges and snowcapped mountains as it leaves Lower Green River Lake. It gets up to 30 feet wide.
Tips: Dry flies and streamers produce fish throughout the summer.

The fishing: Due to the length of this river, more specific information is given in the access listings.

Additional information: This description of the upper portion of this river includes the waters from the Daniel Fish Hatchery upstream to Lower Green River Lake. Much of the Green River is on private ground, so be sure to stay on the public lands.

Contact: Wyoming Game and Fish Department, Pinedale.

108A. Green River Lake Campground

Description: This fee area has 23 units, drinking water, toilets, and a picnic area. Snowcapped mountains cloaked in heavy timber overlook this part of the river.

The fishing: Rainbow trout range from 12 to 14 inches. Spinners, spoons, and nymphs are productive all summer long. Dry fly streamers tend to create more action in late summer. Cutthroat range from 10 to 12 inches. Whitefish range from 10 to 12 inches. Worms and nymphs often produce whitefish.

Directions: From Pinedale, take US 191 north for 5 miles to WY 352. Turn right and drive 40 miles north; the road becomes gravel.

108B. Whiskey Grove Campground

Description: This fee area has 9 units, drinking water, toilets, and a picnic area. Sagebrush flats separate the pine-forested ridges from the river, while thick willow brush line the riverbanks.

The fishing: The same conditions exist here as at site 110A. From Kendall Warm Springs, downstream to the upper limit of the Warren Bridge Access, there is a limit of 2 trout per day, of which only 1 may exceed 20 inches. All trout between 10 and 20 inches must be released. Only artificial flies or lures are allowed.

Directions: From Pinedale, take US 191 north 5 miles to WY 352. Turn right and drive 28 miles north.

108C. Warren Bridge Access

Description: Sagebrush dominates this area. The river is 10 to 20 feet wide here and littered with large boulders. The river bottom is rocky. There are 19 parking areas and primitive camping is available. Access is by a dirt road with steep hills and deep ruts. Trailers are not advised, nor is travel on wet days.

The fishing: Floating is common from this area to a takeout point near Daniel. Float time can vary from 6 to 10 hours and is best attempted from June to September. When water levels drop later in the summer, the float can become very difficult. Access to private land from the river is not allowed, making overnight camping impossible. If you start the float, you must complete it without touching land.

Directions: From Daniel Junction, take US 189/191 north for 9 miles. Cross the bridge to the west bank and turn right onto the improved dirt Warren Bridge Public Access road and select one of the 19 parking areas within the next 7 miles.

108 (Upper) Green River

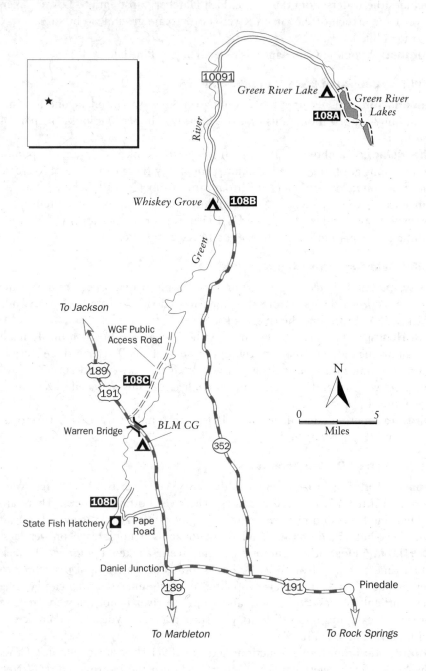

108A Green River Lake / Green River Lakes

10091

River

108B Whiskey Grove

Green

To Jackson

WGF Public Access Road

189

108C

191

Warren Bridge   BLM CG

108D

State Fish Hatchery   Pape Road

Daniel Junction

189

191   Pinedale

To Marbleton

To Rock Springs

352

N

0   5
Miles

108D. Daniel Access

Description: The Wyoming Game and Fish Department manages this area. Camping, toilets, 4 parking areas, and a boat ramp are available. The river has some large islands; the wetlands are home for numerous species of waterfowl.

The fishing: Rainbow trout range from 12 to 14 inches. Wading and floating both produce fish. Spinners, spoons, streamers, nymphs, and standard fly patterns all provide action at various times. Cutthroats range from 10 to 12 inches. The same methods used for rainbows can be effective for these fish. They are less common and caught less often than the rainbows. Whitefish range from 10 to 12 inches. These fish respond well to worms and nymphs.

Directions: From Daniel Junction, take US 189/191 north about 4 miles to Pape Road. Turn left onto this gravel road and travel to 1 of the 4 parking areas in the last 3 miles of this 6-mile-long access.

109 Fontenelle Reservoir

Key species: brown trout, rainbow trout

Description: This 7,000-acre reservoir sits in vast badlands. Sandy beaches and hot summer days make this a pleasant recreation area.

Tips: Fishing with large colorful streamers just off the points in the fall is productive.

The fishing: Rainbow trout range from 12 to 14 inches. Shore anglers do well in the spring with worms, salmon eggs, and Power Bait. As the summer heats up, trolling in deep waters with large lures is the most effective method. Later in the fall, streamers can be productive, but fishing is more likely to be focused on the spawning brown trout. Browns range from 12 to 20 inches; larger ones are often caught. Trolling with a variety of lures produces a few browns during the hot summer days. The best time for these big fish is in the fall. Fishing from the points after sunset with streamers can produce 3- to 4-pound browns.

Additional information: Three camping areas and a marina are available at various locations.

Contact: Wyoming Game and Fish Department, Pinedale.

109A. Fontenelle Creek

Description: This camping area offers a picnic area, a boat ramp, and a marina.

Directions: Fontenelle Reservoir is 74 miles north of I-80/exit 18 (12 miles east of Evanston) on US 189. The Fontenelle Creek Campground is on the west bank, midway between the north and south ends of the reservoir.

109B. Names Hill

Description: This area offers camping and a picnic area.

Directions: Fontenelle Reservoir is 74 miles north of I-80/exit 18 (12 miles east of Evanston) on US 189. This camping area is on the northern end of the reservoir.

109, 110 Fontenelle Reservoir, (Lower) Green River

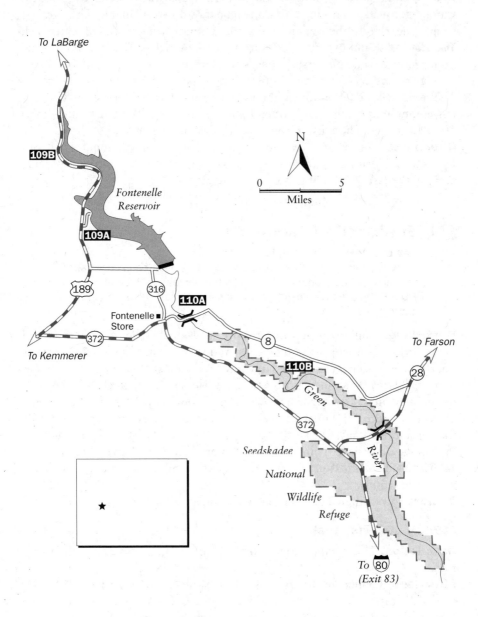

To LaBarge

N

0 — 5
Miles

109B

Fontenelle
Reservoir

109A

189   316

110A

Fontenelle ■
Store

8

110B

To Kemmerer

372

Green

To Farson

28

372

River

Seedskadee

National

Wildlife

Refuge

★

To 80
(Exit 83)

110 (Lower) Green River

Key species: brown trout, rainbow trout, kokanee salmon, whitefish

Description: This section of the river winds its way through a desert landscape. Large cottonwoods line the riverbanks near the upper portions. As the river gains waters from other streams, it becomes cloudy all the way to Flaming Gorge Reservoir.

Tips: Floating is the most effective and appealing method.

The fishing: There are 74 miles of floatable waters on this part of the river. The fishing quality depends on the time of year and the water quality of the river at each location.

Brown Trout range from 10 to 16 inches with much larger ones commonly taken in the fall. These big ones are moving up from Flaming Gorge Reservoir during the fall spawning. A variety of dry flies and large streamers create action.

Rainbow trout range from 10 to 12 inches. These fish populate the clearer waters of the upstream portion near Fontenelle Reservoir, and a few are caught farther downstream. Spinners, flies, and bait take fish in the early spring. Fishing drops off during the summer.

Some kokanee salmon will also move into the river in the fall on their way to spawn. These fish get up to more than 5 pounds. Whitefish range from 10 to 14 inches and are found in the waters closer to Flaming Gorge. Worms and nymphs work well when drifted along the bottom of deep pools.

Additional information: The description of this section includes the waters from below Fontenelle Reservoir downstream to Flaming Gorge Reservoir. There are numerous access points from Bureau of Land Management (BLM) land just off of WY 372, which follows the river. Be mindful of the private lands along the way.

Contact: Wyoming Game and Fish Department, Pinedale.

110A. Fontenelle Dam

Description: This site has 2 camping areas managed by the BLM and a boat ramp. The river is deep and clear as it winds through sagebrush flats and badlands. Cottonwood trees are scattered along the banks.

Directions: Take WY 372 from I-80/exit 83 for 41 miles northwest to the Fontenelle Store. Continue straight ahead on the gravel road to the Tailrace Campground and boat ramp, or turn right onto the gravel road to the Slate Creek Campground, east of the store.

110B. Seedskadee National Wildlife Refuge

Description: This refuge offers access to the Green River at numerous locations from both sides. Be careful of wet roads and avoid trespassing on private ground.

Directions: Take exit 83 off I-80 and head northwest on WY 372 for 23 miles. The refuge includes the next 14 miles upstream toward the Fontenelle Reservoir. East side access can be obtained from County Road 8.

111 North Piney Lake

Key species: cutthroat trout
Description: Steep walls enclose this 66-acre mountain lake.
Tips: Take a of variety of tackle, a big lunch, and your camera.

The fishing: Cutthroat trout range from 7 to 12 inches. Only artificial flies or lures are permitted here. All cutthroat trout under 10 inches must be released. Motorized boats are not allowed. This lake is closed to fishing from June 1 through July 15.

Directions: Take WY 350/Middle Piney Road west out of Big Piney for 17 miles. This paved road will turn to gravel after about 10 miles. Turn right onto the dirt FR 10054 and travel about 0.25 mile to the trail.

Additional information: A difficult, 4-mile trail leads to the lake, where there are no developed camping sites available. Both brook and cutthroat trout are present in local streams. Be sure to consult fishing regulations for current restrictions.

Contact: Wyoming Game and Fish Department, Pinedale.

112 Middle Piney Lake

Key species: cutthroat trout, rainbow trout, mackinaw
Description: Snowcapped mountains rise to 11,000 feet near this 120-acre lake.
Tips: The best action is in early spring with decreasing results the summer.

The fishing: Cutthroat and rainbow trout range from 6 to 8 inches. Worms fished from shore produce some of these trout early in the spring. Flies fished with bubbles tend to create the most action. Mackinaw range from 12 to 20 inches with larger ones reported. These fish tend to be in deep water and are hard to reach. Late in the fall, the lake trout will move into the gravel-bottomed shallows to spawn. If the road is not impassable, this is the best time to fish for them. No motorized boats are allowed, and there are other special regulations. There is a limit of 6 trout per day or 6 in possession. Of these, only 1 may be over 20 inches long and only 2 may be mackinaw.

Directions: Take WY 350 west out of Big Piney for 10 miles to the Middle Piney Road/County Road 111. Stay to the right on this gravel road and drive 10 miles to the Middle Piney Lake Road. Turn left onto this gravel road and travel 3 miles.

Additional information: The Middle Piney Lake Campground is open from July 1 through September 30, weather permitting. There are 5 units and toilets available. Do not attempt to drive the steep parts of the road when they are wet. Additional camping and fishing is available along Middle Piney Creek. Check the current regulations for the stream.

Contact: Wyoming Game and Fish Department, Pinedale.

111-113 North Piney Lake, Middle Piney Lake, LaBarge Creek

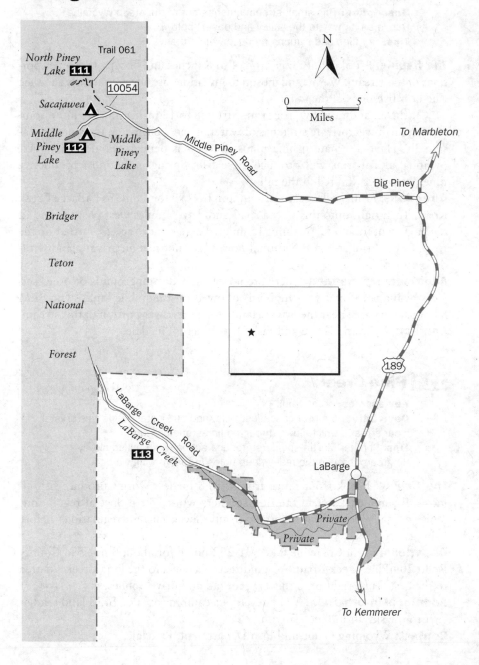

North Piney Lake **111**

Trail 061

10054

Sacajawea

Middle Piney **112**
Lake

Middle Piney Lake

Bridger

Teton

National

Forest

Middle Piney Road

To Marbleton

Big Piney

189

LaBarge Creek Road

LaBarge Creek **113**

LaBarge

Private

Private

To Kemmerer

N

0   5
Miles

113 LaBarge Creek

See map on page 141

Key species: brook trout, cutthroat trout, rainbow trout

Description: This small stream crashes out of the steep Wyoming Range on its way to the valley and desert below.

Tips: Dry flies and nymphs produce well in the fall.

The fishing: Brook trout range from 4 to 8 inches and occupy the upper portions of this stream. Worms and mosquito imitations are effective in early summer. The best fishing is in the fall.

Cutthroat and rainbow trout range from 8 to 12 inches and are more common in the lower, private stretches of water, where permission is granted occasionally. Have alternate fishing plans if access is denied. Standard dry flies, nymphs, and worms will produce these fish. Spring is the most productive time. Success is limited in the fall.

Directions: From LaBarge, head south on US 189 for 1 mile to LaBarge Creek Road. Turn right onto this paved road and drive 3 miles west past the end of the pavement for a total of about 15 miles. There is more access, farther up the road, in the Bridger-Teton National Forest. Do not fish on private land without permission.

Additional information: There are no developed campgrounds or other services available. Primitive camping is allowed on the public lands. The BLM has a parking area near the private land along the lower portion of this stream.

Contact: Wyoming Game and Fish Department, Pinedale.

114 Pine Creek

See map on page 144

Key species: brook trout

Description: A mix of cascades, falls, and still water define this crystal-clear stream, which flows through a limestone canyon.

Tips: Panther Martin spinners produce action when pulled slowly upstream through the many deep holes in fast-moving water.

The fishing: Brook trout range from 6 to 8 inches. Worms produce fish almost all summer. Later in the fall, spinners work better. Special regulations limit the daily possession of brook trout. Check current regulations before fishing.

Directions: From Cokeville take WY 232 north for about 3 miles to County Road 204/Pine Creek Road. A sign directs travelers to the Pine Creek ski area to the east. Turn right onto this gravel road and drive 3 miles.

Additional information: An undeveloped camping area on BLM land is adjacent to the ski lift in Pine Canyon.

Contact: Wyoming Game and Fish Department, Pinedale.

Pine Creek is a crystal-clear brook trout stream which flows through a limestone canyon.

115 Hobble Creek

Key species: brook trout, cutthroat trout
Description: This mountain stream gets up to 6 feet wide before reaching the barren mountains above Smith's Fork.
Tips: Take a of variety of tackle and a large lunch.

The fishing: Brook trout range from 6 to 10 inches. They tend to be larger the farther you are from the most accessible areas. There are special daily limits on brook trout here. Be sure to check the current regulations. Cutthroat range from 8 to 12 inches. Check the special regulations for fishing the portion of Hobble Creek on the Bridger-Teton National Forest. Only artificial flies and lures are allowed and any cutthroat trout 10 inches long or less must be released.

Directions: Take WY 232 north out of Cokeville for 13 miles to the end of the pavement. Bear right at the fork onto what will become FR 10062. It is a steady climb from here on a single-lane road with small, narrow pullouts. Continue on FR 10062 about 8 miles to FR 10066. Stay to the left on this dirt road about 4 miles to FR 10193. Turn left onto this dirt road and travel 10 miles downhill to the campground.

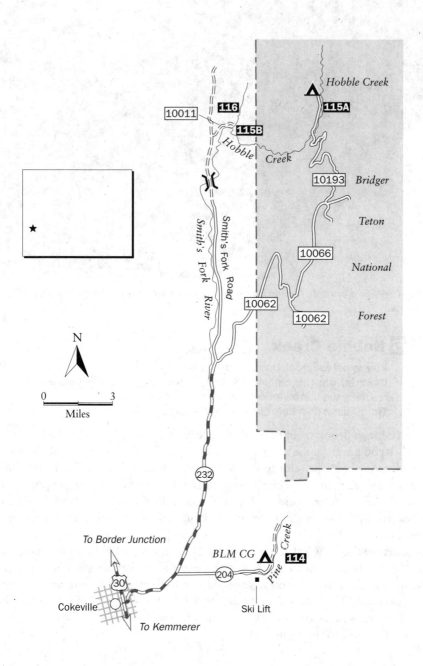

Additional information: Hobble Creek Campground is open from July 1 through October 31, weather permitting. There are 18 units available along with drinking water and toilets. The 240-acre Lake Alice is about 1.5 miles upstream from the campground. Reaching the lake requires some footwork.
Contact: Wyoming Game and Fish Department, Pinedale.

116 Smith's Fork

Key species: brown trout, cutthroat trout, whitefish
Description: Smiths Fork gets up to 30 feet wide as it leaves the pine forest and winds through grazing land. Willows line the banks for nearly the entire length of the stream.
Tips: Fish the ripples leading into any of the many pools.

The fishing: Brown trout range from 10 to 18 inches. Larger ones can be found in the private stretches. A variety of bait and lures will catch the bigger fish late in September and October. Spinners can create some explosive action in the upper ripples of the pools. Cutthroat trout range from 10 to 16 inches. Most of the bigger fish are caught on private stretches of the stream. The trout are present in the Bridger-Teton National Forest though the average length is only 12 inches. Fishing in the national forest on the Smith's Fork drainage is restricted to artificial flies and lures. Cutthroat trout 10 inches or less must be released. Whitefish range from 10 to 14 inches. Worms and nymphs take these fish in deep, slow moving current.

Smith's Fork widens as it leaves the forest and flows into grazing country.

Directions: Take WY 232 north out of Cokeville for 13 miles to the end of the pavement. Smith's Fork parallels WY 232 north of Cokeville. This paved road becomes dirt in about 13 miles while still passing through private lands. Stay to the left on the Smith's Fork Road and travel 16 miles to the national forest boundary.

Additional information: The best fishing is where the stream flows through private lands, but access is uncertain because landowners may not give permission. There are no developed campgrounds in the area.

Contact: Wyoming Game and Fish Department, Pinedale.

117 Viva Naughton Reservoir

Key species: rainbow trout
Description: On the northwest side of this 1,375-acre reservoir, aspen trees grow along the side of a sage-blanketed ridge. The reservoir is surrounded by somewhat barren rolling hills.
Tips: Fish the points on the bottom from shore or by boat.

The fishing: Rainbow trout range from 14 to 18 inches, with larger ones reported. Trollers do well with pop gear throughout the season. Shore anglers who fish the bottom with salmon eggs, Power Bait, and worms also get results. The best shore fishing is in early spring and late fall.

Directions: From Kemmerer, take WY 233 north for 16 miles. The reservoir will be on the left side.

Additional information: There are 2 parking areas with toilets available here, along with a marina. The parking areas are on the south and north ends of the reservoir. The marina is located about midway between the parking areas and has the only boat access. There is a fee of $5 without hookups and $15 with hookups. Camping and cabins are also available at the marina.

Contact: Wyoming Game and Fish Department, Pinedale.

118 Kemmerer City Reservoir

Key species: rainbow trout
Description: Flat land, rolling hills, and high, sage-covered ridges surround this 130-acre reservoir along the Hams Fork River.
Tips: Light colored flies work best when used in dim sunlight or on cloudy days.

The fishing: Rainbow trout range from 12 to 20 inches, with larger ones reported. No motorized boats are allowed. This reservoir is managed as a trophy trout fishery, so it has special regulations. There is a limit of 2 trout per day, of which only 1 may be over 20 inches. Any trout 13 to 20 inches must be released. Fishing is allowed with artificial flies or lures only. Fly fishing with bell boats is popular. Light colored, dry flies tend to be the most productive, especially when used early in the morning or late evening.

117, 118 Viva Naughton Reservoir, Kemmerer City Reservoir

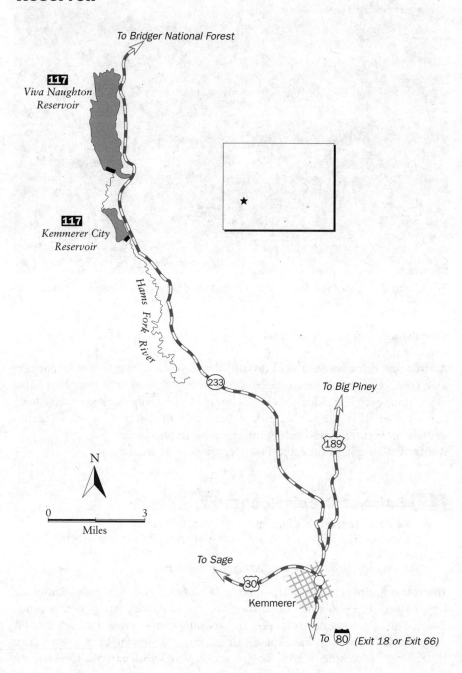

To Bridger National Forest

117
Viva Naughton Reservoir

117
Kemmerer City Reservoir

Hams Fork River

233

To Big Piney

189

N

0   3
Miles

To Sage

30

Kemmerer

To 80 (Exit 18 or Exit 66)

Try fishing the Hams Fork River for browns during your trip to Kemmerer City Reservoir.

Directions: From Kemmerer, take WY 233 north for 15 miles. The reservoir will be on the left side.

Additional information: A short trail leads to this lake. There is parking along the road; a stile crosses the barbed wire fence. The Hams Fork River also offers some excellent fishing. Access is limited to specially marked areas. Check current regulations for the location you choose. Brown trout reach 18 inches and are most often found below the reservoir in late fall.

Contact: Wyoming Game and Fish Department, Pinedale.

119 Sulphur Creek Reservoir

Key species: brown trout, cutthroat trout, rainbow trout
Description: This is a 699-acre reservoir on a windy prairie near the Utah border.
Tips: Anglers do well when fishing from the dam.

The fishing: Brown trout average 12 to 18 inches. Fall is best for catching the bigger ones. The shoreline along the dam gets the most action with worms, Power Bait, salmon eggs, spinners, and spoons. Cutthroat and rainbow trout range from 12 to 16 inches. These fish are more often caught from spring to June. After the weather warms up, the action slows until early October. Shore anglers do well along the dam. The wind here generally blows at the backs of the anglers, which makes casting easier. Boaters have access to a good ramp, but the wind can be a problem once you are out on the lake.

119 Sulphur Creek Reservoir

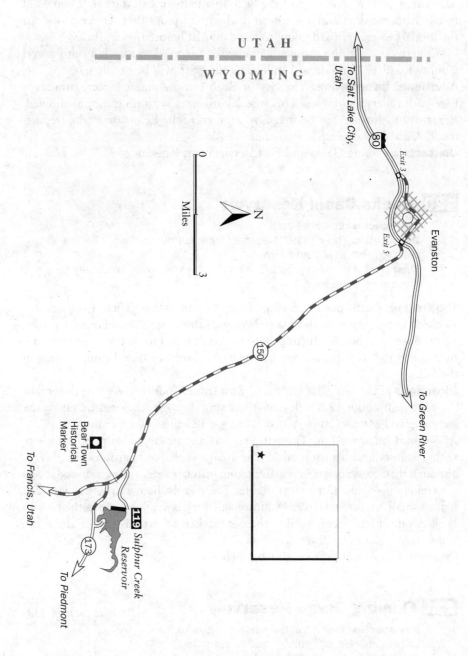

UTAH

WYOMING

To Salt Lake City, Utah

80

Exit 3

Exit 5

Evanston

To Green River

150

Bear Town Historical Marker

To Francis, Utah

173

119 Sulphur Creek Reservoir

To Piedmont

0

Miles

3

N

Directions: Take WY 150 south out of Evanston for about 9.5 miles. The dam will be visible to the left of the Bear Town Historical Marker. If you want to fish from the dam and don't need the boat ramp or other services, look for the unmarked gravel road going to the dam just before this marker.

Otherwise, continue about 0.75 mile past the marker, turn left onto gravel County Road 173 and drive 1 mile. The city park will be on the left.

Additional information: The city of Evanston maintains a recreation area here with toilets and tables. This is a day-use area with no camping allowed. Reservations for use can be made by contacting the Evanston Parks Department. A good boat ramp is available.

Contact: Wyoming Game and Fish Department, Pinedale.

120 Meeks Cabin Reservoir

Key species: cutthroat trout
Description: The Wasatch National Forest surrounds this 137-acre reservoir with BLM land nearby.
Tips: Fishing is fair-to-good in the spring, then drops off drastically for the rest of the season.

The fishing: Cutthroat trout range from 8 to 14 inches. These trout are not stocked, so they are not abundant. Worms, salmon eggs, and Power Bait can all produce fish. Bottom fishing from the bank tends to be the most common fishing method. Limited success can be had fishing dry flies during evening in the fall.

Directions: Take WY 410 south and west from Mountain View to the end of the pavement about 12.5 miles away, passing through Robertson. Stay to the left on gravel Meeks Cabin Access Road for 12 miles.

Additional information: The national forest maintains a campground here with 19 units and 5 group sites. The roads in the campground are paved, although the access road is gravel. Drinking water, toilets, and accommodations for trailers up to 32 feet are available. There is no boat ramp, but you can launch small boats from shore. Additional fishing is available along the Black's Fork River. Public access to this river is marked at various places along the route to Meeks Cabin Reservoir.

Contact: Evanston Chamber of Commerce.

121 Flaming Gorge Reservoir

See map on page 153

Key species: brown trout, rainbow trout, kokanee salmon, mackinaw, catfish, smallmouth bass
Description: The 42,000-acre Flaming Gorge Reservoir stretches about 91 miles into Wyoming and Utah. It is surrounded by steep canyon country.
Tips: Trolling is by far the most productive method. Use large lures, Rapalas, or #3 spinners in deep water.

120 Meeks Cabin Reservoir

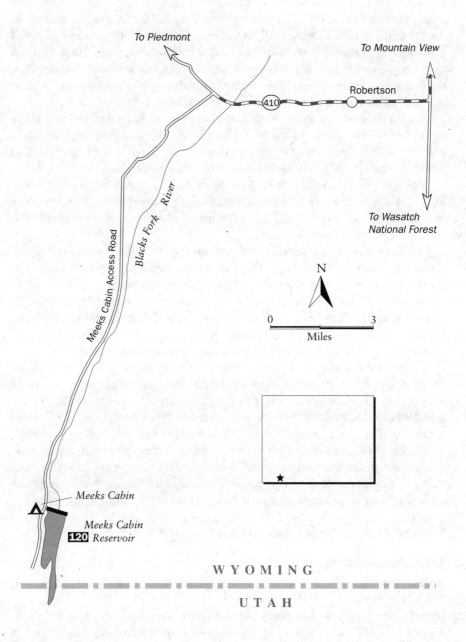

To Piedmont

To Mountain View

Robertson

410

To Wasatch
National Forest

Meeks Cabin Access Road

Blacks Fork River

N

0   3
Miles

Meeks Cabin

Meeks Cabin
120 Reservoir

WYOMING

UTAH

The fishing: This reservoir is managed as a trophy fishery. There is a limit of 6 trout or salmon. No more than 3 may be kokanee salmon, and no more than 3 may be mackinaw. Only 1 mackinaw may exceed 28 inches. Possession or use of gaffs is not allowed. All kokanee salmon caught between October 1 through November 7 must be released. Mackinaw average 20 pounds. A boat and a good fish finder are required to locate these lunkers. Downriggers, trolling with wire line, or jigging produce fish almost all year long, but finding the fish in this large body of water can be difficult.

Brown trout are stocked, but the population seems to be diminishing. There are still some large ones taken by trolling along the shoreline with Rapalas, Flatfish, and #3 spinners. The best time to catch brown trout is at dusk and dawn; the most productive months are April and November.

Kokanee salmon reach up to 5 pounds, though most will be 16 to 18 inches long. Trolling with worms or small lures trailing some type of attractor is the most effective method. During the fall, when the kokanee are getting ready to spawn, jigging will be productive.

Rainbow trout are stocked every year and provide the best shore fishing. These fish generally range from 14 to 18 inches. Spoons, spinners, plugs, and a variety of natural baits are effective for catching rainbows.

Smallmouth bass average 9 to 12 inches in length. Bigger ones are occasionally caught. They are generally found in the rocky coves and respond well to spinner baits, jigs, crayfish imitations, Rapalas, and Rooster Tails. The most productive time of year for bass is from mid-June through August.

Catfish are found in the upper portions of the reservoir including the Green River. Night fishing with worms or cut bait during the summer is the most productive. Some catfish here reach up to 20 pounds.

Additional information: There are more than 600 camping and picnic areas located within this recreation area. These range from modern to primitive, with access both by boat or car. Marinas and boat ramps are also available. The same regulations apply to both Wyoming and Utah; a reciprocal fishing stamp is available which allows anglers with a valid fishing license from the adjoining state to fish in both states. Note: There are additional access points in Utah.

Contact: Flaming Gorge National Recreation Area.

121A. Firehole Canyon

Description: Camping is available with showers, a trailer sanitary station, and a boat ramp.

Directions: Take I-80 east from Green River about 8 miles to exit 99. From exit 99 take US 191 about 12 miles south to Flaming Gorge Road/Road 33. Turn right onto this paved road and drive about 10 miles.

121 Flaming Gorge Reservoir

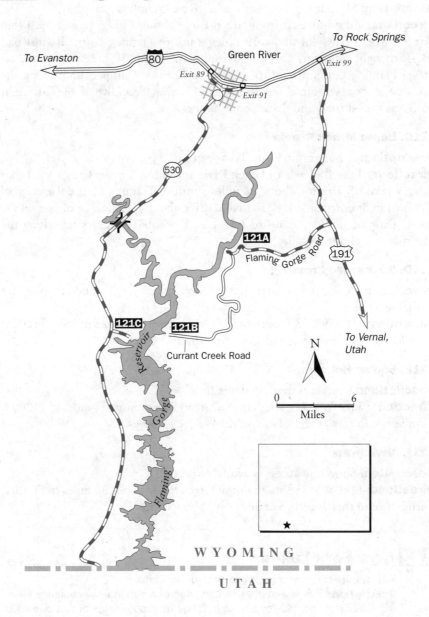

To Evanston

To Rock Springs

80

Green River

Exit 89

Exit 91

Exit 99

530

121A

Flaming Gorge Road

191

121C

121B

Currant Creek Road

Reservoir

To Vernal,
Utah

N

0 — 6
Miles

Flaming Gorge

WYOMING

UTAH

★

121B. Currant Creek

Description: Shoreline access with primitive camping is available.

Directions: Take I-80 east from Green River about 8 miles to exit 99. From exit 99 take US 191 for about 12 miles south to Flaming Gorge Road/Road 33. Turn right onto this paved road and drive about 10 miles. Continue on gravel Flaming Gorge Road/Road 33 past Firehole Campground, along the east side of the reservoir, about 10 miles to Currant Creek/Road 38. Turn right onto this gravel road and drive about 4 miles.

121C. Upper Marsh Creek

Description: A boat ramp is available here.

Directions: Take I-80 east of Green River for about 8 miles to exit 99. From exit 99 take US 191 for about 12 miles south to Flaming Gorge Road/Road 33. Turn right onto this paved road and drive about 10 miles. Continue on the gravel Flaming Gorge Road/Road 33 past Firehole Campground, along the east side, for about 23 miles.

121D. Buckboard Crossing

Description: A marina, a boat ramp, toilets, picnic areas, and camping are available here.

Directions: Take WY 530 south out of Green River about 23 miles to FR 009. Turn left onto this paved road and drive about 2 miles.

121E. Squaw Hollow

Description: A boat ramp is available here.

Directions: Take WY 530 south out of Green River about 31 miles to FR 004. Turn left onto this gravel road and drive about 3 miles.

121F. Anvil Draw

Description: Shoreline access is available here.

Directions: Take WY 530 south out of Green River about 39 miles to FR 001. Turn left onto this gravel road and drive about 3 miles.

122 New Fork Lakes

See map on page 156

Key species: brown trout, rainbow trout, mackinaw
Description: This is actually one lake, due to a very narrow channel of water close to the middle. Although, it has the appearance of two lakes.
Tips: Shore anglers do best in the early spring with worms fished on the bottom.

The fishing: Brown trout range from 12 to 14 inches, with larger ones reported. Late fall tends to be the most productive time for both shore and boat anglers. Spinners and spoons are effective. Rainbow trout range from 10 to 12 inches. Early spring tends to be the best time for shore anglers using worms, salmon eggs, Power Bait, and small spinners. Later in the summer fishing tends to slack off. Dry flies can produce early in the morning or late evening. Mackinaw are the fish of choice with 20-pounders not uncommon. Large Rapalas and Flatfish produce results for trollers in the deeper water.

Additional information: There are 3 developed campgrounds along the lake. The dirt access road from WY 352 is virtually impassable when wet.

Contact: Wyoming Game and Fish Department, Pinedale.

122A. New Fork Lake Campground

Description: This area offers 20 units, a picnic ground, toilets, drinking water and a boat ramp.

Directions: Pinedale is 100 miles north of Rock Springs on US 191. Continue past Pinedale on US 191 for 5 miles to WY 352. Turn right onto this paved road and drive 14 miles. Turn right onto the gravel New Fork Lake road and travel about 3 miles.

122B. Narrows Campground

Description: This fee area offers 19 units, a picnic ground, toilets, drinking water, and a boat ramp.

Directions: Head north from Pinedale on US 191 for 5 miles to WY 352. Turn right onto this paved road and drive 14.5 miles. Turn right onto the gravel New Fork Lake road and travel about 6 miles following the north shore.

123 Duck Creek

Key species: brown trout
Description: This small, clear stream flows through meadows lined with willows.
Tips: Long poles and low profiles work best.

See map on page 156

The fishing: Brown trout average 12 to 18 inches. These wary fish easily spot anglers, so use a careful approach. Grasshoppers will coax some action when they are allowed to drift into promising areas. Worms can produce but are trickier to position correctly. Muddler patterns and mayfly imitations work well when placed carefully.

Directions: From Pinedale, take US 191 north to one of three foot access points between 2 and 3.5 miles away.

Additional information: There are no services at this location. Fence stiles allow foot access to the stream.

Contact: Wyoming Game and Fish Department, Pinedale.

124 Willow Lake

Key species: brook trout, rainbow trout, kokanee salmon, mackinaw
Description: This 1,600-acre lake is surrounded by sagebrush-covered hills in the shadow of the Wind River Mountains.
Tips: Salmon eggs are effective when bottom fishing in the spring.

See map on page 156

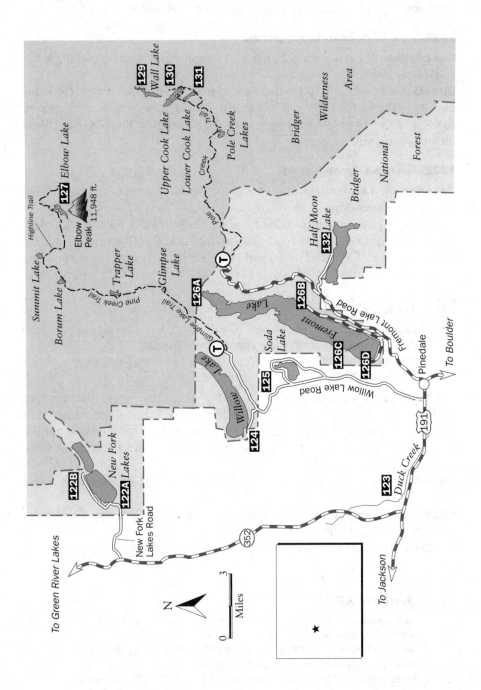

The fishing: Mackinaw average 10 to 13 inches. These popular fish are most often caught by trolling the deep water with Rapalas. Early in the spring, mackinaw can be caught from shore as they move into the shallower water to spawn. Salmon eggs are effective when fished on the bottom from shore. Rainbow trout range from 10 to 16 inches. Early spring, during spawning, provides the most action. Worms, salmon eggs, and Power Bait are effective when fishing from shore. For most of the summer, trolling with Flatfish, Rapalas, and spinners can create some action in the deeper water. Kokanee salmon range from 8 to 10 inches. Bright spinners and worms produce these fish from either shore or boat. Brook trout range from 6 to 8 inches. Worms are commonly fished from shore in the upper portions of the lake. During fall spawning, just about any bait or lure will be effective.

Directions: Near the west end of Pinedale on US 191, turn north onto Willow Lake Road, following the signs to the Soda Lake Wildlife Habitat Management Area. Take this paved road, which will become gravel, for 5 miles to the next access intersection for Soda Lake. Stay left for the next 1.5 miles to Willow Lake Road. Take Willow Lake Road to the left for 4 miles.

Additional information: Willow Lake Campground has 7 units, toilets, a boat ramp, and a picnic area.

125 Soda Lake

Key species: brook trout, brown trout
Description: This is a 312-acre lake in rolling sagebrush country near the Wind River Mountains.
Tips: Jigs work well when bounced along the bottom from either shore or by boat.

The fishing: Brook trout range from 6 to 10 inches. The bubble-and-fly technique produces fairly well, especially in fall. Brown trout average 12 to 16 inches. Jigs, spinners, streamers, and Rapalas are effective. Fall offers shore anglers an opportunity to catch some of the larger ones. Boaters trolling deeper water have the advantage throughout the season. Soda Lake is closed to fishing from October 1 through May 9.

Directions: Near the west end of Pinedale, turn north following the signs to the Soda Lake Wildlife Habitat Management Area. Take this paved road, which soon turns to gravel, for 5 miles to the next access intersection for Soda Lake. Stay left for the next 1.5 miles to the Willow Lake Road. Turn right and travel 0.5 mile.

Additional information: Primitive camping is allowed, with toilets and a boat ramp available. This area is closed from October 1 through May 9. Motorized boats are not allowed from May 10 through May 31.

Contact: Wyoming Game and Fish Department, Pinedale.

126 Fremont Lake

See map on page 156

Key species: rainbow trout, mackinaw, kokanee salmon

Description: Sagebrush dominates the western hills of this 5,000-acre mountain lake while forested foothills stretch eastward into the Wind River Mountains.

Tips: Fluorescent spinners work well for both salmon and rainbow trout in the early spring.

The fishing: Rainbow trout range from 10 to 14 inches. Worms and salmon eggs produce well for shore anglers fishing the bottom. Spinners work as well, but are more effective when trolled. Kokanee salmon range from 10 to 12 inches. These fish are a relatively new addition to this lake and are still in the growth stage. Worms and salmon eggs work well along with small fluorescent spinners fished from shore or boat. Reaching 20 pounds, mackinaw are the most sought after fish here. Boaters take the greatest share of the large fish from deeper waters. Large Rapalas and similar lures work well when trolled. May and June offer more intense action than late summer, but trollers are successful all season.

Additional information: There are various developed campgrounds along the lake. The Lakeside Lodge is a commercial resort on the southern portion of the lake. This is a high wind area and boaters must exercise caution, especially in smaller craft.

Contact: Wyoming Game and Fish Department, Pinedale.

126A. Upper Fremont Lake Campground

Description: This campground is accessed by boat. There are 5 units available.

Directions: The lake is about 9 miles long; most boat launching facilities are on the southern end. The distance to the campground, at the north end of the lake, depends on which boat ramp is used.

126B. Fremont Lake Campground

Description: This fee area has 54 units, a picnic area, drinking water, toilets, and a boat ramp.

Directions: From Pinedale take Fremont Lake Road about 2.25 miles to FR 111. Turn left onto FR 111 and travel about 3.5 miles to the campground.

126C. Sandy Beach

Description: This picnic area is for day use only and has tables and toilets.

Directions: From Pinedale take paved Fremont Lake Road north about 2.25 miles to FR 111. Turn left and travel about 0.25 mile.

126D. Lower Fremont

Description: This location offers a boat ramp and toilets.

Directions: From Pinedale take Fremont Lake Road north about 2.25 miles to FR 111. Turn left onto FR 111 and travel past the Lakeside Lodge to the parking area about 2.25 miles away.

127 Elbow Lake

See map on page 156

Key species: golden trout
Description: This ice-cold, 80-acre mountain lake is surrounded by solid rock. Elbow Mountain towers over the lake on the southern shore. Boulders are scattered over the alpine tundra, like abandoned ammunition from a rock fight among giants.
Tips: Take a variety of small brightly colored spinners and flies. The high elevation of this lake means that the ice melts late in the season. Packing into this area can be a test of endurance, so take light gear and a big lunch.

The fishing: Golden trout range from 8 to 16 inches. These fish respond well to dry fly patterns.

Directions: Near the west end of Pinedale, turn north onto Willow Lake Road, following the signs to the Soda Lake Wildlife Habitat Management Area. Take this paved road, which soon becomes gravel, for 5 miles to the next access intersection for Soda Lake. Stay left for the next 1.5 miles to Willow Lake Road. Take Willow Lake Road to the left for 2.7 miles to the Bridger-Teton National Forest boundary. Just after entering the forest, turn right onto one-lane dirt FR 10053 and travel 2.5 miles to Spring Creek Park Trailhead. Hike up the moderate Glimpse Lake Trail for 6 miles to the Pine Creek Canyon Trail junction at Glimpse Lake. Continue north on the Pine Creek Canyon Trail for 6.5 miles to the Highline Trail junction at Summit Lake. Take Highline Trail south of Summit Lake for 4 miles.

Additional information: This lake is in the Bridger Wilderness Area of the rugged Wind River Mountains. The moderate-to-difficult high altitude trail covers 17.5 miles. A 5- to 7-day trip is advised. A more complete description of the trail is given in the book *Hiking Wyoming's Wind River Range* by Ron Adkison and published by Falcon Publishing.

Contact: Wyoming Game and Fish Department, Pinedale.

128 New Fork River

See map on page 161

Key species: brown trout, rainbow trout
Description: This stream offers about 50 miles of floatable water with fairly slow currents in long runs and a few pools. Willows line the banks. Stream width ranges from 20 feet up to 60 feet in the lower stretches.
Tips: Floating offers the best fishing access since most of this river flows through private land.

The fishing: Brown trout average 10 to 20 inches. Fly fishing is the most popular method. Muddler patterns, mayfly, and grasshopper imitations produce results. Rainbow trout range from 10 to 16 inches. These trout are less abundant than the more sought-after browns. Mayfly imitations, Muddler patterns, and Woolly Buggers do well at various times. The stretch of river from the Mesa Road Bridge downstream to the Boulder Bridge on County Road 136 is subject to special regulations. These include a daily limit of 2 trout, salmon, or grayling, of which only 1 may be over 20 inches long. All trout between 10 and 20 inches must be released. Only artificial flies or lures are allowed on this upper stretch of river. From Boulder Bridge at County Road 136 downstream to the Green River there is a daily limit of 3 trout, of which only 1 may be over 20 inches. Be sure to check current regulations at the time of your visit.

Additional information: There are no services provided along this river. If you choose to fish from spring to late August, be sure to bring insect repellent.

Contact: Wyoming Game and Fish Department, Pinedale.

128A. Mesa Road Bridge

Description: This is floating access only.

Directions: Take County Road 123 south out of Pinedale for 2 miles.

128B. Ecklund Public Access

Description: This area offers foot access for shore fishing. No services are provided and a short hike is required.

Directions: Head north on US 191 from Boulder for 6.5 miles, or 5.5 miles south on US 191 from Pinedale. Turn west onto the dirt road and travel around the south end of the airport runway to parking spots about 0.75 mile away.

128C. Ziegler Float Access

Description: A boat ramp, parking, and toilets are available.

Directions: Head north on US 191 from Boulder about 0.25 mile to County Road 136. Turn left onto this road and travel 0.75 mile to the parking area.

128D. BLM

Description: Primitive camping is allowed here, but there are no services.

Directions: From Boulder, take US 191 south 3 miles to County Road 106. Turn right onto this gravel road and drive 4 miles. Turn right onto the dirt road and travel 0.5 mile to the river.

129 Wall Lake

See map on page 156

Key species: golden trout

Description: This 105-acre lake is locked into the rugged rocks along the backbone of the mountains.

Tips: An assortment of Mepps spinners is effective and easy to pack in.

The fishing: Golden trout range from 8 to 11 inches. Try using spinners in a variety of colors. The bubble-and-fly technique is also effective. The best fishing is in early morning or late evening. Overnight camping is recommended if you choose to fish the late evening hours.

Directions: From Pinedale take the Fremont Lake Road/Skyline Drive north for 15 miles. Signs directing the way to Fremont and Halfmoon lakes help to identify this road, which starts where US 191 curves. The road forks about

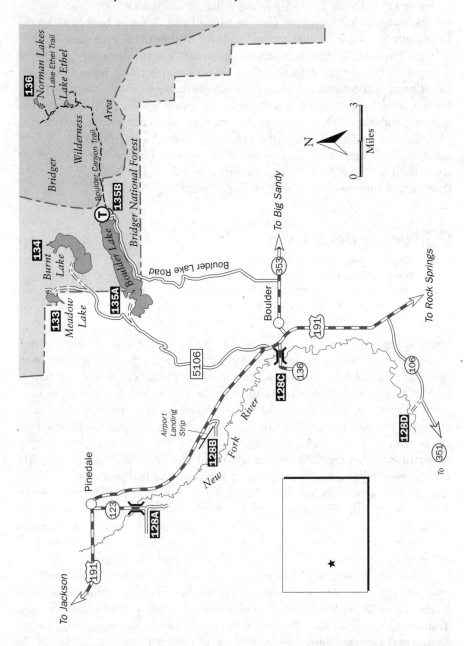

200 yards past the information center. At the end of the road you will see Elkhart Park. The left fork leads to Trail's End Campground and the north parking lot for Pine Creek Canyon Trail. The right fork leads to the parking lot for the Pole Creek Trail. There are toilets and drinking water here.

Follow the Pole Creek Trail past the Miller Lake, Sweeney Lake, and Seneca Lake trails for about 9 miles to the Highline Trail near the Pole Creek Lakes. Take the Highline Trail to the north for about 1 mile to the Fremont Trail. Go to the right and follow this trail past Cook Lakes for about 1.25 miles.

Additional information: This lake is one of the less visited locations in the Bridger Wilderness Area. However, the takeoff point leading to the lake is quite popular; both the campground and parking areas fill to capacity in the summer. The moderate-to-difficult trail covers approximately 22 miles round trip. A more complete description of the trail appears in the book *Hiking Wyoming's Wind River Range* by Ron Adkison and published by Falcon Publishing.

Contact: Wyoming Game and Fish Department, Pinedale.

130 Upper Cook Lake

See map on page 156

Key species: brook trout, golden trout
Description: This 163-acre lake sits in mountains at over 10,000 feet above sea level. The trip into this remote lake is an adventure in itself.
Tips: A spinning rod permits a variety of methods to be used, allowing anglers to select assorted hooks, lures, and flies.

The fishing: Brook trout range from 4 to 8 inches. These trout respond well to worms. Small mosquito imitations are productive, especially in early summer. Later in the fall, Panther Martin and other spinners find some action. Golden trout range from 8 to 11 inches. The golden trout here tend to have quite an appetite. The bubble-and-fly technique, using a variety of dry flies, is effective. The best times of day are early morning, late evening, and when the sky is overcast.

Directions: From Pinedale take the Fremont Lake Road/Skyline Drive north for 15 miles. Signs directing the way to Fremont and Halfmoon lakes help to identify this road, which starts where US 191 curves. The road forks about 200 yards past the information center. At the end of the road you will see Elkhart Park. The left fork leads to Trail's End Campground and the north parking lot for Pine Creek Canyon Trail. The right fork leads to the parking lot for the Pole Creek Trail. There are toilets and drinking water here.

Follow the Pole Creek Trail past the Miller Lake, Sweeney Lake, and Seneca Lake trails for about 9 miles to the Highline Trail near the Pole Creek Lakes. Take the Highline Trail to the north for about 1 mile to the Fremont Trail. Turn right and follow this trail past Lower Cook Lake for about 0.75 mile.

Additional information: This lake is one of the least visited locations in the Bridger Wilderness Area. However, the takeoff point leading to the lake is quite popular; both the campground and parking areas fill to capacity in the

summer. The moderate-to-difficult trail covers approximately 22 miles round trip. A more complete description of the trail appears in the book *Hiking Wyoming's Wind River Range* by Ron Adkison and published by Falcon Publishing.
Contact: Wyoming Game and Fish Department, Pinedale.

131 Lower Cook Lake

See map on page 156

Key species: brook trout
Description: This 82-acre ice-melt lake sits in the same terrain as Upper Cook Lake.
Tips: Small black ant or mosquito imitations work well.

The fishing: Brook trout range from 6 to 9 inches. The lake tends to be over-populated, making the fish quite hungry. There are some periods in the late summer when the feeding is slower, but it picks up in the fall.
Directions: Pinedale is 100 miles north of Rock Springs on US 191. At the only prominent curve in Pinedale, take the Fremont Lake Road/Skyline Drive for 15 miles. Signs directing the way to Fremont and Halfmoon lakes help to identify this road. The road will fork about 200 yards past the information center at the end of the road. At the end of the road you will see Elkhart Park. The Trails End Campground and the Pine Creek Trailhead will be to the left. The Pole Creek Trailhead is to the right. Follow the Pole Creek Trail past the Miller Lake, Sweeney Lake, and Seneca Lake trails for about 9 miles to the Highline Trail near the Pole Creek Lakes. Take the Highline Trail to the north for about 1 mile to the Fremont Trail. Go to the right and follow this trail for about 0.5
Additional information: This lake is one of the least visited locations in the Bridger Wilderness Area. However, the takeoff point leading to the lake is quite popular. Both the campground and parking areas generally fill to capacity during the summer months. The moderate-to difficult-trail is approximately a 22-mile round trip, so adequate planning is required. A more complete description of the trail is given in the book *Hiking Wyoming's Wind River Range* by Ron Adkison and published by Falcon Publishing.
Contact: Wyoming Game and Fish Department, Pinedale.

132 Half Moon Lake

See map on page 156

Key species: rainbow trout, mackinaw
Description: Pine trees shade the southern shore of this 920-acre lake, while mountains line the northern horizon.
Tips: Shore fishing is best in early spring with limited success by boat through the summer.

The fishing: Rainbow trout range from 10 to 16 inches. Worms fished on the bottom can be the most effective method in the spring. Later in the summer and into the fall, small colorful spinners tend to be more productive. Mackinaw range from 12 to 15 inches. Boaters tend to see more action when fishing with Flatfish and Rapalas. There is a daily limit of 6 trout, of which only 1 may be over 20 inches. Of these 6, only 2 may be mackinaw.

Directions: At Pinedale, take Fremont Lake Road north about 6 miles. Turn right onto the gravel road marked as the access and drive about 3 miles.

Additional information: A lodge and a boat ramp are on the north shore of the lake. The Half Moon Lake Campground is also on the same side of the lake. This fee area has 18 units, a picnic ground, toilets, and a boat ramp.

Contact: Wyoming Game and Fish Department, Pinedale.

133 Meadow Lake

See map on page 161

Key species: grayling
Description: This 115-acre lake is nestled in rolling sage-covered hills and aspen groves.
Tips: These fish have small bones; a hard pull to set the hook can break through their jawbone.

The fishing: Grayling range from 12 to 18 inches. Small flies in a variety of patterns produce the most action. The best time is just after the ice melts, usually in May. The bubble-and-fly technique is the most effective, but small spinners also create some action. Meadow Lake is closed to fishing November 15 through April 30.

Directions: From Boulder head north on US 191 to County Road 5106 (10 miles south of Pinedale). Turn right onto this gravel road and drive 7 miles to the Burnt Lake intersection. Turn left onto this gravel road and drive 3 miles to the Meadow Lake intersection. Turn left onto this gravel road and travel 2 miles.

Additional information: There are no developed campgrounds or services in this area.

Contact: Wyoming Game and Fish Department, Pinedale.

134 Burnt Lake

See map on page 161

Key species: rainbow trout, mackinaw
Description: Forest and snowcapped mountains surround this 815-acre lake.
Tips: Salmon eggs are best fished on the bottom in the early spring.

The fishing: Rainbow trout average 12 to 16 inches. The fishing is best in early spring, with salmon eggs, worms, or Power Bait as good bait choices. Small, colorful spinners and an assortment of flies will produce better results later in the season. Mackinaw range from 8 to 12 inches. The fall season finds more action using a variety of baits and lures. Salmon eggs and pop gear tend to be the most effective. Burnt Lake is closed to fishing November 15 through April 30.

Directions: From Boulder head north on US 191 to County Road 5106 (10 miles south of Pinedale). Turn right onto this gravel road and drive 7 miles to the Burnt Lake intersection. Turn left onto this gravel road and drive 3 miles to the Meadow Lake intersection. Turn right at this intersection and travel 1.5 miles

Additional information: There are no developed camping sites or services at this location.

Contact: Wyoming Game and Fish Department, Pinedale.

135 Boulder Lake

See map on page 161

Key species: rainbow trout, mackinaw

Description: This long, 1,400-acre lake stretches from forests to sage-covered hills. The rugged Wind River Mountains offer a spectacular touch to the scenery.

Tips: Salmon eggs work well when fished on the bottom in the early spring. Success is limited in the fall.

The fishing: Rainbow trout range from 12 to 14 inches. Early spring anglers do well with worms and salmon eggs. Later in the season, spinners and a variety of dry flies create most of the action. Mackinaw range from 8 to 11 inches. Fall fishing with Flatfish is the most productive method. Sometimes salmon eggs fished on the bottom create action.

Additional information: There is a primitive camping area located along the northwestern end of the lake as well as a developed campground at the opposite shore. Boulder Lake Campground is on the eastern end.

Contact: Wyoming Game and Fish Department, Pinedale.

135A. County Road 5106

Description: This is a parking area near the dam on the lower north shore.

Directions: From Boulder, head north on US 191 to County Road 5106 (10 miles south of Pinedale). Turn right onto this gravel road and drive 7 miles to the Burnt Lake intersection. Turn right onto this gravel road and travel 0.5 mile.

135B. Boulder Lake Campground

Description: This area has 28 units, a picnic ground, and toilets; it is located on the south shore.

Directions: From Boulder take WY 353 east 2 miles to County Road 125/Boulder Lake Road. Turn left onto this gravel road, which turns into a rough dirt trail, and travel 10 miles north to the Boulder Lake Ranch junction. Stay to the left for 0.2 mile. The road will follow above the south shore of the lake starting about 7 miles north of WY 353.

136 Norman Lakes

See map on page 161

Key species: golden trout

Description: These two lakes are joined by a short beaver run for a total of 41 surface acres of water. A forest fire has transformed the spruce and lodgepole pine to a charred graveyard of dead timber. Large granite domes and boulders lay exposed in the lake.

Tips: White streamers and an assortment of colorful spinners can produce some explosive results.

The fishing: Golden trout range from 8 to 11 inches. Try using flies early in the morning or late in the evening. During the brighter portion of the day, spinners provoke strikes. These fish tend to spawn near the end of June and even as late as July. They will be in the rocky shallows at this time.

Directions: From Boulder take WY 353 east for 2 miles to County Road 125/ Boulder Lake Road. Turn left onto this gravel road, which becomes a rough dirt trail, and travel 10 miles to the Boulder Lake Ranch junction. Stay to the left and travel 0.2 mile to the trailhead. Take the Boulder Canyon Trail about 6 miles to the Lake Ethel Trail. Take the Lake Ethel Trail to the left from the outlet of Lake Ethel for about 1.25 miles, just past a shallow pond settled in a meadow known as Eds Lake. Turn right off the main trail before climbing the switchbacks and going on to Lake Christina. Follow the small stream to the northeast for 0.5 mile to Norman Lakes.

Additional information: This area is reached by foot or horse on a moderate-to-difficult trail. Camping is allowed under certain guidelines, but be aware that this is rugged and wild country. A more complete description of the trail is given in the book *Hiking Wyoming's Wind River Range* by Ron Adkison and published by Falcon Publishing.

Contact: Wyoming Game and Fish Department, Pinedale.

137 Big Sandy Reservoir

Key species: brown trout, rainbow trout

Description: This 800-acre reservoir sits in a wide open sage desert. The beaches are predominately sandy, inviting swimmers. A merciless wind blows most of the time.

Tips: Yellow spoons with brown spots bring on some impressive strikes in the fall when the brown trout are spawning.

The fishing: Brown trout range from 12 to 20 inches. Late in the fall, try using large spoons from shore. Early in the year, trolling with a variety of gear tends to be the only successful method. Rainbow trout range from 12 to 16 inches. Fish close to shore early in spring, either from a boat or the bank. Worms, salmon eggs, Power Bait, and Mepps spinners take their share of strikes.

Directions: From Farson, take US 191 north for 8 miles to Big Sandy Reservoir Road. Turn right onto this gravel road and drive 2 miles.

Additional information: Primitive camping is allowed here, but there are no developed campsites or services.

Contact: Wyoming Game and Fish Department, Pinedale.

137 Big Sandy Reservoir

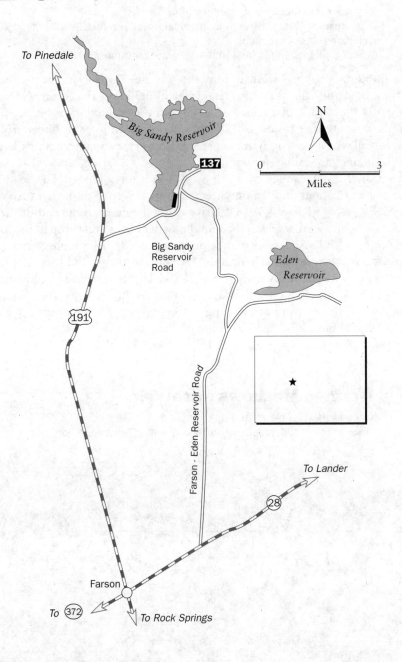

To Pinedale

Big Sandy Reservoir

137

N

0 3
Miles

Big Sandy
Reservoir
Road

Eden
Reservoir

191

★

Farson - Eden Reservoir Road

To Lander

28

Farson

To 372

To Rock Springs

138 Frye Lake

See map on page 170

Key species: brook trout, rainbow trout
Description: This 105-acre mountain lake sits in a rock-infested field with pine trees on all sides.
Tips: Bottom fishing is best, but snags can be frustrating.

The fishing: Brook trout range from 4 to 6 inches. Worms are most effective in the spring and fall. These fish tend to be found in the shallower water and are easily spooked. Some flies work well, but they take quite a bit of effort. Rainbow trout range from 8 to 12 inches. Worms tend to be the most productive bait all year long. The action tapers off later in the summer, making stream fishing a more appealing option.

Directions: From Lander, take 5th Street south for 9 blocks. The road will continue to the right on Fremont Street. Follow this road to the left turn onto the Sinks Canyon Road/WY 131. Drive about 10 miles to the end of the asphalt. Continue on this gravel road up the switchbacks and through the forest for another 6 miles. The lake will be on the right side, with limited parking.

Additional information: There is no developed campground here, but there are several nearby at Sinks Canyon State Park. The local streams that intercept Sinks Canyon Road all offer fishing opportunities. Brook trout dominate, but rainbow and brown trout can be caught. Generally the farther away an angler is from access points, the better the fishing will be.

Contact: Wyoming Game and Fish Department, Pinedale.

139 Worthen Meadows Reservoir

See map on page 170

Key species: brook trout, rainbow trout
Description: Lodgepole pine surrounds this 95-acre reservoir, which

This 95-acre trout-bearing reservoir has a campground, boat ramp, drinking water, and other amenities available for the angler.

has inviting sandy beaches.

Tips: Worms produce throughout the season, though the action is much slower in the summer months.

The fishing: Brook trout range from 4 to 6 inches. Worms and small flies take a good share of these fish from the mouth of the creek that fills the lake. Rainbow trout range from 8 to 10 inches. Worms, salmon eggs, and Power Bait are productive in the early spring and summer. Bobbers work well and tend to avoid the snags on the rocky and sometimes weedy bottom. Later in the season spinners are the most effective, especially when used from a boat.

Directions: From Lander take 5th Street south for 9 blocks. The road will continue to the right on Fremont Street. Follow this road to the left turn onto the Sinks Canyon Road/WY 131. Drive about 10 miles to the end of the asphalt. Continue on this gravel road up the switchbacks and through the forest on FR 300 for another 7 miles to FR 302. Turn right onto this dirt road and travel 3 miles.

Additional information: The Worthen Meadows Campground is a fee area with a camping area and a picnic ground. There are 20 units available in the lakeside division with 8 units in the hillside area. There is a good boat ramp and parking area, along with drinking water, toilets, and accommodations for trailers up to 22 feet. The area is open from July 1 through September 30.

Contact: Wyoming Game and Fish Department, Lander.

140 Fiddlers Lake

See map on page 170

Key species: rainbow trout

Description: There are 57 surface acres of water reflecting snowcapped mountains and tall pines. The shore is littered with boulders and deadfall.

Tips: Small bright flies are effective in the early morning light.

You will find rainbow trout in the waters of 57-acre Fiddlers Lake, surrounded by snowcapped peaks.

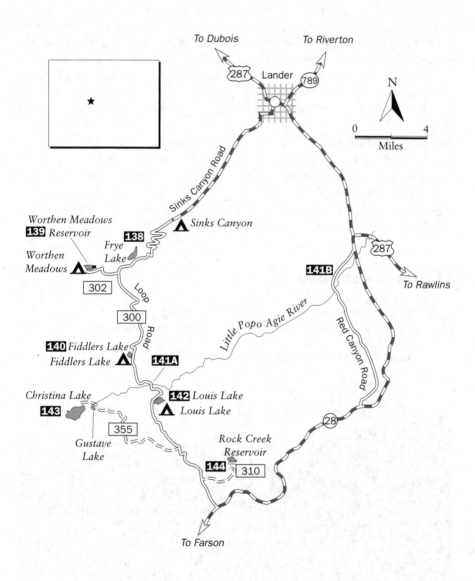

The fishing: Rainbow trout range from 8 to 10 inches. Worms and a variety of flies work well in the early spring. Early morning or late evening are the best times. Later in the fall, colorful spinners can produce some action.

Directions: In Lander take 5th Street south 9 blocks. The road will continue to the right here on Fremont Street. Follow this road to the left turn onto the Sinks Canyon Road/WY 131. Drive about 10 miles to the end of the asphalt. Continue on this gravel road up the switchbacks and through the forest on FR 300 for another 13 miles. The lake will be on the right side.

Additional information: The Fiddlers Lake Campground is a fee area with 13 units, drinking water, toilets, a boat ramp, and can accommodate trailers up to 16 feet. There are also barrier-free areas for the disabled. Only non-motorized boats are allowed.

Contact: Wyoming Game and Fish Department, Lander.

141 Little Popo Agie River

Key species: brook trout, rainbow trout

Description: This river runs fast and deep. The rapids break into whitewater around large rocks while the level grassy-banked areas have deep, inviting pools.

Tips: Small dark flies can provoke attacks when floated into the backwaters by large boulders.

Deep and fast-running, the Little Popo Agie River holds brook and rainbow trout in a forest setting.

The fishing: Brook trout range from 4 to 8 inches. Worms and small mosquito imitations work fairly well throughout the season. These trout dominate the upper reaches of the river, with the larger ones found farther away from any easy access. If grasshoppers are present later in the summer, an angler can create quite a bit of action using grasshopper imitations as bait. Rainbow trout range from 6 to 13 inches. Worms and dry flies work well from spring until the water levels drop in the late July. Grasshoppers and their imitations will produce some fish in the fall. The larger fish are mainly caught in the lower reaches closer to Lander.

Additional information: You can reach this river from the Shoshone National Forest and a public access area near Lander. There is a developed campground with 4 units, a picnic area, and toilets located near the river crossing in the national forest.

Contact: Wyoming Game and Fish Department, Lander.

141A. National Forest

Directions: In Lander take 5th Street south 9 blocks. The road will continue to the right here on Fremont Street. Follow this road to the left turn onto the Sinks Canyon Road/WY 131. Drive about 10 miles to the end of the asphalt. Continue on this gravel road up the switchbacks and through the forest for about 23 miles. There is limited parking where the road crosses the river.

141B. Wyoming Game and Fish Department Access

Directions: Take US 287 south out of Lander for about 10 miles to WY 28. Take this highway for about 2 miles to County Road 235/Red Canyon Road. Turn right onto this gravel road and travel about 0.5 mile to the parking areas.

142 Louis Lake

See map on page 170

Key species: brook trout, rainbow trout, mackinaw
Description: Steep piles of rock surround this 120-acre lake at an elevation of 8,550 feet. Aspen trees and willows encroach on the lake shore.
Tips: Bait works best in the spring. As summer warms up, small fluorescent spinners provoke a limited amount of action.

The fishing: Brook trout range from 4 to 6 inches and are mostly found in the brush-engulfed inlet. Worms are the easiest to use. Small black gnat flies can produce, but may be very difficult to present due to the trees by the shore. Rainbow trout range from 6 to 12 inches. Worms and salmon eggs produce fish just after the ice melts in late spring. During early mornings and late evenings, anglers find action with the bubble-and-fly technique. Boaters will have more action than shore anglers during the summer months by fishing deep with a variety of lures. Mackinaw average 10 to 12 inches. Trollers are the most likely to catch these fish with jigheads and pop gear.

Anglers may find brook trout, rainbow trout, and mackinaw in this beautiful 120-acre lake.

Directions: In Lander take 5th Street south 9 blocks. The road continues to the right on Fremont Street. Follow this road to the left turn onto Sinks Canyon Road/WY 131. Drive about 10 miles to the end of the asphalt. Continue on this gravel road up the switchbacks and through the forest on FR 300 for another 16 miles.

Louis Lake can also be reached from US 28. Take the Loop Road/FR 300 for about 10 miles north of US 28.

Additional information: A picnic area and a campground are at different locations on the lake. The Louis Lake Picnic Area has 18 units, a boat ramp, and toilets. The Louis Lake Campground is a fee area with 9 units, drinking water, toilets, and a boat ramp and can accommodate trailers up to 22 feet long. Both areas are open from July 1 through September 30.

Contact: Wyoming Game and Fish Department, Lander.

143 Christina Lake

See map on page 170

Key species: brook trout, mackinaw
Description: Snowcapped peaks and cool crisp air surround this ice-cold, 340-acre high country lake.
Tips: Early spring offers the best fishing but the worst access conditions because of snow.

The fishing: Brook trout range from 6 to 8 inches. Worms and small mosquito imitations give some results for most of the season. Later in the fall, these trout will be in gravel-bottomed shallow water and will have aggressive appetites. Mackinaw average 8 to 10 inches. Typically, these fish are found in deep water. Salmon eggs work well as bait during the spawning run in late fall when they are in shallow water. The rugged trail into the area limits boating.

There is a limit of 6 trout, per day, of which only 1 may be over 20 inches. Of these 6 trout, only 2 may be mackinaw.

Directions: In Lander, take 5th Street south for 9 blocks. The road will continue to the right here on Fremont Street. Follow this road to the left turn onto Sinks Canyon Road/WY 131. Drive about 10 miles to the end of the asphalt. Continue on this gravel road up the switchbacks and through the forest on FR 300 for another 24 miles to Christina Lake Road. Take this four-wheel-drive trail to the right for 10 miles to the lake. The Christina Lake road can also be reached from US 28. Take the Loop Road/FR 300 for about 4 miles north of US 28.

Additional information: You can reach this lake by foot, horseback, or four-wheel-drive (including ATVs) over about 10 miles of mountain trail. There are no developed campgrounds at the lake, but primitive camping is allowed within certain guidelines.

Contact: Wyoming Game and Fish Department, Lander.

144 Rock Creek Reservoir

See map on page 170

Key species: rainbow trout
Description: This 75-acre reservoir sits in a pine-forested canyon in rocky country. It is a deep drop in and a steep climb out.
Tips: Worms work well on the bottom in early spring.

The fishing: Rainbow trout range from 8 to 10 inches. Worms, salmon eggs, and Power Bait work well fished on the bottom in the early spring. Results are more limited in the fall. Fishing drops off drastically in the summer with some strikes on bright spinners and spoons. Dry flies work on occasion in the shadows of late evening toward fall.

Directions: Take US 287 south out of Lander for about 10 miles to WY 28. Turn right and drive about 18 miles to the Loop Road/FR 300. There will be a large parking area here with an information booth on the right side of the highway. Turn right onto this gravel road and travel 2 miles to FR 310. Turn right onto this four-wheel-drive trail and travel 2 miles.

Additional information: A four-wheel-drive vehicle is required to reach this area on a trail that runs through some private land. Primitive camping is allowed. No motorized boats are allowed.

Contact: Wyoming Game and Fish Department, Lander.

145 Sweetwater River

Key species: brook trout, brown trout
Description: This mountain stream begins in the Wind River Mountains. Spruce, pine, aspen, and willow line its banks as it flows to the high desert below and on to Pathfinder Reservoir, west of Casper.
Tips: Bucktail Mepps spinners have hooked some large brown trout in late August.

145 Sweetwater River

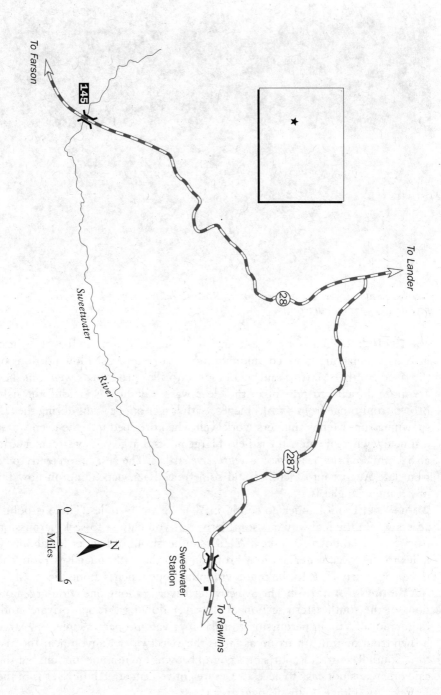

To Farson

145

Sweetwater

River

To Lander

28

287

Sweetwater
Station

To Rawlins

0
Miles
6

N

Nestled in pine-forested canyon country, Rock Creek Reservoir has a good population of rainbow trout.

The fishing: Brook trout range from 4 to 8 inches. Worms are best for these little fish, which are more commonly found in the upper, shallow portions of the river. Panther Martins and small mosquito flies produce as well, but they are more difficult to present in the clear waters without spooking the fish. Brown trout range from 8 to 14 inches, with larger ones caught during the fall spawning run. Mepps spinners work well when dropped into the deep water just below where it enters the riffles of large pools. Large yellow streamers can also tempt the browns into some aggressive strikes. The best action tends to be from late August into October and sometimes later, depending on how far upstream an angler is.

Directions: From Lander go south on WY 28 for 44 miles. There is public access where the highway crosses the river. If you choose to seek permission from private landowners, take WY 287 southeast out of Lander for about 50 miles to the Sweetwater Station. From here to the Pathfinder Reservoir, the river stays fairly close to the road, with numerous ranches along the way.

Additional information: The Sweetwater River is a long one with large portions of the southeastern section of the river flowing through private land. Inquire locally about permission to fish on private property. Some very large brown trout migrate upstream as far as the Sweetwater Canyon near the historic South Pass area. Reports of 8 pound browns are not uncommon, but the canyon area is not easy to access. A more convenient stretch of river is in the Jeffrey City (Home on the Range) area.

Contact: Wyoming Game and Fish Department, Lander.

Southeast

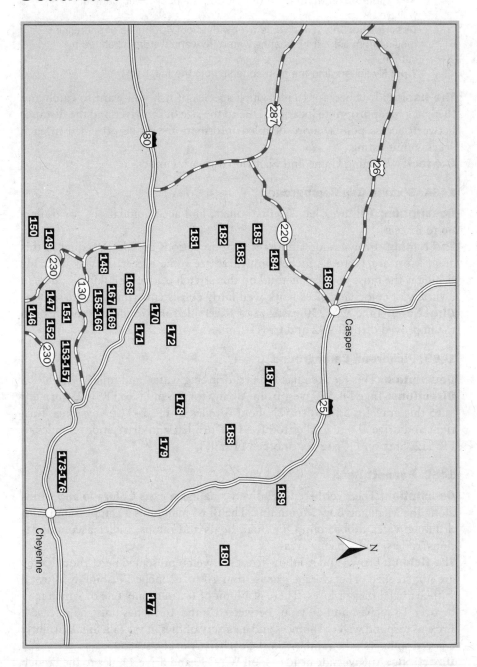

146 (Upper) North Platte River

Key species: brown trout, cutthroat trout, rainbow trout, catfish, walleye

Description: This is a diverse river with about 400 miles of shoreline ranging from cold, trout-bearing waters to warm waters inhabited by catfish.

Tips: Fly fishers find the best conditions in the fall.

The fishing: It is best to decide which species of fish you want to catch and then pick an appropriate location. Due to the size of this river and the distance between access points, more detailed information will be provided in each access point listing.

Contact: Wyoming Game and Fish Department, Lander.

146A. Sixmile Gap Campground

Description: This area has 7 units, toilets, and accommodations for trailers up to 32 feet.

The fishing: Brown and rainbow trout populations are almost equal in this area. Most are 10 to 12 inches, but there are some bigger ones as well. Fly fishing is the most popular method on this stretch of river. Elk Hair Caddis in a variety of colors and sizes work well fairly consistently through the season.

Directions: Take WY 230 east out of Riverside for 25 miles. Turn left onto the improved dirt FR 492 and travel 2 miles.

146B. Pickaroon Campground

Description: This fee area has 8 units, drinking water, and toilets.

Directions: Take FR 500 west from Albany for 2.5 miles to FR 542. Turn left onto this gravel road and travel about 5 miles to FR 543 at Keystone. Turn right and drive about 2 miles to FR 511. Turn left and drive about 3 miles to FR 512. Stay on FR 512 for another 11 miles.

146C. Bennett Peak

Description: The river here is relatively small as it exits Colorado and winds along the Medicine Bow Mountains. The BLM maintains a campground with drinking water, a boat ramp for small boats and ramps, trailer accommodations, toilets, and a picnic area.

The fishing: Brown and rainbow trout are well represented here, though they are not stocked. The average size is from 10 to 12 inches. Fishing is allowed with artificial flies or lures. There is a limit of 6 trout, only one of which may be over 16 inches, and all trout between 10 and 16 inches must be released. Browns respond well to spinners and a variety of flies in the fall. Small brightly colored spinners take rainbow in the early part of the season.

Directions: At Riverside head east on WY 230 and drive 4 miles to the French Creek Road/CR 660. Turn left and stay on this road for 13 miles to BLM Road 3404. Turn left onto this improved dirt road and travel 6 miles.

146 (Upper) North Platte River

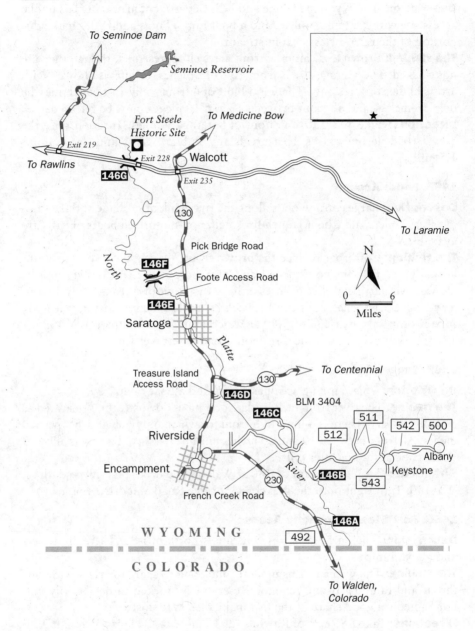

To Seminoe Dam

Seminoe Reservoir

Fort Steele
Historic Site

To Medicine Bow

Exit 219

To Rawlins

Exit 228

Walcott

146G

Exit 235

To Laramie

130

Pick Bridge Road

146F

Foote Access Road

North

146E

Saratoga

Platte

N

0   6

Miles

Treasure Island
Access Road

130

To Centennial

146D

146C

BLM 3404

Riverside

512

511

542   500

Encampment

146B

Albany

Keystone

French Creek Road

230

543

River

WYOMING

146A

COLORADO

492

To Walden,
Colorado

146D. Treasure Island

Description: The Wyoming Game and Fish Department maintains this public access site with camping, toilets, and a boat ramp. Pools and riffles make this portion of the river a classic trout stream.

The fishing: Brown and rainbow trout are well represented, though they are not stocked. The average size is from 10 to 12 inches. Fishing is allowed with artificial flies or lures only. There is a limit of 6 trout, only 1 of which may be over 16 inches, and all trout between 10 and 16 inches must be released.

Directions: Take WY 230 south out of Saratoga 9 miles. Turn left onto the gravel road designated as Treasure Island Public Access and drive about 1.5 miles.

146E. Foote Access

Description: Large cottonwoods along the riverbank offer shade at this camping area. Toilets and a boat launch for small, non-motorized boats or rafts are available.

The fishing: Cutthroat replace the brown trout, sharing the river with rainbows. These fish are not stocked and average 10 to 12 inches. Fishing is allowed with artificial flies or lures only, with a limit of 6 trout. Only 1 trout may be over 16 inches. All trout between 10 and 16 inches must be released.

Directions: Take exit 235 off I-80 at Walcott and drive south on WY 130 for 17 miles. Turn right onto the dirt Foote Road and travel 1 mile.

146F. Sanger Access

Description: This camping area has toilets and a boat ramp.

The fishing: The river from Pick Bridge for 5 miles downstream is operated as a trophy fishery. There is a limit of 6 trout, of which only one may be over 20 inches. All trout between 10 and 20 inches must be released. Fishing is allowed with artificial flies or lures only.

Directions: Take exit 235 off of I-80 at Walcott and drive 14.5 miles south on WY 130. Turn right onto the gravel Pick Bridge Road and drive 4 miles.

146G. Fort Steele/Rochelle Access

Description: The Fort Steele Historic Site is north of I-80. There are toilets and a boat ramp.

The fishing: The water warms up here, and walleye share the river with cutthroat and rainbow trout. Seminoe Reservoir is stocked rather heavily and undoubtedly a good share of the fish make their way upstream.

Directions: Take I-80 east of Rawlins for 15 miles to the Fort Steele exit 228. There is access to the river on both sides of the interstate.

147 French Creek

Key species: brook trout, brown trout, rainbow trout

Description: This little stream flows out of the forest in the Medicine Bow Mountains to join the North Platte River just east of Riverside. Tall pines line the clear, cold stream up to the grassy ranchland where it joins the North Platte River.

Tips: Worms are best in the spring while grasshoppers are preferred in the fall.

The fishing: Brook trout range from 4 to 8 inches. The biggest ones are in the less accessible areas. Worms work well in the spring with lesser success in the summer. As fall spawning starts, almost anything works. Brown trout average 8 to 12 inches. Spinners and hopper imitations tighten lines in the fall. Rainbow trout range from 8 to 12 inches. Worms and nymphs work well in the spring. Later in the summer dry flies have some results in the late evening shadows. Grasshoppers or their imitations are best used in the late fall for all trout here.

Directions: From Riverside head east on WY 230 and drive 4 miles to the Holmes Road/French Creek Road/CR 660. Turn left and stay on this all-weather road for 16 miles.

Additional information: The French Creek Campground has 11 units, toilets, and accommodations for trailers up to 32 feet. The campground is open from June 1 to October 1.

Contact: Wyoming Game and Fish Department, Laramie.

148 Saratoga Lake

Key species: brown trout, rainbow trout

Description: This fairly shallow, 284-acre lake sits in the open, grassy plain west of the Medicine Bow Mountains.

Tips: Shore fishing around the dam area seems to produce the most action during late summer.

The fishing: Brown trout range from 16 to 24 inches, but some 5 pounders are taken occasionally. These trout are most commonly caught late in September, but they are fussy. Rainbow trout range from 8 to 16 inches. Early spring or just after the ice melts is the most productive time for either shore or boat anglers. Worms, salmon eggs, and marshmallows generate action along with spoons and a variety of flies. In the fall, trollers do better with small spinners, but shore anglers take a few with flies or bait early in the morning or late in the evening. The weeds become thick in the fall and many fish are lost after tangling the line in the weeds near shore. Use a strong line if you are shore fishing in the fall.

Directions: Take WY 130 south from Walcott for 19 miles, or 1 mile north of Saratoga. Turn east onto the gravel road marked as the access to the Saratoga Lake Campground and drive about 0.5 mile.

Additional information: The city of Saratoga operates a fee campground along

147, 148 French Creek, Saratoga Lake

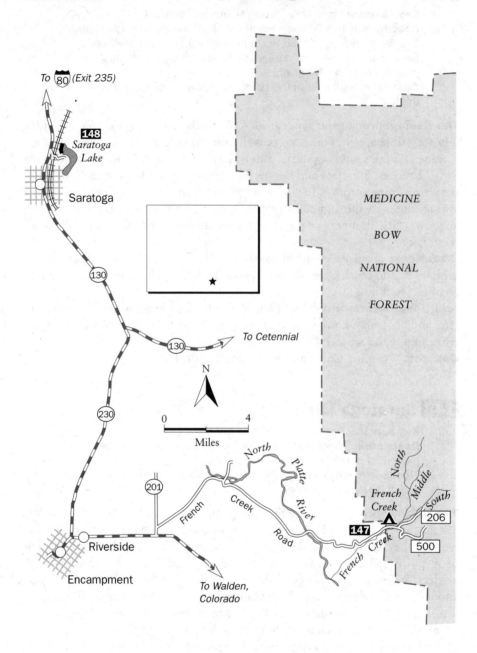

To (80) (Exit 235)

148
Saratoga
Lake

Saratoga

130

To Cetennial

N

230

201

0   4

Miles

North Platte River

French Creek Road

MEDICINE

BOW

NATIONAL

FOREST

North Middle South

French Creek

147

206

500

Riverside

Encampment

To Walden,
Colorado

Anglers occasionally take 5 pound brown trout out of Saratoga Lake.

the southern shore of the lake. There is drinking water, electrical hookups, toilets, and picnic tables. Fishing is allowed from the dock at the boat ramp, but boats have priority.

Contact: Wyoming Game and Fish Department, Laramie.

149 Encampment River

Key species: brown trout
Description: This clear, coldwater river flowing out of Colorado is shaded by high mountains and evergreens.
Tips: Grasshopper imitations are dynamite in the late summer and early fall.

The fishing: Brown trout range from 8 to 16 inches. The larger fish tend to be found in the lower stretches until fall spawning moves them upstream. Caddis and mayfly patterns work well for most of the season, with the best results early in the morning or late in the evening.

Directions: Take WY 70 west through Encampment to the last house on the left. Turn left on a well-traveled dirt road (County Road 353) and follow this over a small creek and through a narrow cattle guard to the junction of the Encampment Trail Head/CR 3407. Stay to the left on CR 3407 and drive another 1.25 miles. The Encampment trail follows the Encampment River for about 10 miles through historic mining camps. The trail runs roughly north and south with trailheads at Encampment and about 1 mile southeast of Hog Park Reservoir.

Additional information: Camping is available at the north access near Encampment.

Contact: Wyoming Game and Fish Department, Laramie.

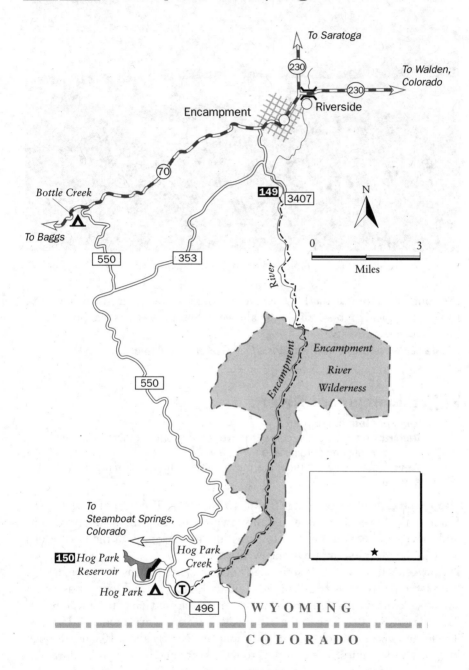

To Saratoga

To Walden, Colorado

Encampment

Riverside

Bottle Creek

To Baggs

Encampment River Wilderness

River

To Steamboat Springs, Colorado

150 Hog Park Reservoir

Hog Park Creek

Hog Park

WYOMING

COLORADO

N

0   3
Miles

The deep waters of 695-acre Hog Park Reservoir produce trout all season long.

150 Hog Park Reservoir

Key species: brook trout, rainbow trout
Description: The 695 surface acres of Hog Park Reservoir may be reduced a great deal by late September. The steep, heavily forested ridges surrounding the reservoir, at 8,000 feet, contain lodgepole pine and other conifers. Be prepared for cool weather, even in the summer.
Tips: The deeper waters along the dam are the most productive all season.

The fishing: Brook trout range from 4 to 6 inches. These trout are more commonly found near the inlet. Worms and small mosquito imitations are effective all season. Rainbow trout range from 6 to 14 inches. Worms, salmon eggs, and Power Bait fished from shore create good action in the early spring. Boaters have the most success in late September using a variety of spoons and spinners. Trollers usually take the biggest fish year-round. When the fishing gets slow in the reservoir, anglers find 8- to 10-inch trout in the stream below the dam.

Directions: From Encampment, head west on WY 70 for 6 miles to FR 550. Turn left onto this gravel road and travel 15 miles. Stay to the left and continue on FR 496 for 1 mile. Turn right at the sign for the Lakeview Campground and drive 1 mile.

Additional information: The Lakeview Campground is a fee area with 50 units, toilets, a boat ramp, and accommodations for trailers up to 30 feet. The campground is open from June 15 to October 31.

Contact: Wyoming Game and Fish Department, Laramie.

151 Rob Roy Reservoir

Key species: Brook trout, brown trout, rainbow trout, splake
Description: A dense lodgepole pine forest stands on the shoreline of this 800-acre reservoir. The campground is at 9,500 feet elevation.
Tips: Worms work best when fished on the bottom in early spring.

The fishing: Brook trout range from 6 to 8 inches. Worms are the most commonly used bait. These fish tend to be caught incidently while fishing for other species. Brown trout range from 7 to 12 inches and, as with brook trout, tend to be caught when fishing for the more common rainbow. Rainbow trout range from 8 to 13 inches; much larger ones can be found in the fall. Bottom-fishing worms, salmon eggs, Power Bait, and marshmallows from shore just after ice-out works well. Trollers create some action with spinners when the weather warms up and the trout move into deeper water. Splake range from 6 to 10 inches. Spinners and spoons take these fish from either shore or by boat.

Directions: Take WY 130 west out of Laramie for 24 miles to WY 11. Turn left onto this paved road and drive 11 miles to Albany. Take FR 500 west of Albany for 11 miles.

Additional information: The Rob Roy Campground is a fee area with 65 units, drinking water, toilets, a boat ramp, and accommodations for trailers up to 35 feet. This area is open from June 15 to October 1. Additional fishing is available in local streams.

Contact: Wyoming Game and Fish Department, Laramie.

152 Lake Owen

Key species: Brook trout, brown trout, rainbow trout
Description: A lodgepole pine forest encloses this 121-acre high country lake. At 9,000 feet, this place can get cold when the sun goes down, even in the summer.
Tips: The deeper drop-offs along both the dam and the railroad tracks are the most productive areas.

The fishing: Brook trout range from 6 to 8 inches. Worms generally produce the largest number of these trout. Brook trout are not the primary quarry here and are more often caught while trying to hook one of the other species present in the lake. Brown trout range from 8 inches to 24 inches. Worms tend to be the food of choice for these trout. Shore fishing from late August through September provides the most action. Rainbow trout range from 10 to 17 inches. The bubble-and-fly method is effective either from shore or by boat. Most of the rainbow are taken shortly after ice-out in the early spring.

Directions: Take WY 130 west from Laramie 24 miles to WY 11. Turn left and drive 8 miles to FR 311. You will see a sign with directions to the Forbes/Sheep Mountain Wildlife Habitat Management Area. Turn left onto the gravel FR 311 and drive 2 miles to FR 517. Stay to the right on this single lane, gravel road with pullouts for 2 miles to FR 540. Turn left onto this wider gravel road and travel 2 miles. The lake is on the left side.

151-157 Rob Roy Reservoir, Lake Owen, Sodergreen Lake, Meeboer Lake, Lake Hattie Reservoir, Gelatt Lake, Twin Buttes Lake

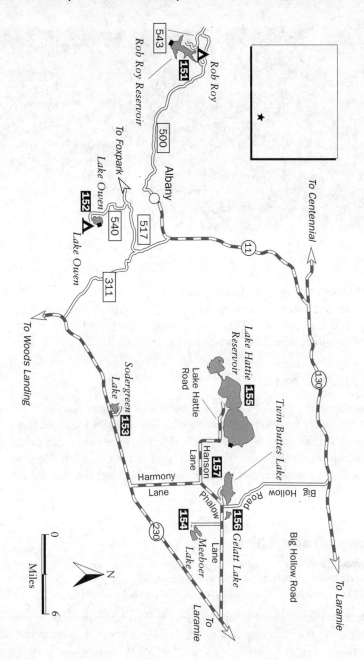

Lake Owen is nestled at 9,000 feet and is surrounded by pines. It holds brook, rainbow, and brown trout.

Additional information: The Lake Owen Campground is a fee area with 35 units, drinking water, toilets, a picnic area, a boat ramp, and accommodations for trailers up to 22 feet long. This area is open from June 1 to October 15. **Contact:** Wyoming Game and Fish Department, Laramie.

LARAMIE PLAINS LAKES

This vast plain covers a great deal of territory southwest of Laramie. The virtually flat grassland offers no resistance to the heavy winds that blow for most of the day. Early morning and late evening will give some relief, but in the lake areas the mosquitoes take over from early spring into mid-fall. Boating can become a challenge when the wind kicks up, so be aware of conditions and distances.

153 Sodergreen Lake

See map on page 187

Key species: rainbow trout
Description: The wind blasts this 72-acre lake.
Tips: Worms work well when fished on the bottom in early spring.

The fishing: Rainbow trout range from 6 to 9 inches. Catchable trout are stocked here early in the spring and grow quickly. However, later in the summer the fishing is not as productive. Streamers work well in the spring when fished with a bubble. Worms, salmon eggs, and Power Bait are effective when fished on the bottom. The wind will often determine the technique to use. Late in September, the fishing picks up a little with spoons and small spinners providing the better part of the action.

Directions: Take WY 230 southwest from Laramie 22 miles. The lake is on the right.

Additional information: No camping facilities are available.

Contact: Wyoming Game and Fish Department, Laramie.

154 Meeboer Lake

See map on page 187

Key species: rainbow trout
Description: As with the other plains lakes, the wind blows hard on 119-acre Meeboer Lake.
Tips: The bubble-and-fly method offers the best action in the early morning or late evening.

The fishing: Rainbow range from 6 to 14 inches. Catchable trout are stocked every year and tend to grow very fast. Winter kill can devastate the fish population, resulting in smaller fish. If they live, they can reach up to 20 inches. Streamers work well when fished with bubbles in the early spring. During the summer, worms, salmon eggs, and Power Bait fished on the bottom tend to be most productive. In October, trollers do well with worm harnesses. Some action can be had by fishing with spinners and spoons from a boat.

Directions: Take WY 230 southwest out of Laramie for 7.5 miles to Phalow Lane/CR 422. Turn right and drive 5 miles to CR 41/Meeboer Road. Turn left onto this gravel road and drive 1.5 miles.

Additional information: Camping is allowed. Toilets, a boat ramp, and disabled access is available.

Contact: Wyoming Game and Fish Department, Laramie.

155 Lake Hattie

See map on page 187

Key species: brown trout, cutthroat trout, rainbow trout, kokanee salmon, mackinaw, perch.
Description: There are 1,500 surface acres of windswept water on this lake. Far off, snowcapped mountains offer scenery but no wind resistance.
Tips: Fish the points by either boat or shore, especially in the fall.

The fishing: Brown trout range from 10 to 12 inches; 10-pounders are caught from time to time. Trolling with plugs and large spoons after dark works well from September through October. The fish tend to be near the points and peninsulas.

Cutthroat trout range from 10 to 14 inches. Hornberg, Renegade, and other related flies work well with the bubble method in the spring. Shore anglers do well with salmon eggs, Power Bait, and worms early in the spring and in the fall. The greater part of the summer tends to find trollers having the most success.

Rainbow trout range from 10 to 14 inches, and 6-pounders are caught occasionally. The same techniques used for cutthroat are effective for these fish. Fall fishing can produce some of the bigger fish, but spring is the best all-round time.

Kokanee salmon average 16 inches, though some reach 10 pounds. Trollers have the best opportunity using cowbells in deep water during the autumn.

Mackinaw range from 2 pounds on up to the 10-pound class. Trollers tend to catch the majority of these fish using sucker meat early in the morning or late evening. Fall is the best season with a few mackinaw caught on worm harnesses in the late summer.

Perch range from 7 to 10 inches. These tasty fish feed in schools and finding them can be a challenge. Be prepared for some fast, furious action when you do find them. Small jigs, worms, and leeches are usually productive all season.

Directions: Take WY 230 southwest of Laramie for 15 miles to Phalow Lane. Turn right onto this paved road and drive 3.5 miles to Hanson Lane. Turn left onto this paved road and drive 5 miles.

Additional information: This windy area is not the most pleasant place to camp, but it is allowed. A boat ramp is present but may not be usable due to low water later in the year.

Contact: Wyoming Game and Fish Department, Laramie.

156 Gelatt Lake

See map on page 187

Key species: cutthroat trout, rainbow trout
Description: Weeds can take over this 34-acre lake toward the end of summer.
Tips: Plan to fish this lake early and take a variety of tackle.

The fishing: Cutthroat and rainbow trout range from 8 to 12 inches. The most productive fishing time is just after the ice melts in May and June. These fish can respond to anything from worms to wet flies and spinners. Bring plenty of lures, flies, bait, and patience.

Directions: Take WY 230 southwest of Laramie for 7.5 miles to Phalow Lane/ CR 422. Turn right onto this paved road and drive 5 miles.

Additional information: Camping is available along with parking, toilets, and a boat ramp.

Contact: Wyoming Game and Fish Department, Laramie.

157 Twin Buttes Lake

See map on page 187

Key species: brown trout, rainbow trout, perch
Description: Lake Hattie feeds this 250-acre, windswept lake.
Tips: Work the points, especially late in the summer.

The fishing: Brown trout range from 12 to 18 inches. Trollers do well with worm harnesses around the peninsulas late in the fall. Shore fishing with streamers in the spring can produce some fish, but the better action is in late September.

Rainbow trout range from 12 to 16 inches. Streamers, worms, and salmon eggs produce a few trout in the spring. The summer does not produce many of these fish, though fishing improves slightly in the fall. Perch range from 7 to 9 inches. These fish school when feeding and provide the angler with a feast or famine. Jigs and worms can be effective when an angler is in the right spot at the right time; be ready.

Directions: Take WY 230 southwest of Laramie for 7.5 miles to Phalow Lane/ CR 422. Turn right onto this paved road and drive 5 miles. Go straight ahead onto the gravel access road and travel 1 mile.

Additional information: Camping is available along with parking, toilets and a boat ramp.

Contact: Wyoming Game and Fish Department, Laramie.

THE SNOWY RANGE

The Snowy Range Scenic Byway heads to the lakes and streams in this section. This road travels through wide-open grassy valleys, densely forested mountains, and barren, permanently snow-covered peaks. Although the road may stay open from Memorial Day to the end of October, the first snow in early September may still be present the following July. The elevation reaches 10,847 feet at the road's highest point, with mountaintops climbing dramatically nearby.

The area is divided into the east and west sections administered by two different Forest Service ranger districts.

158 Nash Fork Creek

Key species: brook trout
Description: This creek crashes over some large boulders on its way through the pine forest.
Tips: Look for the undercut washouts near the larger rocks.

The fishing: Brook trout range from 6 to 9 inches. Worms are the most productive when allowed to drift into deeper parts of the creek. Snags can be frustrating and will quickly claim tackle; be sure to take plenty.

Directions: Take WY 130 west out of Laramie about 40 miles.

Additional information: The Green Rock Picnic Area is a fee area with 9 units and foot access to the creek.

Contact: Wyoming Game and Fish Department, Laramie.

159 Big Brooklyn Lake

Key species: brook trout, cutthroat trout
Description: This 36-acre alpine lake is near timberline. Huge snowcapped peaks loom over the tall fir trees, making them look significantly smaller.
Tips: Small, dark flies fished with bubbles find action in the shadows and dim light throughout the season.

158–165 Nash Fork Creek, Big Brooklyn Lake, Towner Lake, Libby Lake, Lewis Lake, Lookout Lake, Mirror Lake, Silver Lake

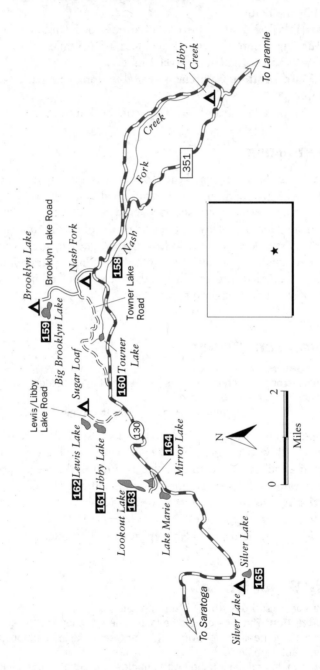

The fishing: Brook trout range from 6 to 8 inches. Worms, along with mosquito and black gnat imitations, will create some activity. Cutthroat range from 7 to 11 inches. These fish tend to respond to worms in the early spring. Later in the summer, they tend to get pickier.

Directions: Take WY 130 west of Laramie for 40 miles to the Towner Lake Road. Turn right onto this narrow, paved road and drive 1.5 miles.

Additional information: Brooklyn Lake Campground is a fee area with 17 units, drinking water, toilets, and accommodations for trailers up to 22 feet. This area, at 10,500 feet, is open from July 15 to September 10, weather permitting. Only non-motorized boats are allowed. Nearby, Little Brooklyn Lake also offers fishing opportunities for brook trout.

Contact: Wyoming Game and Fish Department, Laramie.

160 Towner Lake

Key species: brook trout

Description: This shallow, 9-acre, alpine lake is within the fir and pine forest of the Snowy Range.

Tips: Watch your position to avoid alerting the fish.

The fishing: Brook trout range from 6 to 10 inches. The clear waters help alert them when your shadow passes in their line of sight. Worms can be effective when placed to avoid alarming them.

Directions: Take WY 130 west out of Laramie for 40 miles to the Towner Lake Road. Turn right onto this narrow, paved road and drive 1 mile. Turn left onto the single lane improved dirt road going directly past Little Brooklyn Lake and travel about 1 mile. The lake will be on your left.

Additional information: There are no services at this location, but camping and other related amenities are nearby.

Contact: Wyoming Game and Fish Department, Laramie.

161 Libby Lake

Key species: brook trout, cutthroat trout

Description: This alpine lake has 26 surface acres of ice-cold water.

Tips: Worms work almost all season with faster action in early summer.

The fishing: The trout here range from 6 to 11 inches. Smaller brook trout tend to be more plentiful. Small mosquito imitations and worms create action from July until the first part of September.

Directions: Take WY 130 west of Laramie for about 44 miles to the Lewis/Libby Lake Road. Turn right onto this gravel road and travel about 0.75 mile.

Additional information: Nearby Sugarloaf Campground offers 16 units with drinking water, toilets, and accommodations for trailers up to 22 feet. This fee area is open from July 15 to September 10. A picnic area is also available with

4 units. The elevation is 10,700 feet, so be prepared for cool temperatures. Boating is allowed, but there is no boat ramp.

Contact: Wyoming Game and Fish Department, Laramie.

162 Lewis Lake

See map on page 192

Key species: brook trout, brown trout, cutthroat trout, rainbow trout, splake

Description: Lewis Lake is 19 surface acres of water sitting in the hard rock of the Snowy Range. The elevation is the same here as at Libby Lake so be prepared for cool weather.

Tips: Worms are productive for the whole season.

The fishing: Brook trout range from 4 to 8 inches. Worms tend to be the most effective all year long. Small, size 18 mosquito imitations tend to take a few later in the spring in early morning or late evening. Brown trout range from 8 to 14 inches. Worms provide the most action from shore, especially later in the summer. Cutthroat and rainbow trout range from 6 to 16 inches and respond well in the spring to most baits and lures. Later in the summer, spinners and spoons dominate their interest. In the fall, worms, salmon eggs, and Power Bait find renewed interest from these somewhat fussy eaters. Splake range from 6 to 12 inches. Spinners create some action along with minnow imitation lures.

Directions: Take WY 130 west of Laramie for about 44 miles to the Lewis/Libby Lake Road. Turn right onto this gravel road and travel about 1.25 miles.

Additional information: The Sugarloaf Campground is described in the previous site. The Lewis Lake picnic ground offers 4 units and has drinking water available.

Contact: Wyoming Game and Fish Department, Laramie.

163 Lookout Lake

See map on page 192

Key species: brook trout

Tips: Pack some warm gear and lots of film.

Description: This high alpine lake holds 35 acres of melted ice with some very deep areas. The snow capped Snowy Range is almost to close to take pictures and is still awesome in size.

Fishing: Brook trout range from 6 to 8 inches in length. Worms and small flies, such as mosquito imitations are productive with the better fishing in the later part of summer. Fall does comes early to this high country with the first snow to be expected around the first of September.

Directions: Take Wyoming Highway 130 west of Laramie for about 49 miles to the Mirror Lake Picnic Ground road. Turn right onto this gravel road and travel 0.75 miles. Take the moderate Lookout Lake trail for about 0.75 miles.

Additional information: Lookout Lake is located in a nonmotorized access area. Foot access is by the Mirror Lake Picnic Area.

Contact: Wyoming Game and Fish Department, Laramie.

Brook and rainbow trout can be had in scenic Mirror Lake, which is accessible by trail from Mirror Lake Picnic Ground.

164 Mirror Lake

See map on page 192

Key species: brook trout, rainbow trout
Description: Year-round snow rests on the mountains that loom over the 26 surface acres of ice water that is Mirror Lake. Fir trees, lodgepole pines and giant boulders are scattered along the shore.
Tips: Worms work best when used with bobbers.

The fishing: Brook trout range from 6 to 9 inches. Worms dangling under a bobber can take fish in the spring. Small flies fished early in the morning can be productive. Fishing is better for these fish in the fall, when spawning makes them aggressive. Rainbow trout range from 7 to 11 inches. Early spring finds these fish at their hungriest. Worms and salmon eggs are good producers. Spinners create some explosive action in the spring and can also hook a few from the deeper water later in the summer.

Directions: Take WY 130 west of Laramie for about 49 miles to the Mirror Lake Picnic Ground road. Turn right onto this gravel road and travel 0.75 mile.

Additional information: The Mirror Lake Picnic Ground is a day-use fee area with 12 units, drinking water, toilets, and accommodations for trailers. The Lakes Trail #296 starts at this picnic area with an additional foot trail to Lake Marie. Both brook and rainbow trout are available in Lake Marie. Going the opposite direction from Mirror Lake, anglers can access Lookout Lake. Brook trout are present in the lake's deep waters. The trailhead for Lookout Lake is at the Mirror Lake Picnic Ground.

Contact: Wyoming Game and Fish Department, Laramie.

165 Silver Lake

See map on page 192

Key species: brook trout
Description: Silver Lake is 17 surface acres of sapphire blue water set between cupped ridges.
Tips: As with the previous site, worms with bobbers work best.

The fishing: Brook trout range from 6 to 10 inches. Worms dangled under bobbers can be effective in the spring. Later in the fall, when spawning takes place, small black gnat imitations can create some explosive action along with a variety of other baits such as grasshopppers and worms.

Directions: Take WY 130 west of Laramie for about 59 miles to the Silver Lake Campground access road. Turn left and drive 1 mile.

Additional information: Silver Lake Campground is a fee area with 19 units, drinking water, toilets, and accommodations for trailers up to 32 feet. The campground is open from July 1 to September 15, weather permitting. Non-motorized boats are allowed on the lake, but there is no boat ramp.

Contact: Wyoming Game and Fish Department, Laramie.

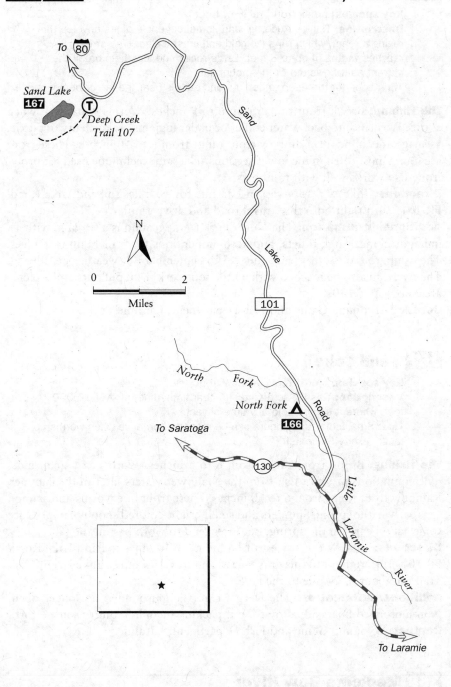

166 North Fork Little Laramie River

See map on page 197

Key species: brook trout, rainbow trout
Description: Thick spruce, fir, and some lodgepole pines envelop this raging stream, which runs ice cold and crystal clear. The stream reaches widths of up to 8 feet. Large rocks and logs help break the current as it flows out of the mountains.
Tips: Look for the deep undercuts and eddies near the larger boulders.

The fishing: Brook trout range from 6 to 9 inches. Worms work well when allowed to drift into backwater eddies or under logjams. Take plenty of tackle, as snags are abundant. Rainbow trout range from 6 to 10 inches. These trout are found most often in the lower sections. The same technique used for brook trout also works well with rainbows.
Directions: Take WY 130 west of Laramie for 40 miles to Sand Lake Road/ FR 101. Turn right onto this gravel road and drive 1 mile.
Additional information: The North Fork Campground is a fee area with 16 units, drinking water, toilets, and accommodations for trailers up to 30 feet. The campground is open from June 15 to September 30, weather permitting. The river can also be reached with a little footwork from pullouts and a picnic area along WY 130.
Contact: Wyoming Game and Fish Department, Laramie.

167 Sand Lake

See map on page 197

Key species: brook trout, rainbow trout
Description: This 92-acre lake sits near timberline, at over 10,000 feet, where it can be cold any time of year.
Tips: Small colorful spinners can be a good alternative when worms no longer excite these fish.

The fishing: Brook trout range from 6 to 8 inches. Worms and small mosquito imitations produce fish from the shallower waters later in the summer. Rainbow trout range from 6 to 10 inches. These trout like worms and salmon eggs early in the spring. Spinners and small bright-colored spoons can produce some action early in the spring, but lures tend to work best in the fall.
Directions: Take WY 130 west of Laramie for 40 miles to Sand Lake Road/ FR 101. Turn right onto this gravel road and travel 15 miles. Take Deep Creek Trail for about 0.75 mile to the lake.
Additional information: The Deep Creek Campground is no longer open. Non-motorized boats are allowed, but packing them in requires some effort.
Contact: Wyoming Game and Fish Department, Laramie.

168 Medicine Bow River

Key species: brook trout
Description: Downed timber and huge rocks litter the path of this

168, 169 Medicine Bow River, East Fork Medicine Bow River

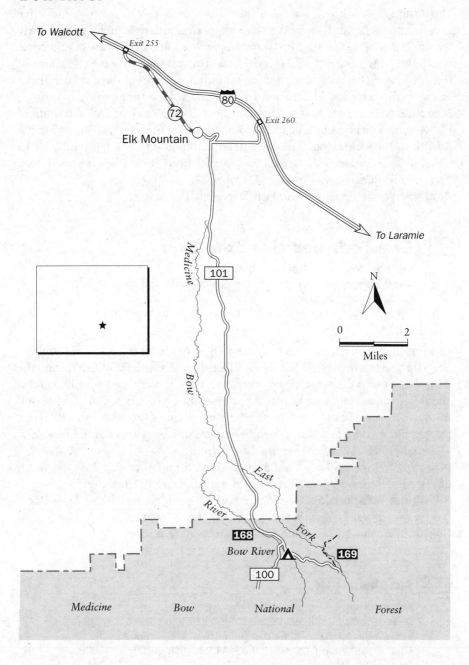

stream as it flows out of the Snowy Mountains to the wide plains below, creating some deep, turbulent holes.

Tips: Take plenty of tackle.

The fishing: Brook trout range from 6 to 8 inches. Worms are productive almost all year long. During the spawning period in late September and early October, the action heats up. Grasshoppers or look-alikes can be effective. Rainbows range from 8 to 10 inches. Worms produce the biggest share of these fish. Wet flies work too, but the multitude of snags in the river can make this a costly endeavor. The most intense action will be found in early spring.

Directions: Take I-80 west of Laramie about 50 miles to exit 260. Go south of Elk Mountain on gravel Medicine Bow Ranger Station Road/CR 101 for 12 miles.

Additional information: The Bow River Campground is a fee area with 13 units, drinking water, toilets, and accommodations for trailers up to 32 feet. This area is open from May 24 to October 31.

Contact: Wyoming Game and Fish Department, Laramie.

169 East Fork Medicine Bow River

See map on page 199

Key species: brook trout, rainbow trout

Description: This raging creek dodges boulders and downed timber on its way to join the main river.

Tips: Let your worm float naturally along the bottom with minimal direction into possible hiding areas.

The fishing: Brook trout range from 4 to 6 inches. Late fall is the best time to fish for these tasty morsels. Worms produce the biggest share of fish during the year. The crystal-clear water lets them see anglers very easily so be careful about your approach. Rainbow trout range from 8 to 10 inches. As with brook trout, worms are the most productive bait and perhaps the easiest to use. These fish are likely to be found in the eddies and foamy backwater along boulders. They tend to be less wary than the brook trout.

Directions: Take I-80 west of Laramie about 50 miles to exit 260. Go south of Elk Mountain on gravel Ranger Station Road/CR 101 for 14 miles.

Additional information: There is camping available nearby at Bow River Campground, but no services are provided at this location.

Contact: Wyoming Game and Fish Department, Laramie.

170 Rock Creek

Key species: brown trout, rainbow trout

Description: After it leaves the mountains, this stream meanders through the open country along the edge of the Laramie plains.

Tips: Grasshoppers or their imitations take fish quickly from late summer through fall.

The fishing: Brown trout range from 8 to 12 inches. Worms or grasshoppers are productive, especially in the fall. Spinners and brightly-colored spoons can

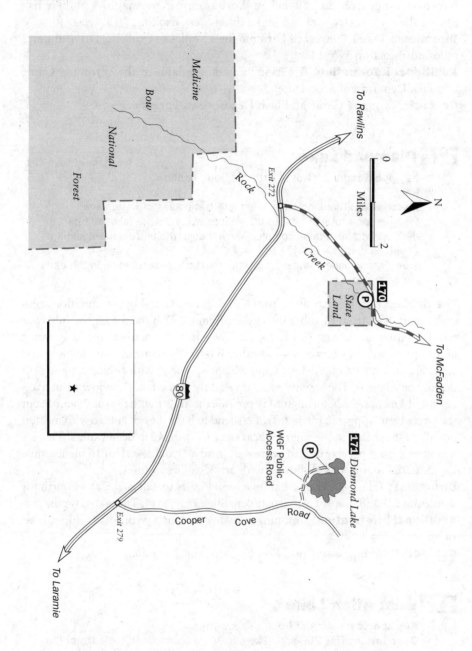

create some explosive action as well, but they require more persistence. Rainbow trout range from 8 to 10 inches. Worms bring in the majority of these fish during the spring. Dry flies can make things very exciting.

Directions: Take I-80 west of Laramie for 41 miles to exit 272. Drive about 2 miles northeast on WY 13.

Additional information: A parking area is available at the Wyoming Game and Fish Department access site.

Contact: Wyoming Game and Fish Department, Laramie.

171 Diamond Lake

See map on page 201

Key species: brook trout, cutthroat trout, rainbow trout

Description: Diamond Lake is actually two bodies of water joined together for a total of about 200 surface acres. These lakes are part of the vast Laramie Plains complex, even though the better known lakes are some distance away.

Tips: Fly-and-bubble anglers have the most consistent action in the early spring and late fall.

The fishing: Brook trout range from 6 to 9 inches. Grasshopper imitations generally work well from October through November. Fish them near the inlet waters. Cutthroat range from 8 to 12 inches. These trout are active in the early spring and respond well to Hornbergs and other related fly patterns. Spin anglers find some action with Panther Martin and Mepps spinners, with fishing tapering off during the summer. The activity picks up slightly in the fall. Rainbow trout average 8 to 14 inches. April through May provide the angler with the most action, but the larger trout appear in the fall. Trollers tend to have the advantage with most, if not all, of the strikes in the summer heat since the fish are in deep waters. There is a limit of 2 trout per day or 2 in possession, and all trout less than 16 inches must be released. Fishing is only allowed with artificial flies or lures.

Directions: Take I-80 west of Laramie for 34 miles to exit 279. Travel north for 4 miles on CR 15/Cooper Cove Road/Bengough Hill Road. The lake is on the left.

Additional information: Camping is available along with toilets and a boat ramp.

Contact: Wyoming Game and Fish Department, Laramie.

172 East Allen Lake

Key species: cutthroat trout, rainbow trout

Description: This 259-acre lake sits in the badlands at the edge of the Laramie Plains.

Tips: Bottom fishing is best in the early spring; weeds limit fishing as the water warms up.

The fishing: Both cutthroat and rainbow trout range from 12 to 16 inches. Power Bait, salmon eggs, and cheese work well when fished from the bottom

172 East Allen Lake

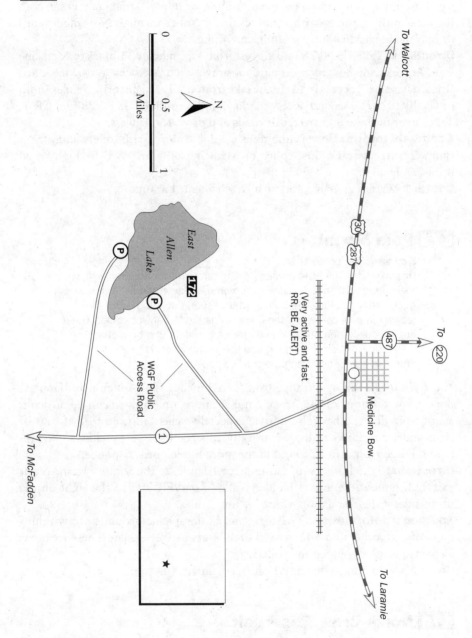

in the early spring. As the weeds mature, bottom fishing comes to a close and fly-and-bubble techniques take over. Trolling with small spinners takes over in the heat of the summer with some results. October through November tends to find the bigger fish hitting almost anything.

Directions: Take US 30/287 northwest from Laramie for 51 miles to Medicine Bow. At Medicine Bow turn left onto the gravel CR 1/Medicine Bow/McFadden Road. There are 2 access roads to the lake from CR 1. The first is 1.5 miles south of US 30/287. The second access road is 2 miles south of US 30/287 on CR 1. Take either of these improved dirt roads and drive 1 mile west.

Additional information: Camping is available along with toilets and a boat ramp. The train tracks just south of Medicine Bow are used by high speed trains, so be alert.

Contact: Wyoming Game and Fish Department, Laramie.

173 Pole Mountain

Key species: brook trout
Description: The little creeks flowing through this area range from 2 feet wide to 10 feet deep, with numerous beaver ponds. Willow brush is thick and high along the banks, while aspen thickets border the lodgepole pine-covered ridges, known as the Vedauwoo rocks. These huge, odd-shaped and stacked granite boulders can be a climbing adventure for both the young and the young at heart.
Tips: Go slow. These fish are easily spooked.

The fishing: Brook trout range from 4 to 9 inches. The 4-inch fish dominate the narrow portions of the stream, and sneaking up on them can be difficult. Worms provide the best alternative, especially when allowed to drift out of sight under cut-banks or logs. Naturally, this results in lost tackle, so be prepared. Large trout can be found in the more hidden beaver ponds.

Directions: Take I-80 east of Laramie for 10 miles to the Summit Rest Area at exit 323. Follow the gravel Hidden Valley Road/FR 705 to the right on the north side of the rest area parking lot for 5 miles.

Additional information: The Blair and Wallis picnic grounds are within 5 miles of each other and offer a total of 30 units between them. These fee areas also have drinking water and toilets.

Contact: Wyoming Game and Fish Department, Cheyenne.

174 North Crow Reservoir

Key species: rainbow trout
Description: This ice-cold, 75-acre, manmade reservoir weaves in and out of granite ridges. The sandy beaches are bordered by sagebrush, grass, and lodgepole pine.
Tips: Fish the points in the early morning and late evening.

The fishing: Rainbow trout range from 6 to 14 inches. Worms, salmon eggs,

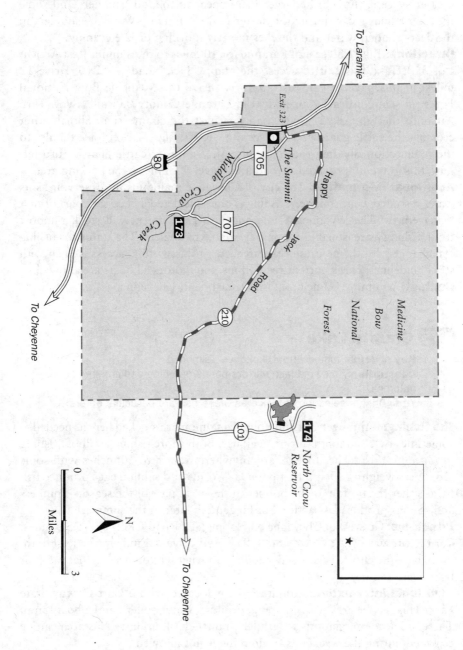

and Power Bait work well when fished from the bottom. Early spring offers greater success, though the larger fish appear in the fall. Spinners and some flies sometimes work during the hotter part of summer. Work the spinners in the deep, shaded water and the flies in early morning or late evening.

Directions: Take I-80 east of Laramie for 10 miles to the Summit Rest Area at exit 323. Take this exit to access the Happy Jack Road/WY 210. Drive 12 miles on this paved road. Just after you leave the Medicine Bow National Forest, a sign confirms your arrival in Laramie County 0.7 mile away. Turn left onto the unmarked gravel road just past the county sign. Shortly after crossing the cattle guard you will see the CR 101 sign. Travel for 2.8 miles to the intersection dividing the road, just after another cattle guard. Turn left onto this gravel/improved dirt road and travel 0.5 mile to the parking area.

Additional information: The city of Cheyenne maintains this reservoir as its water resource. Unfortunately, fishing is not considered a necessary part of that management. The Wyoming Game and Fish Department will stock rainbow trout as long as reasonable access is available to anglers. The status for fishing can change with the politics of the area. As of this writing, access is open with strict guidelines; check current regulations. No motorized boats are allowed.

Contact: Wyoming Game and Fish Department, Cheyenne.

175 Granite Lake

Key species: rainbow trout, kokanee salmon
Description: This cold lake mirrors ponderosa pine and granite outcrops.
Tips: Bring a selection of tackle as these fish are particular eaters.

The fishing: Rainbow trout and kokanee salmon are stocked here as needed—sometimes twice a month during peak use. Both shore fishing and boat fishing produce nice fish. The stockers are anywhere from 8 to 10 inches with some old timers weighing in at 3 to 4 pounds. Worms and salmon eggs produce fish from either the bottom or by bobber in the early part of the season. Spinners and spoons produce less action but bigger fish later in the summer.

Directions: Go west of Cheyenne on Happy Jack Road/CR 210 for 23.5 miles. Turn left toward Curt Gowdy State Park and drive 0.5 mile to the fee booth. From here the choice is yours, depending on whether you need a boat ramp or trailer parking.

Additional information: Granite Lake is located within Curt Gowdy State Park. This is a fee area with camping, drinking water, toilets, and a boat ramp. There are accommodations for trailers, but they fill up fast. This area can be crowded during the weekends. Swimming is not allowed.

Contact: Curt Gowdy State Park.

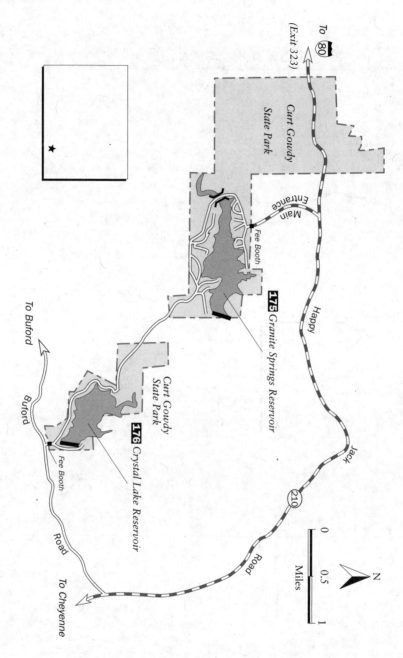

To 80 (Exit 323)

Curt Goudy State Park

Main Entrance

Fee Booth

Happy

175 Granite Springs Reservoir

Curt Goudy State Park

To Buford

Buford

Fee Booth

176 Crystal Lake Reservoir

Jack

210

Road

Road

To Cheyenne

0   0.5   1

Miles

N

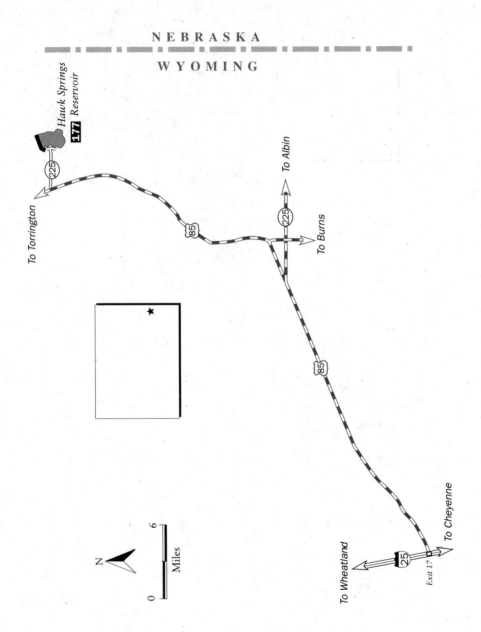

NEBRASKA

WYOMING

Hawk Springs Reservoir

177

225

To Torrington

85

225

To Albin

To Burns

85

To Wheatland

25

Exit 17

To Cheyenne

N

Miles

0   6

176 Crystal Lake

See map on page 207

Key species: brown trout, rainbow trout, mackinaw
Description: This small lake sits in a pine-covered canyon with plenty of shade.
Tips: Bottom-fishing from the shore with worms, Power Bait, or salmon eggs is best.

The fishing: Rainbow trout and some kokanee salmon are stocked here. Rainbow trout up to 4 pounds or more are occasionally caught. There are bigger brown trout here, but they are less common. The mackinaw get up to 15 pounds or more and are found in the deeper water near the dam. Boats are a necessity for catching these lunkers. Fly fishing can be productive either from shore or a boat.

Directions: Go west of Cheyenne on Happy Jack Road/CR 210 for 10 miles to the Crystal Lake turnoff. Turn left onto this gravel road and travel 6 miles to the fee booth on your right.

Additional information: This lake is located in Curt Gowdy State Park. Camping, drinking water, toilets, and a boat ramp are available.

Contact: Curt Gowdy State Park.

177 Hawk Springs Reservoir

Key species: catfish, walleye, largemouth bass
Description: This shallow, manmade reservoir is within sight of some impressive prairie bluffs. A few cottonwood trees furnish shade at the camping area.
Tips: Catfish are most often found along the dam in the early part of the summer.

The fishing: Walleye are the most sought after fish. These fish are stocked twice a year, along with largemouth bass. Any bass caught must be released if they are fewer than 12 inches long. The water gets fairly low and warm in the summer months, making shore fishing rather limited. The catfish stay close to the dam area and are caught regularly with bait in the early summer. The Wyoming Game and Fish Department requires that enough of the skin be left intact on transported fish to identify the species. There is a combined limit of 6 fish.

Directions: Go north out of Cheyenne on I-25 to exit 17. Take US 85 north for 51 miles to the Hawk Springs turnoff. Turn right onto gravel CR 225/K4 and drive 3 miles.

Additional information: There are 24 camping units, toilets, and accommodations for trailers. A boat ramp and parking area are available. This is a popular area in the summer and the campsites fill quickly on weekends and holidays.

Contact: Hawk Springs State Recreation Area.

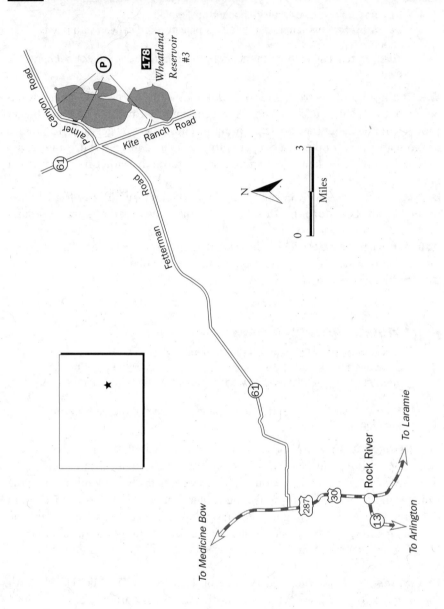

178 Wheatland Reservoir #3

Key species: cutthroat trout, rainbow trout
Description: There are about 760 surface acres of water in this badlands prairie reservoir.
Tips: Trollers tend to catch most of the large fish.

The fishing: Cutthroat and rainbow trout average between 16 and 18 inches. Shore anglers have limited success with a variety of baits including worms, salmon eggs, and Power Bait. Bubble-and-fly techniques result in some action later in the fall. The boaters do best in these waters. Trolling with cowbells and worm harnesses is the most commonly used method. The best time for catching fish here is in the mornings, April through May.

Directions: Take US 30/287 north out of Laramie for 42 miles or about 3 miles past Rock River. Turn right onto gravel Fetterman Road/CR 61 and travel about 18 miles to the intersection with Kite Ranch Road and Palmer Canyon Road. The reservoir can be reached from either of these roads; notice that Fetterman Road turns left at this intersection away from the reservoir.

Additional information: Camping is available with toilets and a boat ramp. Nearby Wheatland Reservoir #2 is often confused for this lake. Reservoir #2 is on private land. Take care to arrive at Wheatland Reservoir #3 and avoid the hassle of trespassing.

Contact: Wyoming Game and Fish Department, Cheyenne.

179 Johnson Creek Reservoir

See map on page 212

Key species: rainbow trout
Description: This 7-acre reservoir is in a rugged canyon.
Tips: Worms take trout with varying success all season.

The fishing: Rainbow trout range from 6 to 10 inches. Catchable trout are stocked here. Worms, salmon eggs, and Power Bait produce fish through the early spring with some success in the late summer. Small spinners and colorful spoons can create some action when the trout are not interested in worms.

Directions: Take US 30/287 north out of Laramie for 18 miles to WY 34. Turn right onto this paved road and drive 26 miles to the Sybille/Johnson Creek Access. Turn left onto this dirt road and travel 1 mile.

Additional information: Camping is available with toilets. The reservoir is located within the Sybille/Johnson Creek Access Area. Only non-motorized boats are allowed.

Contact: Wyoming Game and Fish Department, Cheyenne.

180 Grayrocks Reservoir

See map on page 214

Key species: largemouth bass, smallmouth bass, catfish, crappie, tiger musky, perch, walleye
Description: The Laramie River fills this 3,500-acre manmade reservoir located in a vast prairie.

179 Johnson Creek Reservoir

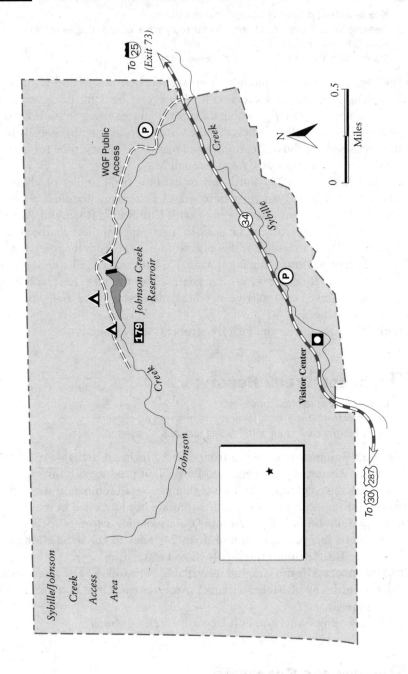

To 25 (Exit 73)

WGF Public Access

P

Creek

Sybille

34

P

N

0   0.5
Miles

Johnson Creek Reservoir

179

Creek

Johnson

Visitor Center

To 30 287

Sybille/Johnson Creek Access Area

Tips: Boats offer the best opportunity to find the particular fish an angler desires.

The fishing: Both largemouth and smallmouth bass range from 8 to 14 inches. June offers the best action in the upper portion of the reservoir when these fish start moving into the weedy sections to spawn. Spinner baits, floating plugs, plastic worms, and plastic salamanders produce attacks. All bass less than 12 inches must be released.

Catfish range from 1 to 10 pounds. These fish are found in the deeper water near the lower portion of the dam. Night fishing in the late summer with worms, sucker meat, and stink bait tends to be successful.

Crappie range from 8 to 10 inches. Small jigs and worms produce results along the cliffs on the north side of the reservoir. There is a limit of 15 crappie per day or 15 in possession.

Tiger musky average 10 to 20 pounds, but they occasionally reach 30 pounds. These fish respond well to minnow imitations. Their aggressive strikes can erupt into an exciting experience. Tiger muskies tend to be in the upper portions of the reservoir.

Perch range from 8 to 10 inches. Just about anything an angler offers is acceptable. Catching the larger ones will take some persistence since the smaller ones are quicker to notice an angler's offering.

Walleye average 1 to 3 pounds. May through July finds good success with nightcrawlers and jigs. As the heat bears down toward the first part of August, these fish tend to move into deeper water. Trolling during the day with minnow imitations produces the best results. Late in the afternoon, walleye will move into the shady shallows.

Directions: Take exit 80 off I-25 at Wheatland and drive east toward town about 1 mile. Turn left, following the sign directing you toward the Laramie River Power Station. Follow this paved road for 20 miles. The reservoir is on the left.

Additional information: Camping is available with limited facilities, including toilets and 2 boat ramps. This a large, popular reservoir that gets crowded at these access areas, especially on holidays and weekends.

Contact: Wyoming Game and Fish Department, Cheyenne.

181 Seminoe Reservoir

See map on page 216

Key species: brown trout, rainbow trout, walleye
Description: This large, deep body of water has sandy beaches to the south and steep mountains to the north.
Tips: The trout tend to be more concentrated along the North Platte portion of the reservoir, starting at the dam and moving steadily upstream over the course of the summer.

The fishing: Brown trout average 1 to 3 pounds and reach up to 8 pounds. Trolling spinners, spoons, and Rapalas in the fall produces the biggest fish most consistently. The browns tend to be found moving upstream into the North Platte River during this time.

180 Grayrocks Reservoir

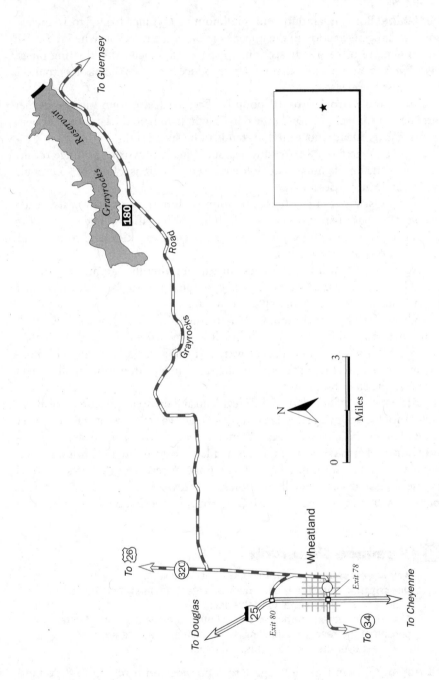

Rainbow trout average 1 to 2 pounds. June and July are best for shore anglers. Worms, marshmallows, and Power Bait fished from the bottom produces both the most and the largest fish. Though trollers catch trout through these months, late summer and early fall are better. Worm harnesses and cowbells work well. The bigger fish tend to concentrate from Coal Creek Bay upstream to the North Platte River. Flies can be productive in early morning or late evening as the fish begin to surface in the shady areas.

Walleye range from 12 to 14 inches. Shore anglers are not very successful. April through May produces walleye from the bottom with minnows, crawfish, and sometimes nightcrawlers. The Medicine Bow Arm of the reservoir holds the greater concentration of walleye. The east side of the reservoir also yields more walleye than trout. Trollers or boaters using jigs have the best results from June to early July.

Additional information: This 21,000-acre reservoir is in Seminoe State Park. Campgrounds, picnic areas, and boat facilities are available.

Contact: Seminoe State Park.

181A. Sand Mountain

Description: This day-use fee area along Coal Creek Bay offers picnic facilities, drinking water, and toilets.

Directions: Take exit 219 off I-80 at Sinclair and drive north on Seminoe Road/CR 351 for 25 miles. Turn right onto the paved road marked as access for Sand Mountain and travel 2 miles.

181B. Sunshine Beach

Description: Camping is available in this fee area along with a picnic ground and toilets. Four-wheel-drive vehicles are recommended for reaching the area. Large campers and trailers are not allowed.

Directions: Take exit 219 off of I-80 at Sinclair and drive north on Seminoe Road for 32 miles. Turn right onto the trail and travel about 1 mile.

181C. South Red Hills Area

Description: This fee area has a campground, picnic area, drinking water, playground, toilets, and a boat ramp.

Directions: Take exit 219 off of I-80 at Sinclair and drive north on Seminoe Road for 34 miles. The paved road becomes gravel for the last 3 miles.

181D. North Red Hills Area

Description: This fee area has a campground, picnic area, drinking water, toilets, playground, and a boat ramp. The headquarters for the park is also found here.

Directions: Take exit 219 off of I-80 at Sinclair and drive north on Seminoe Road for 34 miles. The paved road will turn to gravel for the last 4 miles.

181E. Medicine Bow Access

Description: This access area is maintained by the Wyoming Game and Fish

181–185 Seminoe Reservoir, North Platte River (Miracle Mile), Dome Rock Reservoir, Alcova Reservoir, Pathfinder Reservoir

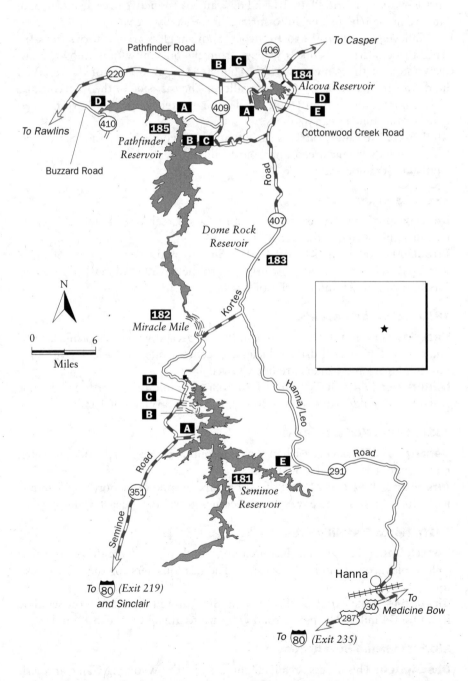

Department and offers toilets, a parking area, and a boat ramp.

Directions: From Hanna, take CR 291/Hanna Leo Road north and then west for 22 miles. At the Wyoming Game and Fish Department access sign, turn left and travel on this improved dirt road about 2 miles. CR 291 becomes gravel outside of Hanna.

182 North Platte River (Miracle Mile)

Key species: brown trout, rainbow trout, walleye

Description: The North Platte meanders through this mountain-bordered desert and is up to 25 feet wide with plenty of current. The granite mountains are barren of trees, but the canyons and hidden draws are not. Willow brush and a few large cottonwoods line the banks. The desert to the east is open and windy.

Tips: Though fish may be caught at any time of day, evenings are more productive.

The fishing: Brown trout range from 12 to 24 inches in this blue-ribbon river. July to September provides the most action, with intensity increasing toward September. A variety of techniques produce results, including Mepps spinners and colorful spoons. Fly fishers find large nymphs and grasshopper imitations appealing later in the summer as well. Rainbow trout average 12 to 16 inches. April through May is the most productive time. Use salmon eggs. Later in the summer, spinners and flies create some action. Walleye range from 8 to 10 inches, though larger ones are sometimes reported. Worms and sucker meat are effective in the river just above Pathfinder. A few walleye strike at lures being offered to the more sought after trout. This area is closed to night fishing (8 P.M. to 6 A.M.) for the month of April. There is a limit of 2 trout per day or 2 in possession, of which only 1 may be over 20 inches.

Directions: From Casper, head west 8.5 miles from the junction with WY 487 to the Alcova Store on the south side of WY 220. At the store, turn left onto CR 407/Kortes Road. Follow this paved and gravel road for 34 miles.

Additional information: This area covers several miles between Seminoe and Pathfinder reservoirs and is accessible from Sinclair. The road north of Seminoe Reservoir should not be attempted in foul weather. There is a gate on the road that is locked when conditions are bad. Camping is available, along with parking areas and toilets, at various points on both sides of the river.

Contact: Wyoming Game and Fish Department, Casper.

183 Dome Rock Reservoir

Key species: rainbow trout

Description: This 9-acre lake is in a remote, isolated countryside of granite outcroppings and rolling sagebrush desert.

Tips: Heavy test line can save the day when a fish gets tangled in the weeds.

The fishing: Rainbow trout range from 12 to 20 inches; larger ones are occasionally taken. There is a limit of 1 trout per day or 1 in possession, which must be 20 inches or longer. Only artificial flies or lures are allowed. Early spring is the best time to fish. The bubble-and-fly method gets results while avoiding most of the weeds.

Directions: From Casper, head west 8.5 miles from the junction with WY 487 to the Alcova Store, on the south side of WY 220. At the store, turn left onto CR 407/Kortes Road/Cottonwood Road. Follow this paved and gravel road 19 miles. The reservoir is to the left of the road.

Additional information: There are no services or facilities provided, other than a parking area.

Contact: Wyoming Game and Fish Department, Casper.

184 Alcova Reservoir

See map on page 216

Key species: brown trout, rainbow trout, walleye
Description: Alcova Reservoir has 2,260 surface acres of water backed into colorful badlands and cliffs.
Tips: Fish the rocky points.

The fishing: Brown trout range from 12 to 20 inches. Spoons such as Dardevle and other similar lures work best along the rocky points late in October and into November. Both trolling and shore fishing result in some action. Rainbow trout range from 10 to 12 inches. Anglers fishing from shore with worms, salmon eggs, and Power Bait catch fish off the bottom. April through May tends to be the most productive time, but September and October also give some action. Trollers do fairly well with cowbells almost all season; it slows down in the summer months, but not nearly as much as for shore anglers. Walleyes range from 1 to 8 pounds and seem to be most active from June through July. Later in the summer, baited jigs produce some results in the canyon area. Otherwise, worm harnesses top the list for effectiveness.

Additional information: Camping and picnic facilities are available at different places along the reservoir. Special regulations apply for ice fishing, allowing anglers to use up to 6 lines under certain guidelines.

Contact: Wyoming Game and Fish Department, Casper.

184A. Fremont Canyon

Description: This site offers camping, a boat ramp, and toilets.

Directions: Take WY 220 west out of Casper for 34.5 miles to Alcova Lake Park. Turn left onto the paved CR 406/Lakeshore Drive and go about 5 miles.

184B. Lakeshore Drive

Description: This site has a marina offering boat rentals, a restaurant, lounge, store, and gas. Other available services include camping, a picnic area, and toilets.

Directions: Take WY 220 west out of Casper for 34.5 miles to Alcova Lake Park. Turn left onto CR 406/Lakeshore Drive and go 4 miles.

184C. Okie Beach

Description: This popular site offers camping, picnicking, toilets, group shelters, and wheelchair access.
Directions: Take WY 220 west out of Casper for 34.5 miles to Alcova Lake Park. Turn left onto the paved CR 406/Lakeshore Drive and go 3.5 miles.

184D. Cottonwood Creek

Description: This site offers more than water recreation; an interpretive trail leads through a dinosaur bed. Collecting fossils is not allowed, but walking the trail is informative and interesting. Other available facilities include camping, picnicking, group shelters, toilets, and a boat ramp.
Directions: Take WY 220 west out of Casper for 30 miles to the Alcova Store. Turn left onto CR 407/Kortes Road and drive 6.3 miles past the store. Turn right onto gravel Cottonwood Creek Road and travel 1.5 miles.

184E. Black Beach

Description: This site offers camping, picnicking, group shelters, toilets, a boat ramp, and wheelchair access.
Directions: Take WY 220 west out of Casper for 30 miles to the Alcova Store. Turn left onto the paved CR 407 and drive past the store about 11 miles. Turn right onto the gravel access road and travel about 3.5 miles.

185 Pathfinder Reservoir

See map on page 216

Key species: brown trout, rainbow trout, walleye
Description: Pathfinder Reservoir is a 22,000-acre desert lake. Around the reservoir, granite outcroppings and sagebrush-covered hills stretch far into the distance. At certain times, the lighting makes the whole landscape feel like another planet.
Tips: The brown trout move into both the Sweetwater River and the North Platte River in late fall; bright streamers can be effective during this time.

The fishing: Brown trout range from 12 to 24 inches. Generally, the big browns don't show up until November near the inlets. Bright pink or purple streamers offer results at either the North Platte or the Sweetwater entrance. Rainbow trout range from 10 to 12 inches. May to early June seems to be the best time. Use worms, salmon eggs, or Power Bait. Later, through the summer and into the fall, the bubble-and-fly method produces some action. Trollers tend to have better results later in the year using spinners and cowbells. Walleye average 10 to 14 inches. Minnows and jigs provide results from June through July. Boaters tend to have the best access and more success.
Additional information: This is a large reservoir with limited road access.
Contact: Wyoming Game and Fish Department, Casper.

185A. Bishop's Point

Description: This site offers camping, picnicking, toilets, and a boat ramp.

Directions: Take WY 220 west out of Casper 40 miles to CR 409/Pathfinder Road. Turn left and drive 3.5 miles to the Bishop's Point access road. Turn right onto this gravel road and travel 4 miles.

185B. Weiss

Description: This site offers camping, picnicking, group shelter, toilets, and a boat ramp.

Directions: Take WY 220 west out of Casper for 40 miles to CR 409/Pathfinder Road. Turn left and travel 7 miles.

185C. Diabase

Description: There is a marina here along with camping, picnicking, group shelter, toilets, and a boat ramp.

Directions: Take WY 220 west out of Casper for 40 miles to CR 409/Pathfinder Road. Turn left and travel about 9 miles.

185D. Sweetwater Access

Description: There are no services located here and low water levels may make fishing difficult without a boat.

Directions: Take WY 220 west out of Casper for 50 miles to the Buzzard Road/CR 410. Turn left onto this gravel path, which becomes dirt, and travel 2.5 miles.

186 (Middle) North Platte River

Key species: brown trout, rainbow trout

Description: The river is wide and deep with water levels closely regulated by a series of upstream dams. A variety of plants and trees line the banks and wide open spaces and distant mountains are never far from view.

Tips: Floating is the most effective method because it allows anglers access to the greatest number of fishing opportunities.

The fishing: The Bureau of Reclamation flushes the river from Gray Reef Dam downstream in October to help clear the silt. When this is being done, the fishing tends to be very poor except in the clear section above Gray Reef Dam and below Alcova Reservoir. Brown trout range from 10 to 12 inches, though 10-pounders are hooked from time to time. These trout are less prominent than the rainbow and thus receive less attention. Late fall is the best time for browns except when the silt is being flushed from the river. Small spinners and weighted nymphs are productive. Rainbow trout range from 12 to 16 inches, with 3-pounders showing up fairly consistently. Drifting nightcrawlers in early spring is the most productive. Some artificial flies create some action such as the Crane fly, Caddis fly, and the North Platte Special, the may fly. Later, in the heat of the summer, spinners tend to take more fish.

Additional information: There is a variety of camping and other services available at different locations. Details are given in the access description. Floaters will find red triangles along the river indicating private land and blue triangles designating public lands. Approximate float times are listed below although they may vary with fluctuation in river flows, weather, and style of floating.

Gray Reef	to	Lusby	4.5	hours
Lusby	to	Government Bridge	2.0	hours
Government Bridge	to	By-The-Way	1.0	hours
By-The-Way	to	Sechrist	5.0	hours
Sechrist	to	Bessemer Bend	2.5	hours
Bessemer Bend	to	Morad	7.0	hours
Morad	to	Platter River Parkway	2.25	hours
Platter River Parkway	to	Riverview Park	0.75	hours
Riverview Park	to	Evansville	1.75	hours
Evansville	to	Edness Kimball	2.5	hours

Contact: Wyoming Game and Fish Department, Casper.

186A. Gray Reef Reservoir

Description: This small reservoir is managed by the Bureau of Reclamation. It is used to regulate water flow from the Alcova Power Plant. Camping is available, along with toilets and a boat ramp.
Directions: Take WY 220 west out of Casper about 29 miles to CR 419. Turn left onto this gravel road and travel about 1 mile.

186B. Lusby

Description: Two parking areas are available, as well as a boat ramp.
Directions: Take WY 220 west out of Casper for about 21.5 miles. Turn left onto the dirt road and travel 2 miles.

186C. Trappers Route

Description: This area offers shore fishing and limited boating with no ramp.
Directions: Take WY 220 west out of Casper for about 21 miles to Trapper Road/CR 319. Turn right onto this gravel road and travel about 2 miles.

186D. Government Bridge

Description: This area offers shore fishing and limited boating with no ramp.
Directions: Take WY 220 west out of Casper about 20 miles.

186E. Bolton Creek

Description: This area offers shore fishing and limited boating with no ramp.
Directions: Take WY 220 west out of Casper for about 19.5 miles to the Bolton Creek Road. Turn left onto this gravel road, which turns to dirt, and travel about 1 mile. Bear to the right for about 1 mile along the river.

186 (Middle) North Platte River

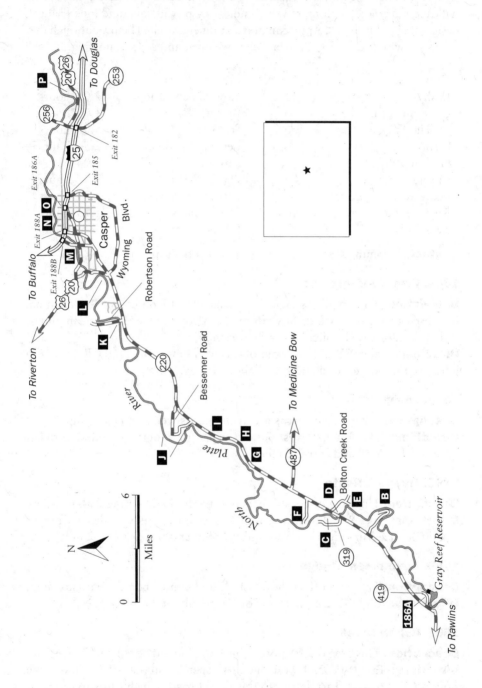

186F. By-The-Way

Description: This area offers shore fishing access.
Directions: Take WY 220 west out of Casper for about 18 miles to the access road. Turn right onto this dirt road and travel 1.75 miles.

186G. Sechrist

Description: This area offers shore fishing, toilets, and a boat ramp.
Directions: Take WY 220 west out of Casper about 16.25 miles to the access road. Turn right onto this dirt road and travel 0.25 mile.

186H. Schmitt

Description: A parking area is provided for shore fishing in this area.
Directions: Take WY 220 west out of Casper for 15 miles. The parking area will be on the right side.

186I. The Narrows

Description: This area offers shore fishing access.
Directions: Take WY 220 west out of Casper for about 14.5 miles.

186J. Speck/Bessemer/Hartnett

Description: This area offers shore fishing from two parking areas.
Directions: Take WY 220 west out of Casper for 10 miles to the Bessemer Road. Turn right onto this gravel road. The first parking area is near the highway and the second is about 2 miles farther.

186K. Paradise Valley/Robertson Road

Description: This area has 2 separate parking areas and offers shore fishing and limited boating, but no boat ramp.
Directions: Paradise Valley is just outside the southwest portion of Casper. Take WY 220 west to the Roberston Road. Turn right onto this paved road and travel 0.25 mile to the bridge access parking on the left. Continue past this parking area for a total of 1 mile to the other parking area on the right.

186L. Morad Park

Description: This park offers shore fishing and a boat ramp.
Directions: This park is located in the northwest corner of the intersection of Wyoming Boulevard and WY 220, within the Casper city limits.

186M. Platte River Parkway

Description: This area offers picnicking, hiking, biking, toilets, and a boat ramp.
Directions: The access area is located in Casper along the Yellowstone Highway just south of Business US 20/26 near the AMOCO Oil Refinery.

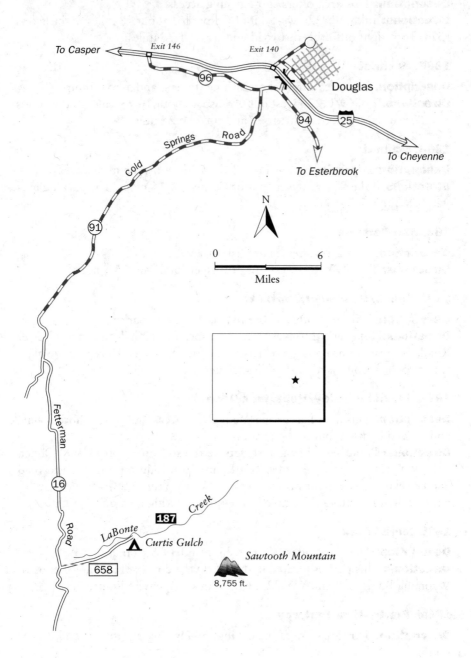

To Casper

Exit 146

Exit 140

Douglas

96

94

25

To Cheyenne

To Esterbrook

Cold Springs Road

91

N

0   6
Miles

★

Fetterman

16

LaBonte Creek

187

Road

Curtis Gulch

658

Sawtooth Mountain
8,755 ft.

186N. Riverview Park

Description: This park offers a group shelter, a boat ramp, and shore fishing.
Directions: This area is located on M Street in the north central part of Casper. Take Exit 188A off of I-25 and proceed north to M Street.

186O. North Casper Park

Description: This park offers a group shelter and shore fishing.
Directions: Exit I-25 at exit 186B and travel north about 2 miles to the river. The park is on the left.

186P. Edness K. Wilkins State Park

Description: This is a fee area with group shelters, drinking water, phone, playground, toilets, picnic area, boat ramp, and wheelchair-accessible fishing.
Directions: Take WY 256 north of exit 182 just east of Casper on I-25 for about 1 mile. Turn right onto US 20/26 and drive about 2 miles to the park entrance on the left.

187 LaBonte Creek

Key species: rainbow trout
Description: This small stream crashes through a steep, granite canyon. In addition to fishing, the area is popular for climbing and photography.
Tips: Worms work best

The fishing: Rainbow trout range from 7 to 8 inches. These catchable fish are stocked yearly by the Wyoming Game and Fish Department. Worms produce the most fish in the spring; the fish population drops by fall.
Directions: Take WY 91 south out of Douglas 20 miles to the Fetterman Road/CR 16. Turn left on this road, which becomes gravel, and drive 14 miles to FR 658. Turn left onto this gravel road and travel 4 miles.
Additional information: Curtis Gulch Campground has 6 units, drinking water, toilets, and accommodations for trailers up to 22 feet. There is no trash collection in this area so be prepared to pack out what you pack in.
Contact: Wyoming Game and Fish Department, Casper.

188 North Laramie River

Key species: brown trout, rainbow trout
Description: Rugged granite forms the backbone of this country. Beginning in a steep, narrow canyon, the North Laramie River widens and slows in its lower reaches.
Tips: Pack light gear and heavy lunches.

The fishing: Brown trout range from 8 to 15 inches. These fish tend to be found in the slower portions, downstream from the canyon's faster water.

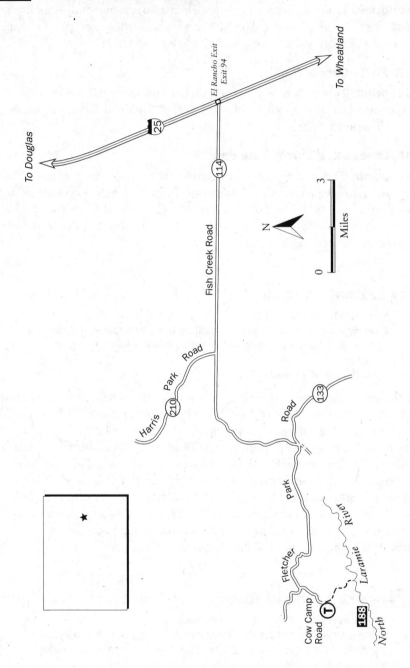

To Douglas

To Wheatland

El Rancho Exit
Exit 94

25

114

Fish Creek Road

N

Miles

3

0

Harris Park Road

210

133

Road

Park

Fletcher

Laramie River

Cow Camp Road

T

188

North

Worms, a variety of flies, and spoons produce results primarily in the fall. Rainbow trout range from 6 to 10 inches. Worms are the most productive bait, but flies work too. The action in late spring and early summer is in the fast water of the upper reaches.

Directions: Take I-25 14 miles north out of Wheatland to El Rancho Road/ Exit 94. From this exit, take the Fish Creek Road/CR 114 west 13.5 miles to Fletcher Park Road. Turn right on this gravel road and drive about 5 miles. Look for and follow the signs to the North Laramie Public Access from the Cow Camp Road for about 1 mile to the trailhead.

Additional information: The only service offered here is parking. Dispersed camping is allowed, but there are no designated sites. The difficult hiking trail is 2.5 miles long and drops 1,000 feet to the river.

Contact: Wyoming Game and Fish Department, Casper.

189 Glendo Reservoir

Key species: walleye, catfish
Description: Winding, colorful cliffs border this large warm-water reservoir. Cottonwood trees offer shade at various camping areas.
Tips: In the late spring or early summer, bottom bouncers or jigs produce the larger walleyes.

The fishing: Walleyes up to 13 pounds are consistently caught here. There is some shore fishing along Whiskey Gulch, but boating is the most productive way to fish here. Catfish are found toward the mouth of the reservoir and range from 1 to 3 pounds. Stink baits work well at night. Yellow perch are numerous, although they tend to end up as food for walleye and do not have time to get very large.

Additional information: Glendo Reservoir is located within Glendo State Park. It has camping, boat ramps, toilets, and accommodations for trailers. The marina has boat rentals, boat sales and service, a cafe and motel, gas, propane, fishing equipment, and licenses.

Contact: Glendo State Park.

189A. Elk Horn Access

Description: A boat ramp and toilets are available.
Directions: Take exit 111 off of I-25 and drive into Glendo. After crossing the railroad tracks, turn left and drive about 5 miles on WY 319. Turn right onto this gravel road and travel about 1.5 miles.

189B. Red Hills Area

Description: About 30 sites are in this windy area with a few shade trees and a rocky shoreline. There is a protected bay for tying boats, a picnic area, toilets, and drinking water.
Directions: Take exit 111 off of I-25 and drive into Glendo. After crossing the railroad tracks, turn left and drive about 1.5 miles to the Red Hills turnoff.

Turn right onto this gravel road. After passing through the fee booth, continue for 3 miles to the camping area.

189C. Reno Cove Campground

Description: Reno Cove Campground has a boat ramp and about 20 camping sites. A protected bay offers shelter for tying boats, but the camping sites get hit with wind. There are a few shade trees, as well as a picnic area, drinking water, and toilets.

Directions: Take Exit 111 off of I-25 and drive into Glendo. After crossing the railroad tracks, turn right and follow the signs to the state park road. Drive east of Glendo about 1.5 miles to the main fee booth. Continue east of the booth for 2.8 miles to the Reno Cove turnoff. Turn left onto this gravel road and travel 3.5 miles.

189D. Custer Cove Campground

Description: There are 40 well-shaded sites here along with a protected bay for tying boats. A picnic area and toilets are also available.

Directions: Take Exit 111 off of I-25 and drive into the town of Glendo. After crossing the railroad tracks, turn right and follow the signs to the state park. Go east out of Glendo on the state park road, about 1.5 miles, to the main fee booth. Continue east of the booth for 2.8 miles to the Reno Cove turnoff. Turn left onto the gravel road and travel 1.8 miles.

189E. Whiskey Gulch Campground

Description: There are about 100 sites here with lots of shade trees and level spots. There is also good wind protection, so bank fishing is popular. Group shelters, a picnic area, drinking water, a boat ramp, and toilets are available.

Directions: Take Exit 111 off of I-25 and drive into Glendo. After crossing the railroad tracks, turn right and follow the signs to the state park. Go east out of Glendo on the state park road for about 3 miles.

189F. Shelter Point Campground

Description: Group shelters, a picnic area, drinking water, and toilets are available here.

Directions: Take Exit 111 off of I-25 and drive into the town of Glendo. After crossing the railroad tracks, turn right and follow the signs to the state park. Go east out of Glendo on the state park road for about 4 miles.

189G. Sandy Beach Campground

Description: This large, sandy beach has about 2 miles of shoreline, depending on the water level. Cottonwoods provide abundant shade. There is no protection from the wind in this area, which can be a major problem.

Directions: Take Exit 111 off of I-25 and drive into the town of Glendo. After crossing the railroad tracks, turn right and follow the signs to the state park. Go east out of Glendo on the state park road. Follow this road across the dam and continue north to the north side of the reservoir. The campground is 13.2 miles from the main fee booth.

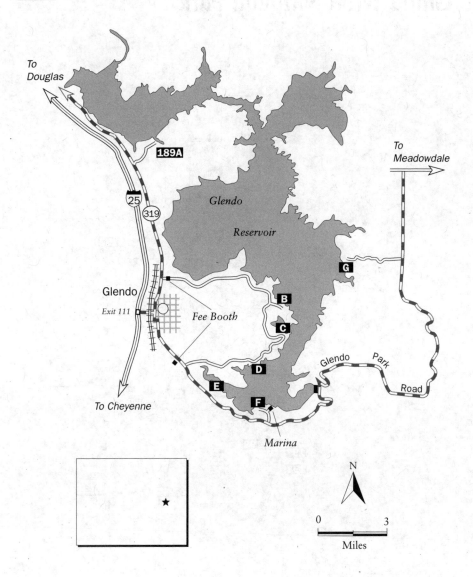

To
Douglas

189A

25

319

To
Meadowdale

Glendo

Reservoir

G

Glendo

Exit 111

Fee Booth

B

C

D

Glendo   Park

E

Road

F

To Cheyenne

Marina

N

0   3

Miles

Grand Teton National Park

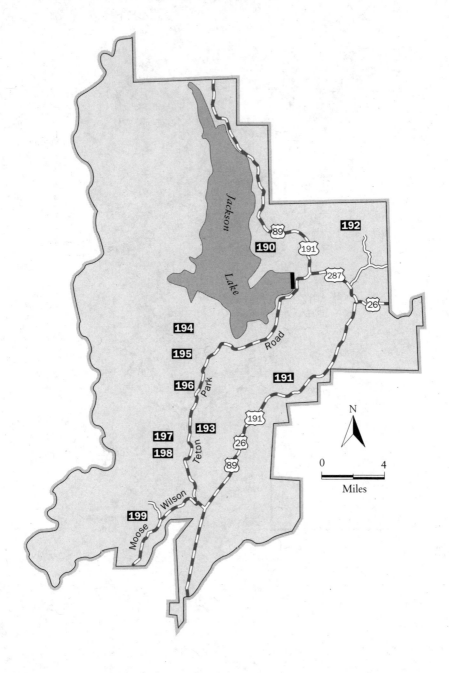

Grand Teton National Park

This majestic park does not seem to have the same demand for overnight camping as nearby Yellowstone National Park. The 5 camping areas within Grand Teton National Park do not fill up as fast. If they are found at capacity, there are campgrounds just outside the park that do not fill, such as the Gros Ventre Campground northeast of Jackson.

The majority of facilities and recreation are found along Jackson Lake. The vast size of this lake offers a lot of exploration and naturally, fishing. The lodge at Jenny Lake also provides a variety of services and is a good starting point to the backcountry.

190 Jackson Lake

Key species: cutthroat trout, mackinaw, whitefish

Description: When you enter this country and see it firsthand, you can easily understand why it is so popular. Photographs cannot capture the magnitude of this extraordinary area. There are 25,730 acres of water available for fishing adventrue and postcard-type photos. The Grand Teton Mountains plunge into the west shore of Jackson Lake in an awesome display of geology.

Tips: Trolling is generally most productive in the summer months.

The fishing: Cutthroat range from 10 to 14 inches. Bottom fishing worms from the bank works well in the spring. Fishing tapers off drastically through summer. Mackinaw range from 14 to 18 inches. Bigger ones are not uncommon and anglers have hooked 50-pounders in the past. Bank fishing does produce some fish, although the larger ones are caught by trollers. Large Rapalas and Flatfish take mackinaw year-round. The secret is to fish at the correct depth. The hotter the water is, the deeper the fish will be. Ice fishing is another popular method for taking these whoppers. Whitefish range from 8 to 12 inches. These fish respond well to worms and some spinners. When the cutthroat quit biting, whitefish take over.

Additional information: Camping, picnicking, and other related facilities are located along the lake. Boating facilities are available at marinas at Colter Bay, Leeks Lodge, and Signal Mountain Lodge. Jackson Lake is closed to fishing from October 1 to October 31.

Contact: Grand Teton National Park.

190A. Lizard Creek Campground

Description: This fee area has 60 units, modern comfort stations, and can accommodate trailers and RV's. There are no utility hookups. The area is open from June 8 through September 8. The units are filled on a first-come, first-served basis and generally fill by 2 P.M.

Directions: From Moran Junction, take US 287/89/191 north about 16 miles.

The 13,770-foot Grand Teton scrapes the western skyline of Grand Teton National Park.

An angler would have a difficult time finding a more spectacular setting than Jackson Lake, in the heart of Grand Teton National Park.

190B. Picnic Area

Description: This day-use area offers tables, toilets, and allows fires within the provided grates.
Directions: From Moran Junction, take US 287/89/191 north for about 13 miles.

190C. Leeks Lodge

Description: A marina is present at this location with meals, groceries, and a boat ramp.
Directions: From Moran Junction, take US 287/89/191 north for about 9.5 miles. Turn left and follow the signs.

190D. Colter Bay

Description: A marina, meals, groceries, and a boat ramp are available, along with a large campground. The Colter Bay Campground is a fee area with 310 units, showers, laundry facilities, modern comfort stations, and accommodations for trailers and RV's. The campground is open from May 17 through September 23 on a first-come, first-served basis. This area generally fills by noon.
Directions: From Moran Junction, take US 287/89/191 north for about 8.5 miles. Turn left and follow the signs.

190 Jackson Lake

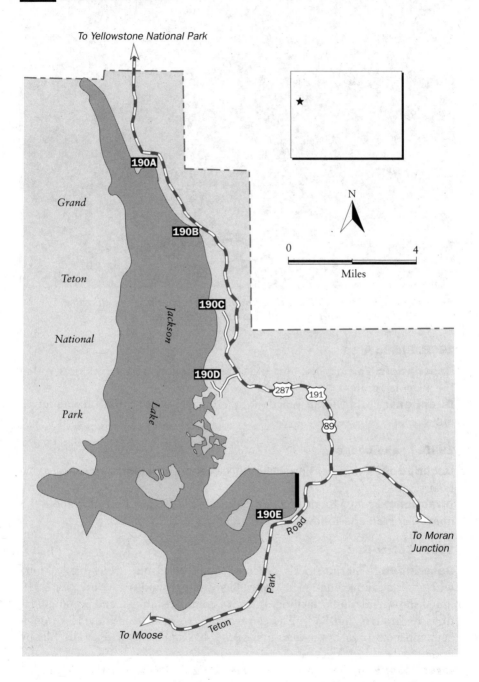

To Yellowstone National Park

190A

190B

190C

190D

287 191

89

Grand

Teton

National

Park

Jackson

Lake

190E

Road

Park

Teton

To Moose

To Moran
Junction

N

0   4
Miles

190E. Signal Mountain Lodge

Description: This fee area has 86 units with modern comfort stations. A marina and lodge are nearby with meals, groceries, a boat ramp, and lodging.
Directions: Moran Junction is 30 miles north of Jackson on US 26/89/191. At Moran Junction, take US 287/89/191 north for about 3 miles to Jackson Lake Junction. At the junction, turn left onto the Teton Park Road and drive 2.5 miles.

191 Snake River

Key species: cutthroat trout, whitefish
Description: The Snake River, which is up to 150 feet wide in places, passes numerous islands and scenic views along its course. Heavy runoff from rain and snow creates new channels virtually every year
Tips: Fishing is best from August to October. Fly fishing is the most productive method.

The fishing: Cutthroat trout average 8 to 18 inches. Stonefly nymphs tend to produce fish throughout the season. Grasshopper imitations improve the action in late fall. Special regulations apply from 1,000 feet below the Jackson Lake Dam to the Wilson Bridge. Of the 6 trout creel limit, only 1 may be over 18 inches; and all trout between 11 and 18 inches must be released immediately. Only artificial flies and lures are allowed on this stretch. The river is closed to trout fishing from November 1 to March 31. Whitefish range from 11 to 14 inches. These fish are found in the deeper spots and respond well to nymphs. The creel limit is 50 whitefish per day or 50 in possession.
Additional information: There are developed campgrounds and picnic areas nearby, but they fill to capacity early in the day during the summer. Wading is limited due to the size, swiftness, and depth of the river. Floating is the best approach.
Contact: Grand Teton National Park.

191A. Pacific Creek

Description: Parking area with access by foot
The fishing: Wading is an option at this put-in/take-out area when water levels drop from late July through October.
Directions: From Moran Junction, take US 287/89/191 north about 1 mile. The access is on the left side.

191B. Deadman's Bar

Description: Parking area with access by foot
The fishing: Wading is an option at this put-in/take-out area when water levels drop from late July through October.
Directions: Take US 26/89/191 north out of Jackson about 20 miles. Turn left onto the gravel access road and travel about 0.75 mile.

191 Snake River

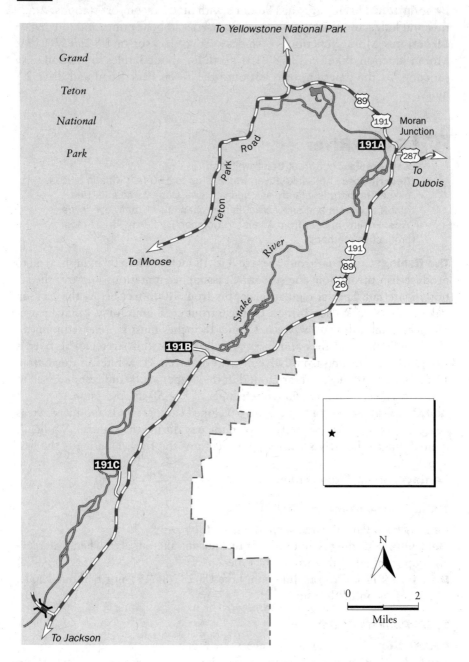

Grand

Teton

National

Park

To Yellowstone National Park

89

191

Moran
Junction

191A

287

To
Dubois

Teton Park Road

To Moose

Snake River

191

89

26

191B

191C

N

0   2
Miles

To Jackson

191C. Schwabacher's Landing

Description: Parking area with access by foot

The fishing: Wading is an option at this put-in/take-out area when water levels drop from late July through October.

Directions: Take US 26/89/191 north out of Jackson about 15.5 miles. Turn left onto the gravel access road and travel about 1 mile.

192 Two Ocean Lake

Key species: cutthroat trout

Description: Spruce trees and panoramic views of the Tetons surround this 625-acre lake. A 6-mile, easy-to-moderate trail circles the lake.

Tips: Worms work best when fished on the bottom in early spring.

The fishing: Cutthroat trout average 10 to 16 inches. Worms work best in the spring. Later in the summer, the action drops off drastically. Flies or colorful spinners in the early morning or late evening might create some action. Grasshoppers are the preferred bait in the fall. There is a limit of 6 trout per day, of which only 1 may be over 20 inches.

Directions: From Moran Junction, take US 287/89/191 north 1 mile. Turn right onto the unpaved Pacific Creek Road and drive about 2 miles to Two Ocean Lake Road. Turn left onto this improved dirt road and travel about 2.25 miles to the trailhead.

Additional information: Motorized boats are not allowed. The lake is open year-round. Nearby Pacific Creek offers some fishing within certain guidelines, as defined by Wyoming state fishing regulations. The best fishing in the creek is upstream in the Bridger-Teton National Forest.

Contact: Grand Teton National Park.

193 Cottonwood Creek

See map on page 240

Key species: cutthroat trout

Description: This mountain stream flows into the large, grassy meadow of the Jackson Hole area, beneath the Tetons which loom to the west.

Tips: Be prepared for some footwork and respect the wildlife.

The fishing: Cutthroat trout range from 8 to 10 inches. Worms can produce anytime, but grasshoppers and their imitations work best since the fishing season does not open until late summer. The usually abundant grassphoppers are the food of choice at this time. An assortment of flies work at varying times. Of the 6 trout daily limit, only 1 may be over 20 inches. Cottonwood Creek is closed to fishing from November 1 through July 31. The portion from the outlet of Jenny Lake downstream to the second bridge south of the Jenny Lake parking area is permanently closed to fishing.

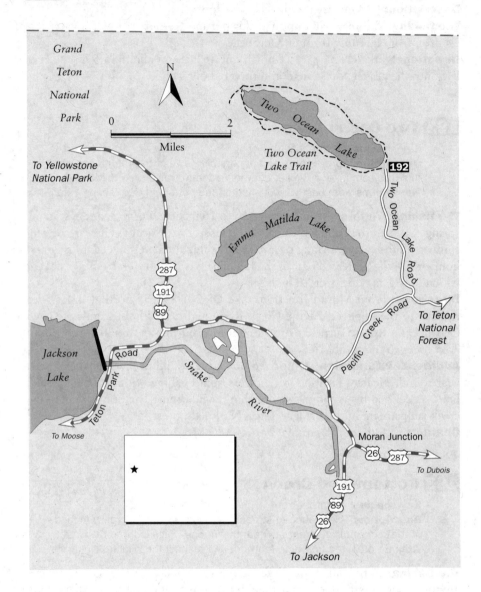

Grand
Teton
National
Park

N

0   2
Miles

To Yellowstone
National Park

Two Ocean Lake

Two Ocean
Lake Trail

192

Two Ocean Lake Road

Emma Matilda Lake

To Teton
National
Forest

287
191
89

Pacific Creek Road

Jackson
Lake

Teton Park Road

Snake River

To Moose

★

Moran Junction

26 287
To Dubois

191
89
26

To Jackson

Directions: Take US 26/89/191 north out of Jackson 12 miles to Moose Junction. Turn left onto the paved Teton Park Road and proceed through the Moose Entrance Station on the other side of the Snake River. Continue for 2.25 miles on the Teton Park Road to the Cottonwood Creek Picnic Area. The creek crosses the road here.

Additional information: The Cottonwood Picnic area offers an easy access point near the Bradley and Taggart Lake Trailhead. Camping is not available along the creek, but Jenny Lake Campground is nearby (see directions for site 196).

Contact: Grand Teton National Park.

194 Leigh Lake

See map on page 241

Key species: cutthroat trout, mackinaw
Description: The Tetons loom over 1,229-acre Leigh Lake. Sandy beaches and shallow water dominate the eastern shore.
Tips: The western shoreline offers the deepest water and the best opportunity for mackinaw.

The fishing: Cutthroat range from 14 to 18 inches. Worms fished on the bottom work well in the spring. Grasshoppers have the greatest success later in the summer, though worms will still take a few fish. If you canoe to the lake, fly fishing can be very good in the early morning or late evening. The Woolly Bugger, Hopper, and leech patterns create some activity. Mackinaw average 8 to 12 inches. The big ones tend to be found in the shallow water during the spawning season, late in the fall. Worms and minnow imitations can produce some action. There is a limit of 6 trout per day, of which only 1 may be over 24 inches.

Directions: Take US 26/89/191 north out of Jackson 12 miles to Moose Junction. Turn left and proceed north past Moose on Teton Park Road, 11 miles to North Jenny Lake Road. Turn left onto this paved road and drive about 1.5 miles to the String Lake parking area. Turn right onto this paved area and drive about 0.5 mile to the north end to access the trailhead. Leigh Lake is about 1 mile away on an easy trail. An alternative is to put in a canoe at this point.

Additional information: This lake can be reached by canoe with a portage or by foot. Camping and other services are available nearby. Jenny Lake is the closest campground. Backcountry camping sites are available at the lake as well. Prior arrangements need to be made before using these sites. Camping permits can be obtained at Moose Visitor Center, Jenny Lake Ranger Station, or Colter Bay Visitor Center. Motorized boats are not allowed.

Contact: Grand Teton National Park.

193, 197, 198 Cottonwood Creek, Bradley Lake, Taggart Lake

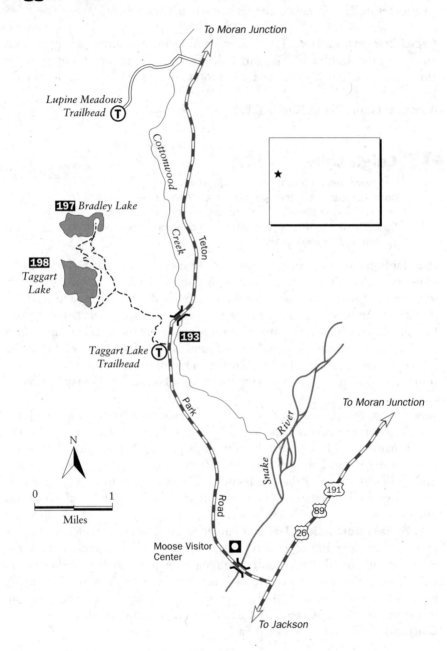

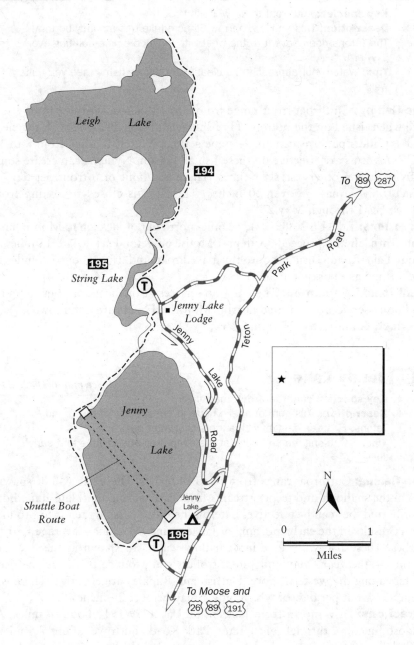

Leigh Lake

194

To 89 287

195
String Lake

T

Jenny Lake
Lodge

Park Road

Teton

Jenny Lake

Jenny

Lake

Shuttle Boat
Route

Jenny
Lake

196

T

N

0   1
Miles

To Moose and
26 89 191

195 String Lake

See map on page 241

Key species: cutthroat trout, whitefish
Description: This shallow, narrow 30-acre lake has a sandy bottom. The Tetons rise above it to the west with lodgepole pine pointing ever skyward.
Tips: Watch your approach; the clear water allows fish to see you quite well.

The fishing: Cutthroat trout range from 8 to 12 inches. Worms can be effective when fished on the bottom. Fly fishing can be challenging with the clear water. Caddis patterns can create some action. Whitefish range from 8 to 12 inches. Worms are effective on these fish all season. Nymphs can create some activity during otherwise slow times. There is a limit of 6 trout per day, of which only 1 may be over 20 inches. This area is closed to fishing from November 1 through May 20.

Directions: Take US 26/89/191, 12 miles north out of Jackson to Moose Junction. Turn left and proceed north past Moose on Teton Park Road, 11 miles to Jenny Lake Road. Turn left onto this paved road and drive about 1.5 miles to the String Lake parking area.

Additional information: There are no services at this location, but camping and other services are located nearby. Motorized boats are not allowed.
Contact: Grand Teton National Park.

196 Jenny Lake

See map on page 241

Key species: cutthroat trout, mackinaw
Description: This gem of a lake rests in the shadow of the Grand Tetons. Fir trees elegantly cloak this coldwater beauty.
Tips: Fish along the shoreline at the deep drop-offs in June and early July.

The fishing: Cutthroat range from 12 to 14 inches. These fish will be spawning in the shallows and feeder streams from early spring until late June. Both worms and flies can be effective. Later in the fall, fly fishing tends to produce better results in the early morning or late evening. Mackinaw average 8 to 12 inches. These fish will move into shallow waters to spawn in the late fall. Earlier in the year (May and June), trollers can produce fish from the deep waters along the western shore. Flatfish and Rapalas are effective. There is a limit of 6 trout per day, of which only 1 may be over 24 inches.

Directions: Drive north from Jackson on US 26/89/191 about 14 miles. At Moose Junction, turn left onto Teton Park Road and travel about 7.5 miles. This lake can also be reached from the one-way road starting at the Jenny Lake Junction, 11 miles north of Moose.

Additional information: Jenny Lake Lodge is accessed by following the one-way road from Jenny Lake Junction. The Jenny Lake Campground has modern comfort stations and 49 units. These units are restricted to tents. A boat ramp is available, but motorized boats must have less than 15 horsepower. There is a shuttle boat that will take you across the lake for a fee.

Contact: Grand Teton National Park.

197 Bradley Lake

See map on page 240

Key species: cutthroat trout

Description: Bradley Lake is 60 surface acres of ice-cold water shimmering beneath the Teton Mountains. A forest fire burned many of the trees in this area, but new growth provides an abundance of food for wildlife.

Tips: Pack a big lunch and light gear. And don't forget film for your camera.

The fishing: Cutthroat trout range from 7 to 14 inches. Worms can be productive. The bubble-and-fly technique is effective in early morning or late evening. The lake is closed to fishing from November 1 through May 20. Bears and moose wander this area.

Directions: Take US 26/89/191 north out of Jackson for 12 miles to Moose Junction. Turn left onto Teton Park Road and pass through the Moose Entrance Station on the west side of the Snake River. Continue for 2 miles on Teton Park Road to the Taggart Creek parking area. Bear right and travel on the foot trail about 2.2 miles.

Additional information: A moderate trail leads to this lake; the 4.4-mile roundtrip hike takes about 3 hours. A backcountry camping area is available, but a backcountry permit is required for all overnight camping. Permits can be obtained at Moose Visitor Center, Jenny Lake Ranger Station, or Colter Bay Visitor Center.

Contact: Grand Teton National Park.

198 Taggart Lake

See map on page 240

Key species: cutthroat trout

Description: Rugged mountains and timber encircle this 163-acre lake. The fire mentioned above took a greater toll here.

Tips: Pack a big lunch and light gear. And don't forget film for your camera.

The fishing: Cutthroat trout range from 8 to 16 inches. Worms can be effective, but as with any lake where packing is required, the tradeoff between taking worms or more lunch meat may be a deterrent. The bubble-and-fly technique is productive. The lake is closed to fishing from November 1 through May 20.

Directions: Take US 26/89/191 north out of Jackson 12 miles to Moose Junction. Turn left onto Teton Park Road and pass through the Moose Entrance Station on the west side of the Snake River. Continue 2 miles on the Teton Park

It is just a short, pleasant hike into Taggart Lake, where there is some excellent cutthroat trout fishing. Nearby Bradley Lake offers good fishing for these native Wyoming trout as well.

Road to the Taggart Creek parking area. Follow the trail from the parking lot for 0.2 mile. At the junction, take the trail to the right for 1.1 miles. From this next junction, take the trail to the left for 0.5 mile to Taggart Lake.

Additional information: This lake is reached by foot on a moderate trail. The 3.6-mile round trip takes about 2 hours.

Contact: Grand Teton National Park.

199 Phelps Lake

Key species: cutthroat trout, mackinaw
Description: This 525-acre lake is nestled between mountain ridges. Lodgepole pines, fir, spruce, and aspen trees make up the surrounding forest.
Tips: Plan ahead; reaching this lake can be difficult.

The fishing: Cutthroat trout range from 12 to 18 inches. The bubble-and-fly technique creates some action in early morning and late evening. Colorful spinners can produce some action in the deep water later in the summer. Mackinaw average 8 to 12 inches. These fish are found in the shallow waters during the late fall spawning period. Jigs and pop gear can create some action for the persistent angler.

Directions: Take US 26/89/191 north out of Jackson 12 miles to Moose Junction. Turn left onto Teton Park Road and travel across the Snake River. Turn

199 Phelps Lake

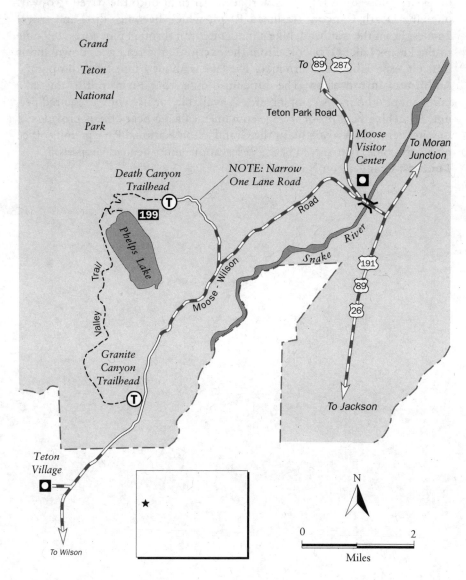

Grand

Teton

National

Park

To 89 287

Teton Park Road

Moose
Visitor
Center

To Moran
Junction

Death Canyon
Trailhead

NOTE: Narrow
One Lane Road

199

Phelps Lake

Road

Snake

River

191

Moose - Wilson

89

26

Valley

Trail

Granite
Canyon
Trailhead

To Jackson

Teton
Village

To Wilson

★

N

0   2

Miles

left onto the paved Moose-Wilson Road and drive 3 miles. No trailers, RVs, or buses are allowed on this narrow road. Turn right onto the paved two-way, one-lane Death Canyon Trailhead Road, which becomes dirt, and travel 2 miles. From the trailhead, hike a moderate trail through pine forest 0.9 mile to the Phelps Lake Overlook. From the overlook, the trail goes down and is difficult, especially the return hike. The lake is about 1 mile from this point.

Additional information: The difficult, 4-mile, round-trip trail to this lake takes about 4 hours. A camping area is available for use with a required permit. A latching bear proof storage container, called a bear box, is provided at the site. Permits are available at the Grand Teton National Park permits office on a first-come, first-served basis. Reservations must be made in person.

Contact: Grand Teton National Park.

Yellowstone National Park

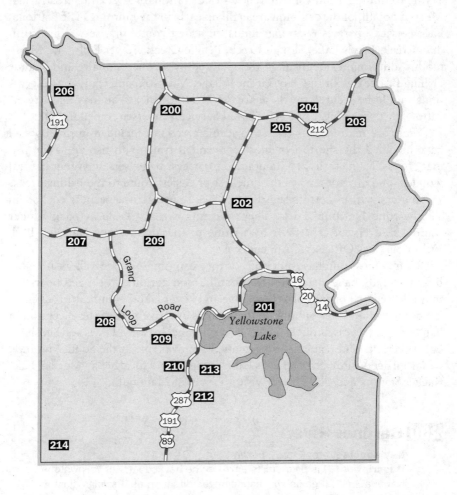

Yellowstone Lake

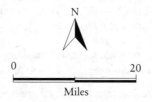

N

0   20

Miles

Yellowstone National Park

Trying to finding a campsite in Yellowstone National Park can be frustrating. Most, if not all, of the camping areas fill up early in the morning. The National Park Service operates 6 campgrounds on a first-come, first-served basis: Indian Creek, Lewis Lake, Slough Creek, Pebble Creek, Tower Falls, and Mammoth. Additional campgrounds are operated by a concessionaire and include Fishing Bridge RV, Bridge Bay, Grant Village, Madison, and Canyon. Reservations should be secured for these areas well in advance. You may make reservations by contacting TW Recreational Services, Inc. (see Appendix A).

There are many access routes to scenic areas not included in this book. I have included the shortest or most convenient trails with fishing as the primary focus. Many trails are maintained for access to geysers and other natural wonders and are not always the quickest or easiest route to the fishing areas.

Anglers within certain age groups need special use permits to fish in Yellowstone National Park. These permits are available at park ranger stations and visitor centers or by writing to the Yellowstone National Park Visitor Services Office (see Appendix A).

Boaters must purchase a permit, or they can obtain a free Yellowstone tag if they already have a transferable Grand Teton permit. Motorized boats are only allowed on portions of Yellowstone and Lewis lakes. Non-motorized boats are permitted on lakes but not on the streams and rivers, with the exception of hand-propelled vessels on the Lewis River channel between Lewis and Shoshone Lakes. Permits and regulation information are available at the South Entrance, Grant Village Visitor Center, Lewis Lake Campground, Bridge Bay Marina, Lake Ranger Station, and the Albright Visitor Center at Mammoth.

200 Gardner River

Key species: brook trout, brown trout
Description: This river starts small in the backcountry of Yellowstone National Park. It gains size and changes direction as it swings north, crashing over boulders in the canyons and meandering through mountain meadows in between. Before getting to the northern border of Yellowstone National Park this ever-widening river cuts a deep, steeply sided canyon, just east of Mammoth.
Tips: Large streamers and nymphs take brown trout in the river's lower portions during the fall spawning.

The fishing: Brook trout range from 8 to 10 inches in the upper river. Fly fishing is the method of choice; grasshopper imitations work well during the last part of summer and into the fall. Brown trout average 10 to 14 inches. These fish are in the lower parts of the river, on their way to spawning grounds, in late August. Artificial flies and lures are the only tackle allowed.

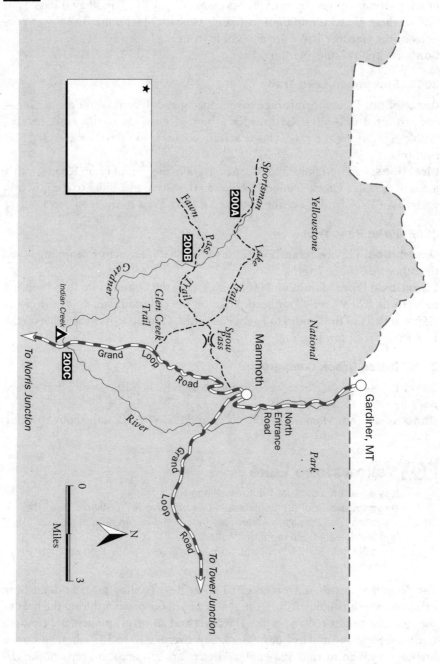

Additional information: Children 12 and under are allowed to use bait in the upper portions of this stream. The Sportsman Lake Trail and Fawn Pass Trail lead to these areas. Camping is available at nearby locations. The lower portions of the Gardner River are accessible from the highway.

Contact: Yellowstone National Park.

200A. Sportsman Lake Trail

Description: This moderate hike covers open meadows with some gentle climbs onto forested ridges. Forest fires have burned portions of this trail, leaving visible signs along the way. This is grizzly country, so take the necessary precautions.

Directions: From Mammoth Hot Springs, take the Grand Loop Road south 5 miles to the Glen Creek Trailhead. Hike on the old road 2 miles to the junction with Fawn Pass Trail. Take the Sportsman Lake Trail to the west for 4 miles.

200B. Fawn Pass Trail

Description: This moderate hike climbs a forested ridge before dropping down the other side to the river.

Directions: From Mammoth Hot Springs, take the Grand Loop Road south 5 miles to the Glen Creek Trailhead. Hike on the old road, which is part of the Glen Creek Trail for 2 miles to Fawn Pass Trail. Continue over the ridge on the Fawn Pass Trail for 2 miles.

200C. Indian Creek Campground

Description: This fee area has 75 units available on a first-come, first-served basis.

Directions: From Mammoth, take the Grand Loop Road south about 10 miles.

201 Yellowstone Lake

Key species: cutthroat trout, mackinaw

Description: Trout are abundant in this massive, 87,000-acre lake. The shoreline runs through a wilderness that includes geothermal geysers and densely forested mountain ridges.

Tips: Bucktail Mepps work well for boat anglers in early June and late September.

The fishing: Cutthroat average 12 to 16 inches. Trolling far from launching areas often results in big fish. Trout tend to be in deep water during the heat of the summer. Bright red and white Dardevls and colorful spinners are productive from the shore and by boat. Mackinaw average 10 to 13 inches, and some are large enough to start spawning. Anglers are required to keep and kill all mackinaw caught in Yellowstone Lake and show them to staff personnel at the ranger stations located in Grant Village, Bridge Bay, or Lake Village.

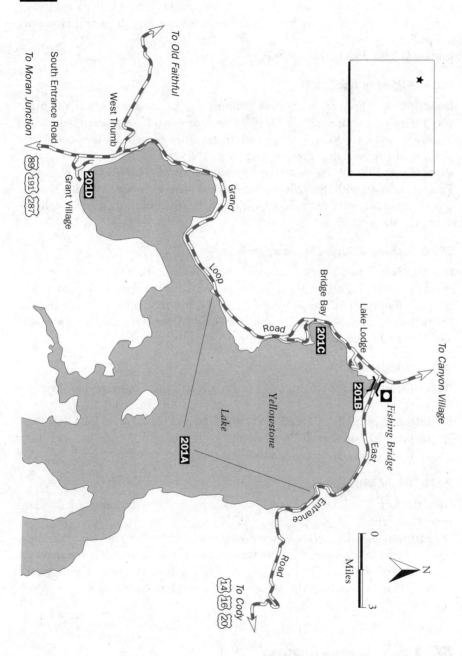

To Old Faithful

To Moran Junction

South Entrance Road

West Thumb

89 191 287

Grant Village

201D

Grand

Loop

Road

Bridge Bay

201C

Lake Lodge

To Canyon Village

201B

Fishing Bridge

East

Yellowstone

Lake

201A

Entrance

Road

To Cody

14 16 20

N

0 Miles 3

Additional information: Mackinaw are unwanted fish in this huge, natural lake. The native Yellowstone cutthroat trout could be severely depleted by the voracious, cutthroat-eating lake trout. Boaters must have a permit issued by the park.

Contact: Yellowstone National Park.

201A. Highway access

Description: There are numerous pullouts and picnic areas where the highway follows the shoreline. US 14/16/20 and the Grand Loop Road from Fishing Bridge to Grant Village offer camping facilities as well. Further details are given below on specific camping areas.

Directions: Take US 14/16/20 west 53 miles from Cody to the East Entrance. The first contact with the Yellowstone Lake shoreline is about 20 miles west of this entrance. From here to Grant Village there are about 30 miles of highway along the shoreline.

201B. Fishing Bridge RV Campground

Description: This fee area allows only hard-sided units; no tents or tent trailers are permitted. This is the only campground offering water, sewer, and electrical hookups. There are 345 units available, but they fill by midmorning.

Directions: Take US 14/16/20 west from Cody 53 miles to the East Entrance. The Fishing Bridge RV area is 27 miles west of this entrance.

201C. Bridge Bay

Description: This fee area has 434 units, a boat ramp, showers, laundry, and toilets.

Directions: Take US 14/16/20 west from Cody 53 miles to the East Entrance. At the Grand Loop Road, 27 miles west of this entrance, turn left and drive about 5 miles toward West Thumb.

201D. Grant Village

Description: This fee area has 428 units, a boat ramp, showers, laundry, and toilets available.

Directions: Take US 14/16/20 west from Cody 53 miles to the East Entrance. At the Grand Loop Road, 27 miles west of this entrance, turn left and drive 21 miles to West Thumb. Turn left onto US 287 and drive about 1 mile to the Grant Village access. Grant Village is about 21 miles north of the South Entrance.

202 Yellowstone River

Key species: cutthroat trout

Description: This river flows out of Yellowstone Lake. Flat surface waters disguise very deep, swift currents gliding over slippery bottoms. The scenery includes wildlife and thick lodgepole pine forest laced with

202 Yellowstone River

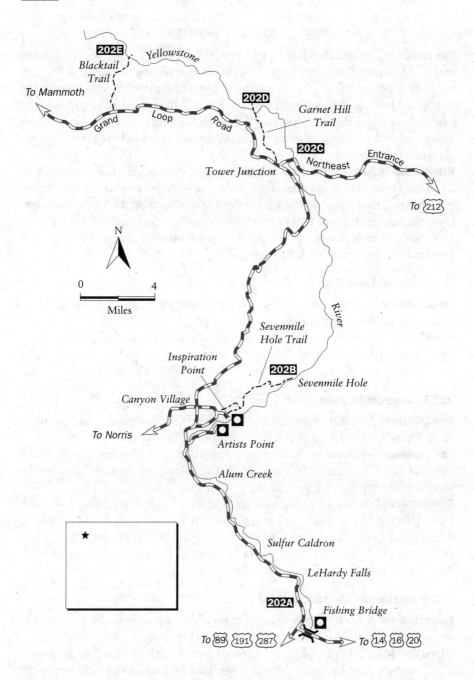

grassy meadows.

Tips: When using nymphs, weighted lines are necessary to reach fish in the deep, swift current. Be aware of the current regulations regarding the use of toxic equipment such as lead sinkers.

The fishing: Cutthroat trout average 14 to 20 inches. Yuk Bugs, Woolly Worms, and other large stonefly imitations are productive for the first part of the season, which opens July 15. As the summer heats up, the trout move closer to the bottom and can be difficult to reach. Dark, small nymphs tend to produce the most action when they are dropped far enough into the water. Some excellent action can be had here. This catch-and-release area is closely regulated by the National Park Service.

Additional information: The most popular portion of this river flows parallel to the Grand Loop Road and offers easy access. Specific areas are permanently closed to fishing, including 1 mile downstream and 0.25 mile upstream from the Fishing Bridge, 100 yards downstream and upstream from LeHardy Falls, and the area downstream from Sulphur Caldron to Alum Creek.

Contact: Yellowstone National Park.

202A. Grand Loop Road

Description: The river here is wide, clear, and deep with multiple pools. There are numerous parking pullouts along the road.

Directions: Take US 14/16/20 west from Cody 53 miles to the East Entrance. Drive past the East Entrance 27 miles, just past Fishing Bridge, and turn right onto Grand Loop Road. The river parallels the highway from here to Canyon.

202B. Sevenmile Hole

Description: Access to this portion of the river is very difficult. The Sevenmile Hole Trail drops nearly 1,500 feet in the last 2 miles of this 5-mile trek.

The fishing: Cutthroat in this section range from 12 to 15 inches. Small Wulff patterns and Elk Hair Caddis are productive during hatches. Otherwise, the small dark nymphs get action along the bottom.

Directions: Take US 14/16/20 west from Cody 53 miles to the East Entrance. Drive past the East Entrance 27 miles, just past Fishing Bridge, and turn right onto Grand Loop Road. Drive 16 miles to the Inspiration Point access. Turn right onto this paved road and travel about 0.25 mile to the Sevenmile Hole Trailhead. From here a 5-mile trail leads to the river.

202C. Northeast Entrance Road

Description: A bridge crosses the river here. A steep drop to the river results in a difficult climb out.

Directions: Take US 14/16/20 west from Cody 53 miles to the East Entrance. Drive past the East Entrance 27 miles, just past Fishing Bridge, and turn right onto Grand Loop Road. Drive 35 miles through Canyon to Tower Junction. Turn right onto the Northeast Entrance Road and drive 1 mile. A parking area is on the northeast side.

202D. Garnet Hill Trail

Description: The river here rages over the many large rocks in the Black Canyon. Wading is dangerous at best. A moderate hike leads to the canyon.

The fishing: Cutthroat trout, rainbow trout, and whitefish occupy this stretch of water. Cutthroat range from 12 to 15 inches. Stonefly patterns work well early in the season. Later, small, dark nymphs get action in the deeper water. Rainbow trout range from 8 to 12 inches. The same techniques for cutthroat will produce these trout as well. Whitefish range from 8 to 14 inches. Dark nymphs fished along the bottom tend to generate action, although whitefish are usually unwanted by anglers.

Directions: Take US 14/16/20 west from Cody 53 miles to the East Entrance. Drive past the East Entrance for 27 miles to the Grand Loop Road, just past Fishing Bridge. Turn right and drive for 35 miles through Canyon to Tower Junction. The Garnet Hill Trail is a short distance past this junction. This moderate trail covers about 4 miles to the suspension bridge crossing the river. Be prepared for quick weather changes and plan to give yourself enough time to get out safely.

202E. Blacktail Trail

Description: This resembles the Garnet Hill area.

Directions: Take US 14/16/20 west from Cody 53 miles to the East Entrance. Drive past the East Entrance 27 miles, just past Fishing Bridge, and turn right

Visitors to Yellowstone National Park can watch native cutthroat trout swim in the Yellowstone River from Fishing Bridge.

onto Grand Loop Road. Drive 35 miles through Canyon to Tower Junction. Continue on the Grand Loop Road toward Mammoth for about 11 miles to Blacktail Pond. This moderate trail leads 4 miles north from the pond to the river.

203 Soda Butte Creek

Key species: cutthroat trout, rainbow trout
Description: This clear, fast creek is 10 feet wide in places. Deep pools and well-defined cutbanks dominate the lower portions.
Tips: Grasshopper imitations are dynamite late in August.

The fishing: Cutthroat range from 10 to 13 inches. Mayflies work well, though grasshopper imitations can create explosive action toward the end of August. Rainbow trout range from 8 to 10 inches. These fish are not as common and are often caught while an angler is seeking the more prominent cutthroat. Anglers are allowed to keep 2 rainbow trout of any size. Cutthroat are subject to special regulations and generally are catch-and-release only. Portions above, and including, Calfee Creek have a limit of 2 cutthroat. Be sure to check current regulations and know where you are.

Directions: Soda Butte Creek parallels the US 212/Northeast Entrance Road for about 7 miles west of the northeast entrance.

Additional information: Camping is available within a reasonable walking distance at Pebble Creek Campground. Highway pullouts are provided at different locations.

Contact: Yellowstone National Park.

204 Slough Creek

Key species: cutthroat trout, rainbow trout
Description: Some pools in Slough Creek are 15 feet wide in the upper stream areas.
Tips: The larger fish tend to be farther from areas of easy access.

The fishing: Cutthroat range from 12 to 16 inches. Clear water can work for you and against you when approaching a promising location; you can see the fish, but they can also see you. Wet flies are productive in the spring. Grasshopper imitations are best in fall. This is a catch-and-release stream, so the fish are well educated and quite challenging to hook. Rainbow trout range from 10 to 12 inches. The same tackle used for cutthroat will produce rainbows. Most of the rainbow are caught by anglers pursuing the colorful cutthroat.

Directions: The Slough Creek Campground road is 24 miles west of the Northeast Entrance or 5 miles east of Tower Junction on US 212/Northeast Entrance Road. Turn north onto this gravel road and drive about 3 miles to the Slough Creek Trailhead. To reach the meadow area, follow the trail about 1.75 miles.

Additional information: Slough Creek Campground is a fee area with 29

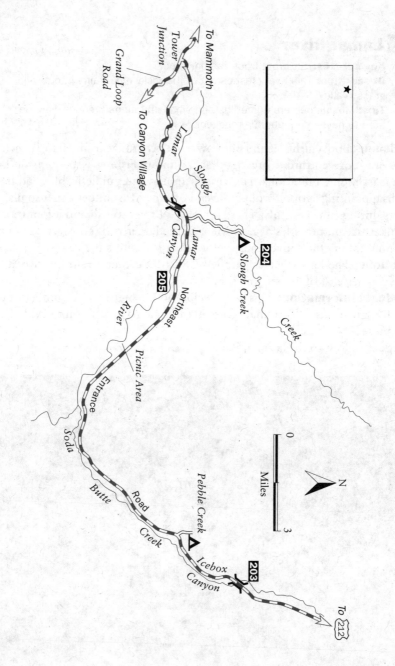

units and toilets. The easier-to-fish pools are reached by foot from the Slough Creek Trail.

Contact: Yellowstone National Park.

205 Lamar River

See map on page 257

Key species: cutthroat trout, rainbow trout
Description: This river crashes out of the rocky mountains into a wide, grassy valley.
Tips: Mosquitoes are numerous and small imitations produce well. Be sure to have adequate bug repellent.

The fishing: Both cutthroat and rainbow trout here range from 10 to 16 inches. There are more cutthroat present than rainbow. Fishing is best in the fall, using grasshopper imitations. The spring runoff creates undesirable conditions and disappointing action through the end of July. Mosquitoes can also plague anglers during June and July. There is plenty of river to fish and a foot trail to the upper stream provides access. Most of the larger fish, however, are in the deep pools along the canyon, just before the river enters the valley.

Directions: The Lamar River parallels US 212/Northeast Entrance Road for about 5 miles east of Tower Junction.

Additional information: This river is close to the highway. A number of potentially dangerous wild animals graze in the area; pay attention to the buffalo and moose.

Contact: Yellowstone National Park.

Anglers fish the deep pools on the Lamar River in search of cutthroat and rainbow trout.

A wide, grassy valley surrounds the Lamar River.

206 Gallatin River

Key species: brook trout, brown trout, cutthroat trout, whitefish
Description: This gravel-bottomed river is 30 feet wide in places as it flows through a grassy valley.
Tips: These fish are not easily fooled; small hooks give anglers a tiny advantage.

The fishing: Cutthroat and rainbow trout both range from 10 to 13 inches. Wading in the stream is refreshing and is the best method for proper positioning in the gentle current. Caddis and mayfly imitations work well. Brown trout range from 10 to 12 inches. These trout are only occasionally caught in late August. Grasshopper imitations are the most productive tackle for in late August. Whitefish range from 10 to 12 inches. Nymphs work best in the deep pools and slower waters.

Directions: The Gallatin River is 35 miles north of West Yellowstone, Montana, on US 191. There are highway pullouts at various locations within the park.

Additional information: There are no facilities along this short stretch of highway. Commercial vehicles such as semi-trucks frequently use this road as a shortcut. If you plan to fish this area make sure to get the necessary permit from the national park service.

Contact: Yellowstone National Park.

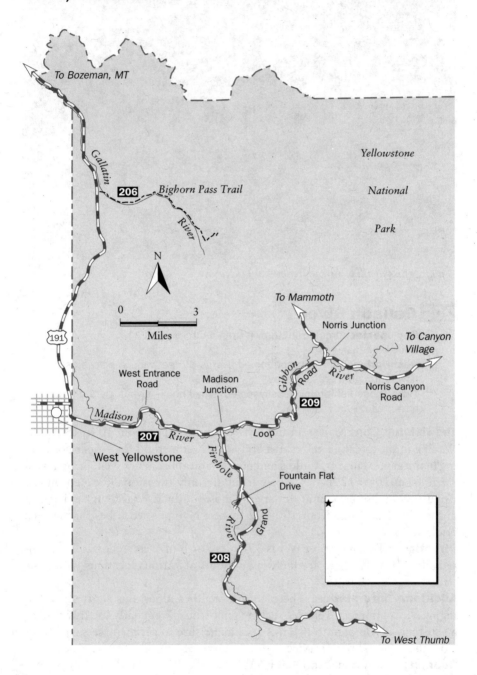

To Bozeman, MT

Gallatin

206 Bighorn Pass Trail

River

Yellowstone

National

Park

N

0   3

Miles

191

To Mammoth

Norris Junction

To Canyon Village

Gibbon

Road

River

West Entrance Road

Madison Junction

Norris Canyon Road

209

Madison

Madison River

Loop

207

West Yellowstone

Firehole

Fountain Flat Drive

River

Grand

208

To West Thumb

207 Madison River

Key species: brown trout, rainbow trout, whitefish
Description: This wide, meandering river has deep courses, numerous riffles, and undercuts.
Tips: Look for trout near the cooler waters of inlets, especially with the Firehole River adding its warm waters from hot springs near Madison Junction.

The fishing: Fly fishing is the only method allowed on this river. Brown trout range from 10 to 16 inches; a 5-pounder is not unheard of. Wet stonefly patterns fished in the deeper runs are productive in the early season for average-size trout. The bigger fish migrate upstream during fall spawning and tend to like large streamers. Grasshopper imitations can be highly effective when a good population of these insects is present. Current regulations allow anglers to keep 2 brown trout, if they are fewer than 13 inches long.

Rainbow trout average 10 to 16 inches. Mayfly and caddis patterns are productive, with the most success in early spring. Dry flies can be difficult to present properly on the river's contrasting surface currents. Wet flies may avoid the surface currents, but you are more likely to catch whitefish by fishing deep. In the future, cutthroat trout may eventually be planted to replace the rainbow, filling the vacancy created by whirling disease.

Whitefish average 8 to 12 inches. These fish tend to stay close to the bottom and are perpetually hungry for wet nymphs. Whitefish are much more common in the lower portions of the river near West Yellowstone.

The Madison River is one of Wyoming's, and the West's, premier trout streams.

Directions: The Madison River parallels the West Entrance Road from West Yellowstone, Montana, east to Madison Junction. There are numerous highway-access pullouts. The river is a short hike from Madison Campground.

Additional information: Wheelchair-accessible fishing is available at the Mount Haynes site, 3.5 miles west of Madison Junction. The boardwalk provides easy wheelchair access for a fly fishing-only stretch of the river. Fishing is allowed from 5 A.M. to 10 P.M. To find out more about this feature, contact the Yellowstone National Park Accessibility Coordinator (see Appendix A). Camping is available at the Madison Campground at Madison Junction. This fee area offers 281 units that should be reserved in advance through TW Recreational Services. The campground is open from May 1 through November 3 if weather and money for upkeep permit.

Contact: Yellowstone National Park.

208 Firehole River

Key species: Brook trout, brown trout, and rainbow trout

See map on page 260

Description: This well-known river starts small, but quickly gains size as other mountain streams flow into it. Hot geysers and springs boil into it, creating summer water temperatures of 80 degrees F. As with the Madison River, the Firehole has an abundance of weeds and insects. The deep cuts, channels, and riffles offer plenty of trout habitat, but the high temperatures result in various migrations; the trout seek cooler water. Most of the river flows through fire-ravaged, forested ridges with a few untouched meadows and stands of trees.

Tips: Small midge, mayfly, and caddis patterns on hook sizes 22 to 16 are almost required for adequate presentation.

The fishing: Fly fishing is the only method allowed on this river. Brook trout range from 4 to 8 inches. These trout are found, primarily, in the stretch of river above Old Faithful. Small mosquito and grasshopper imitations are productive at different times of the season. The hoppers produce better in the late fall. Brown trout average 16 to 18 inches. These fish are extremely wary and difficult to fool. Focus your efforts on coldwater stream inlets in the early morning. Use small flies. Wet flies can be productive but tricky. Rainbow trout average 7 to 14 inches. To catch them, small hooks on a variety of insect imitations are necessary. You can use blue quill, blue dun, midge, and adams. The best fishing for these trout is in the cooler parts of the river during early spring.

Directions: The Firehole River parallels most of the 16 miles along the Grand Loop Road between Madison Junction and Old Faithful, and including Fountain Flat Drive. Many highway pullouts along the river lead to geysers and other attractions. There is also foot access from the highway south of Old Faithful.

Hot springs flowing into the Firehole River can raise its water temperatures into the 80s.

Additional information: Camping is available near the mouth of the Firehole River at Madison Campground, which is described under site 209. Other services and picnic areas are located at different places along the river, including Old Faithful. The section of the river between the road bridge 0.5 mile upstream from Old Faithful to the road bridge at Biscuit Basin is permanently closed to fishing.

Contact: Yellowstone National Park.

See map on page 260

209 Gibbon River

Key species: brook trout, brown trout, rainbow trout, grayling, whitefish

Description: This clear stream is 25 feet wide in places as it flows through forested canyons and wide meadows. Pools are deep and very clear. There are also some violent rapids on the river.

Tips: The riffles offer anglers an opportunity to avoid detection by these wary fish.

The fishing: Grayling range from 6 to 8 inches. These little teasers are found in the upper portions near Grebe Lake. Small black flies from size 10 to 18 work the best. Brook trout range from 4 to 7 inches, with the greatest numbers in the upper waters. Mosquito and grasshopper imitations are productive for these trout. Rainbow trout range from 6 to 10 inches. Small caddis and mayflies work best in the spring and early summer. Brown trout range from 6 to 10 inches in the upper waters. The larger browns can be found near Madison. Large nymphs and streamers are effective on these fish during the fall. Be sure to check current regulations. Only fly fishing is allowed on the lower portions of the river.

Directions: The Gibbon River parallels the Grand Loop Road from Madison Junction and then follows Norris Canyon Road near Norris Junction.

Additional information: Picnic facilities are available along the course of the river. Camping is also available at the Madison Campground near the mouth of the river.

Contact: Yellowstone National Park.

210 Shoshone Lake

Key species: brook trout, brown trout, mackinaw
Description: Lodgepole pines, both burned and alive, surround this 8,000-acre lake.
Tips: Belly boats can be very useful and perhaps the easiest to take into this large body of water.

The fishing: Brook trout range from 6 to 8 inches. These little fish are not the fish of choice here like the brown trout, but small mosquito imitations are effective in catching them. The brook trout tend to be near the mouth of the streams entering this little-fished area. Brown trout range from 16 to 20 inches. Spinners work well late in August from shore and in the areas nearest the outlet. Deep drop-offs and areas farther from shore are more productive in the summer months when fished with jigs and spoons. Mackinaw range from 16 to 20 inches and are found close to shore along the rocky portions of the lake in the early spring. Reaching these deep-water fish usually requires some type of boat.

Additional information: This backcountry lake can be reached by non-motorized boat and by foot. A backcountry permit is required for both day hikes and overnight stays. The Lewis River from Shoshone Lake to Lewis Lake is the only stretch of river in the park where boats are allowed.

Contact: Yellowstone National Park.

210A. DeLacy Creek Trail

Description: This gentle trail follows DeLacy Creek through meadows and pine forest for 3 miles to Shoshone Lake; it is the shortest route to the lake.
Directions: The DeLacy Trailhead is 8 miles east of Old Faithful on the Old Faithful–West Thumb Road/Grand Loop Road.

210B. Dogshead Trail

Description: This moderate hike goes through burned forest and up 200 feet over a ridge to the lake. The 4-mile hike ends at the lake near the Lewis River exit.

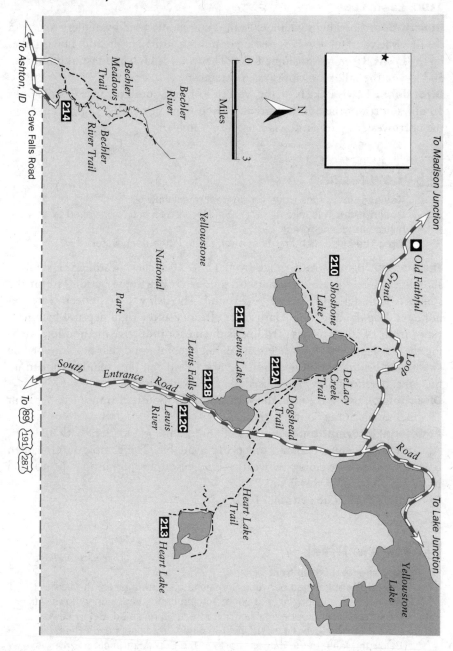

To Ashton, ID

Cave Falls Road

Bechler Meadows Trail

214

Bechler River

Bechler River Trail

Miles

0

N

3

To Madison Junction

Old Faithful

Grand

Loop

210 Shoshone Lake

211 Lewis Lake

DeLacy Creek Trail

212A

Yellowstone

National

Park

Dogshead Trail

Lewis Falls

212B

212C Lewis River

South Entrance Road

Road

To Lake Junction

To 89 191 287

Heart Lake Trail

213 Heart Lake

Yellowstone Lake

Directions: The Dogshead Trailhead is on the South Entrance Road about 15.5 miles north of the South Entrance, just past Lewis Lake.

210C. Lewis Lake

Description: The Lewis Channel Trail is commonly used by anglers to access the Lewis River. This involves rowing or pulling a small craft from Lewis Lake, up the Lewis River, to Shoshone Lake. The water is high and fast in the spring and low in the fall, requiring some portaging.

Directions: Lewis Lake is on the west side of the South Entrance Road, about 10 miles north of the South Entrance. Follow the Lewis River upstream from the northwestern part of Lewis Lake 4 to 5 miles.

211 Lewis Lake

See map on page 265

Key species: brook trout, brown trout, mackinaw
Description: This lake has 5,000 surface acres and is enclosed by a high-country pine forest.
Tips: The bigger fish are most often found in the deep water.

The fishing: Brown trout range from 12 to 20 inches. Wading the shallow shoreline while working spinners or spoons creates some action late in the summer. Trolling is productive year-round. The fish will be in deep water on hot days. Rapalas and large Flatfish are effective at the right depth. Mackinaw range from 14 to 18 inches. Trolling is the most productive method for catching these fish as well. Jigs are effective, but keep in mind that any lure or line containing lead is not allowed in the park. Wind can be a major problem on this lake. Smaller boats are advised to stay away from the middle.

Directions: Lewis Lake is on the west side of the South Entrance Road, about 10 miles north of the South Entrance.

Additional information: Lewis Lake Campground is a fee area with 85 units. A boat ramp, picnic area, and toilets are available. The campground is open from June 7 to November 3, weather and resources permitting. Motorized boats are allowed on this lake.

Contact: Yellowstone National Park.

212 Lewis River

See map on page 265

Key species: brown trout
Description: Located between Shoshone and Lewis lakes, the Lewis River can be challenging and unpredictable during early spring flows. As the water levels drop, a classic trout stream is revealed. Below Lewis Lake, to Lewis River Falls, the river is made up of pools and riffles. Below the falls, to the canyon, north of the South Entrance, the river is up to 75 feet wide with a silty bottom and grassy meadows and timber along its banks.

Tips: The majority of big browns are caught on large streamers in the Lewis River Channel, between Shoshone and Lewis lakes, during the fall spawning.

The fishing: Brown trout average 12 to 20 inches. The big ones are consistently caught in the upper portions of the Lewis River Channel. These trout respond well to large Woolly Buggers, Marabou Muddlers, and other streamers. The farther downstream anglers travel, the smaller the trout will be. The wide, glassy portion between Lewis Falls, downstream to the canyon, is easy to access but holds smaller fish.

Additional information: Camping is available at the south end of Lewis Lake.

Contact: Yellowstone National Park.

212A. Lewis River Channel

Directions: Lewis Lake is on the west side of the South Entrance Road, 10 miles north of the South Entrance. A boat can reach the Lewis River inlet from Lewis Lake. Motorized boats are not allowed in the channel. A foot trail is also available for access just north of Lewis Lake or 15.5 miles north of the South Entrance.

212B. Lewis Lake Campground

Description: This fee area has 85 sites, and restrooms.

Directions: Lewis Lake is 10 miles north of the South Entrance on the South Entrance Road. The lake and campground are on the west side of the highway. The river is accessed by foot from here.

You can catch brown trout up to 20 inches long in the meandering Lewis River.

212C. Highway access

Directions: Take the South Entrance Road north from the South Entrance about 9 miles. The Lewis River is visible on the canyon floor far below. There are numerous pullouts along the highway between the head of the canyon to Lewis Falls.

213 Heart Lake

See map on page 265

Key species: cutthroat trout, mackinaw
Description: A moderate hike leads to this 4,000-acre, heart-shaped lake. Most of the 7-mile walk into the lake is downhill through fire-purged forest. The hot water of Witch Creek will join you shortly after 2 miles of hiking and continue all the way to Heart Lake. An active thermal area is present near the lake providing inspiration and reason for taking caution; both the ecosystem and hiker can suffer irreversible damage. Stay on the trail.
Tips: Belly boats offer the best access to the deep water where the big ones tend to be.

The fishing: Cutthroat trout range from 12 to 16 inches. The bubble-and-fly method works well with best results in the early morning. Mackinaw range from 12 to 14 inches. Rapalas and jigs take these fish, but keep in mind that lures containing lead are not allowed. All mackinaw caught are to be kept regardless of size. This is being done in an effort to preserve the native cutthroat population from decimation by these non-native fish.

Directions: The Heart Lake Trailhead is on the east side of the South Entrance Road, about 15.5 miles north of the South Entrance. The hike from the trailhead to the lakeshore is 7 to 8 miles.

Additional information: A moderate trail leads to this backcountry lake. A permit is required for overnight camping.

Contact: Yellowstone National Park.

214 Bechler River

See map on page 265

Key species: cutthroat trout, rainbow trout
Description: This part of Yellowstone has not experienced the purging of forest fires. The scenery of this southwestern corner makes the added effort to get there pay off. The clear, cold Bechler River has deep channels, rapids, and waterfalls. If you are not planning to camp, be sure to allow plenty of time to return to your vehicle.
Tips: Fish the cutbanks and hidden holes.

The fishing: Cutthroat trout range from 10 to 16 inches. Small, dark nymphs are effective when placed in cutbanks and in the deep water. Rainbow trout average 10 to 14 inches. Wet nymphs work well on these fish in the fast water above deep runs. Fall is the best season for visiting this area, unless you don't mind a muddy hike and multitudes of mosquitoes.

Directions: Take the Cave Falls Road east out of Ashton, Idaho, about 26 miles to the Bechler Ranger Station turnoff. Turn left onto this gravel road and travel about 1.75 miles. Take the Bechler Meadows Trail northeast for 5 miles.

Additional information: Camping is available near Falls Campground. Access to the river involves an easy-to-moderate, 10-mile round trip hike. Because this remote river is not reached by the regular park roads, it is not as heavily visited as other park waters.

Contact: Yellowstone National Park.

Appendix

While in the state of Wyoming the following toll-free numbers can be used to obtain information on fishing.

Jackson	1-800-423-4113
Pinedale	1-800-452-9107
Cody	1-800-654-1178
Sheridan	1-800-331-9834
Green River	1-800-843-8096
Laramie	1-800-843-2352
Lander	1-800-654-7862
Casper	1-800-233-8544
Cheyenne	1-800-842-1934

CHAMBERS OF COMMERCE

Cody Chamber of Commerce
P.O. Box 2777
836 Sheridan
Cody, WY 82414
(307) 587-2777

Evanston Chamber of Commerce
P.O. Box 365
36 Tenth Street
Evanston, WY 82931
(307) 789-2527

Newcastle Chamber of Commerce
P.O. Box 68
921 South Summit
Newcastle, WY 82701
(307) 746-2739

WYOMING GAME AND FISH DEPARTMENT

Casper
Wyoming Game and Fish
2800 Pheasant Drive
Casper, WY 82604
(307) 234-9185

Cheyenne
Wyoming Game and Fish
5400 Bishop Boulevard
Cheyenne, WY 82006
(307) 777-4601

Cody
Wyoming Game and Fish
2820 State Highway 120
Cody, WY 82414
(307) 527-7125

Jackson
Wyoming Game and Fish
P.O. Box 67
Jackson, WY 83001
(307) 733-2321

Lander
Wyoming Game and Fish
260 Buena Vista
Lander, WY 82520
(307) 332-2688

Laramie
Wyoming Game and Fish
528 South Adams
Laramie, WY 82070
(307) 745-4046

Pinedale
Wyoming Game and Fish
P.O. Box 850
Pinedale, WY 82941
(307) 367-4353

Sheridan
Wyoming Game and Fish
P.O. Box 6249
Sheridan, WY 82801
(307) 672-7418

NATIONAL PARKS

Grand Teton National Park
P.O. Drawer 170
Moose, WY 83012
(307) 739-3300

Yellowstone National Park
P.O. Box 168
Yellowstone, WY 83020
(307) 344-7381

NATIONAL RECREATION AREAS

Bighorn Canyon
P.O. Box 487
Lovell, WY 82431
(307) 548-2251

Flaming Gorge
P.O. Box 278
Manila, UT 84046
(801) 784-3445

WYOMING STATE PARKS AND HISTORIC SITES

Boysen State Park
Boysen Route
Shoshoni, WY 82659
(307) 876-2796

Curt Gowdy State Park
1351 Hynds Lodge Road
Cheyenne, WY 82009
(307) 632-7946

Glendo State Park
P.O. Box 398
Glendo, WY 82213
(307) 735-4433

Hawk Springs State Recreation Area
c/o Guernsey State Park
P.O. Box 429
Guernsey, WY 82214
(307) 836-2334

Keyhole State Park
353 McKean Road
Moorcroft, WY 82721
(307) 756-3596

Seminoe State Park
Seminoe Dam Route
Sinclair, WY 82334
(307) 328-0115

WIND RIVER INDIAN RESERVATION

Shoshone and Arapahoe Tribes
Fish and Game Department
P.O. Box 217
Fort Washakie, Wyoming 82514
(307) 332-7207

Reservation permits are available (by town) at:

Dubois
Whiskey Mountain Tackle Shop

Crowheart
Crowheart Store

Ethete
Ethete Station

Fort Washakie
Tribal Texaco

Lander
Ace Hardware; McRaes Drug; Rocky Acre Campground (northwest); Ray Lake Campground (northwest); The Good Place; The Tannery

Pavillion
Basketeria

Pinedale
Wind River Sporting; Great Outdoor Shop

Riverton
Maverick Store; Rocky Mountain Sports; West Route Trading Company

Shoshoni
Trail Town Supply

Thermopolis
Coast to Coast; Wind River Canyon Whitewater

About the Author

Ken Graham was born in Wyoming and worked for 12 years in underground mines there. He came to appreciate the ruggedness and serenity he found on the surface near the isolated mines where he worked. Then, a serious accident on the job forced a career change and he wrote his first FalconGuide, *Rockhounding Wyoming*. This fishing guide is his second effort and he is at work on *Camping Wyoming*. He currently lives in Butte, Montana, but continues to explore the Wyoming backcountry with his wife and son.